THE SEVEN DEADLY SINS
SEVEN DAYS

ORIGINAL STORY BY:
NAKABA SUZUKI
(WEEKLY SHONEN MAGAZINE –
THE SEVEN DEADLY SINS)

LIGHT NOVEL BY:
MAMORU IWASA
(KODANSHA KCDX LIGHT NOVEL –
THE SEVEN DEADLY SINS: SEVEN DAYS)

MANGA BY:
YOU KOKIKUJI

I

You Kokikuji Presents
The Seven Deadly Sins: Seven Days
The Thief and the Saint

contents

You Kokikuji Presents
The Seven Deadly Sins: Seven Days

The Thief and the Saint

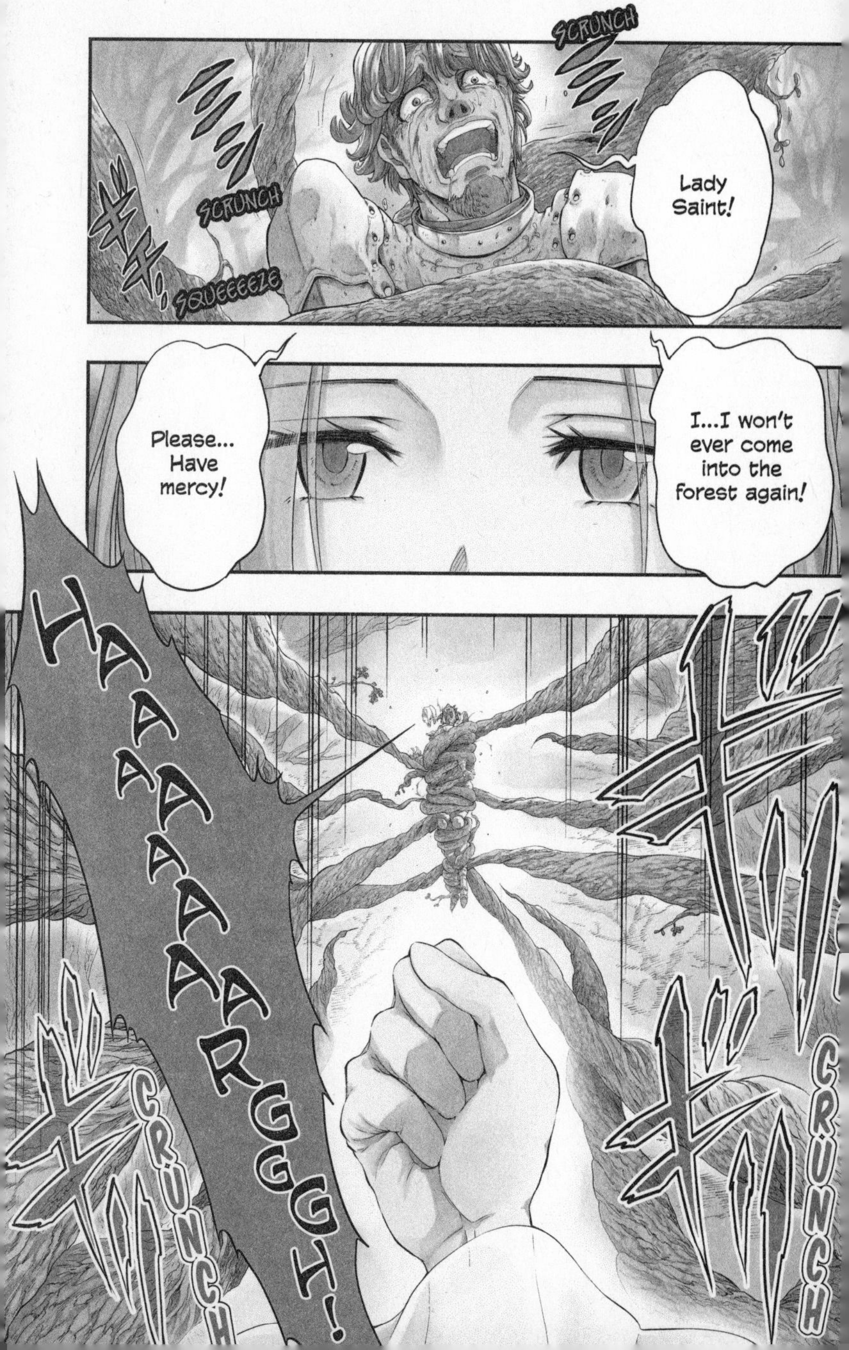
SCRUNCH
Lady Saint!
SCRUNCH
SQUEEEEZE
I...I won't ever come into the forest again!
Please... Have mercy!
HAAAAAAARGGGH!
CRUNCH
CRUNCH

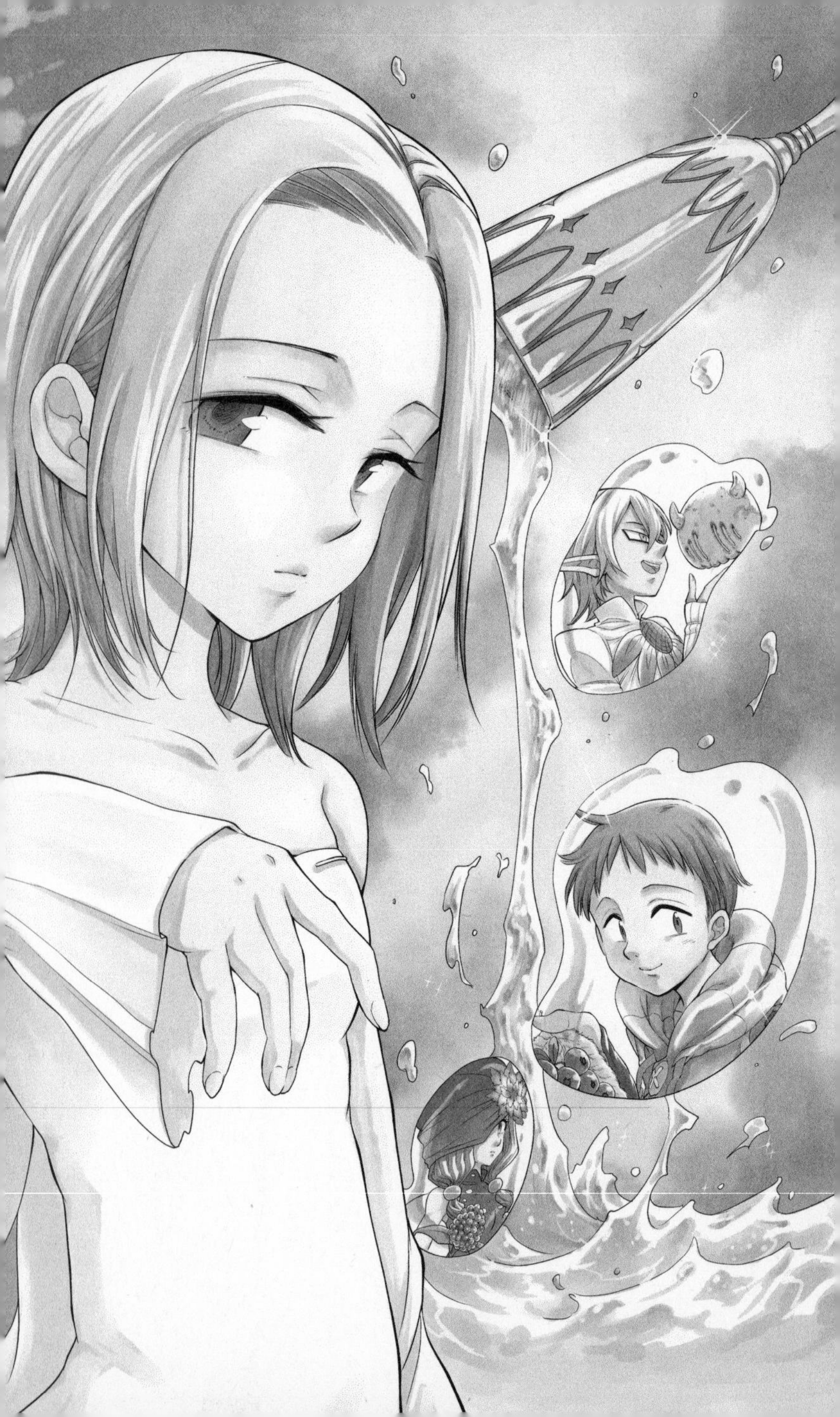

Chapter 1
Seven Hundred Years of Solitude

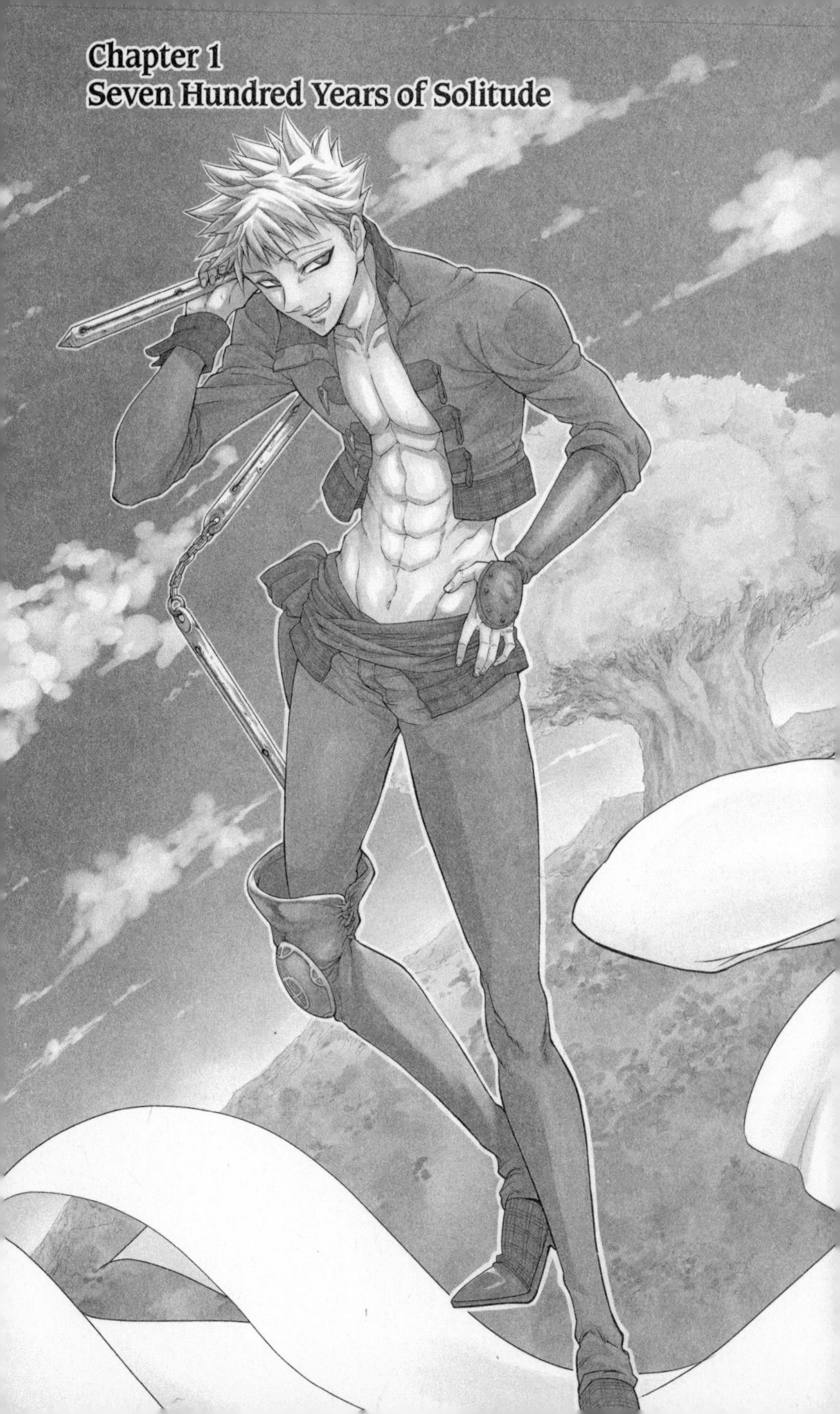

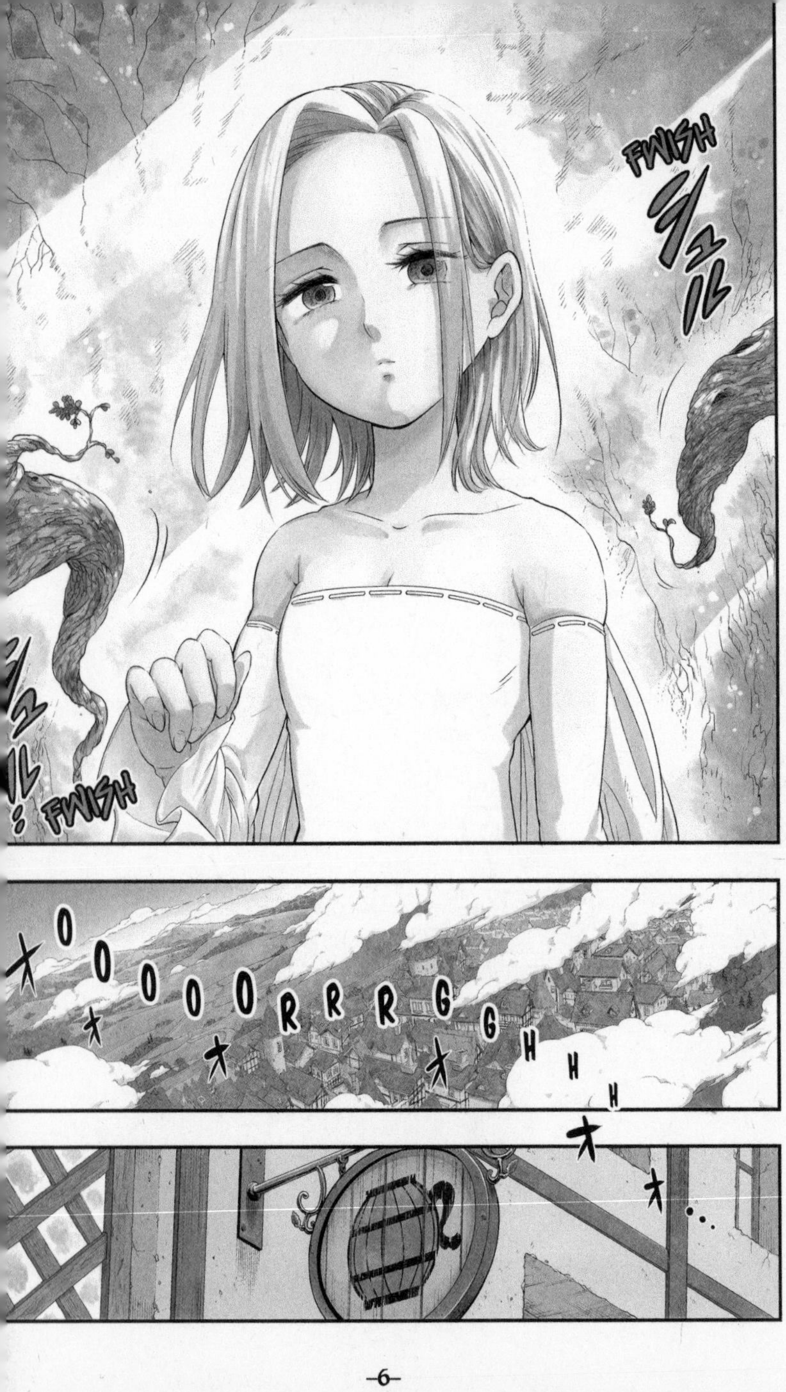
FWISH
シュル
シュル
FWISH
OOOOORRRGGHHH
オオオオオ
オ…

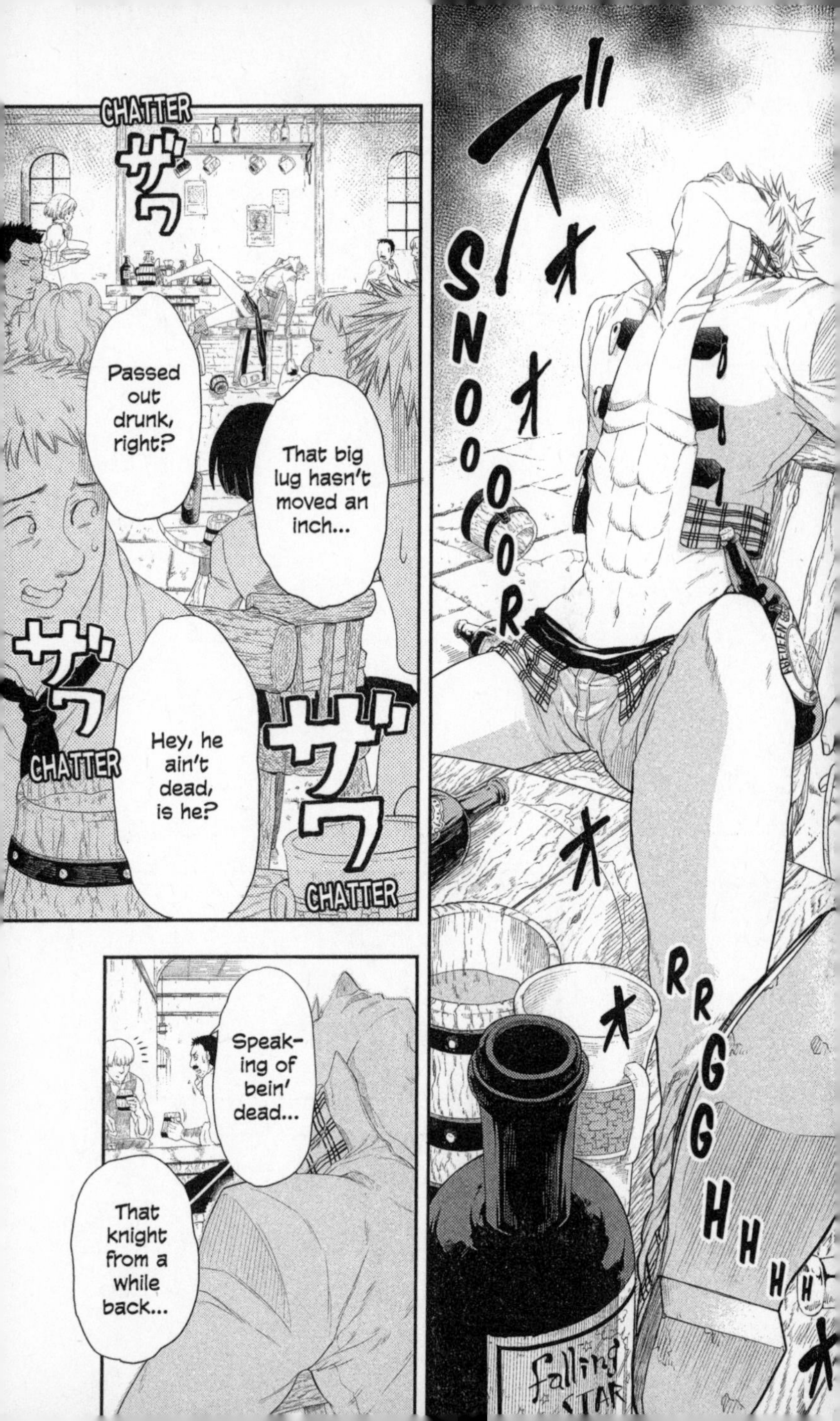
ズオオオ
SNOOOOR
オオ
RRGGHHHH
CHATTER
ザワ
Passed out drunk, right?
That big lug hasn't moved an inch...
ザワ
CHATTER
Hey, he ain't dead, is he?
ザワ
CHATTER
Speak-ing of bein' dead...
That knight from a while back...
Falling STAR

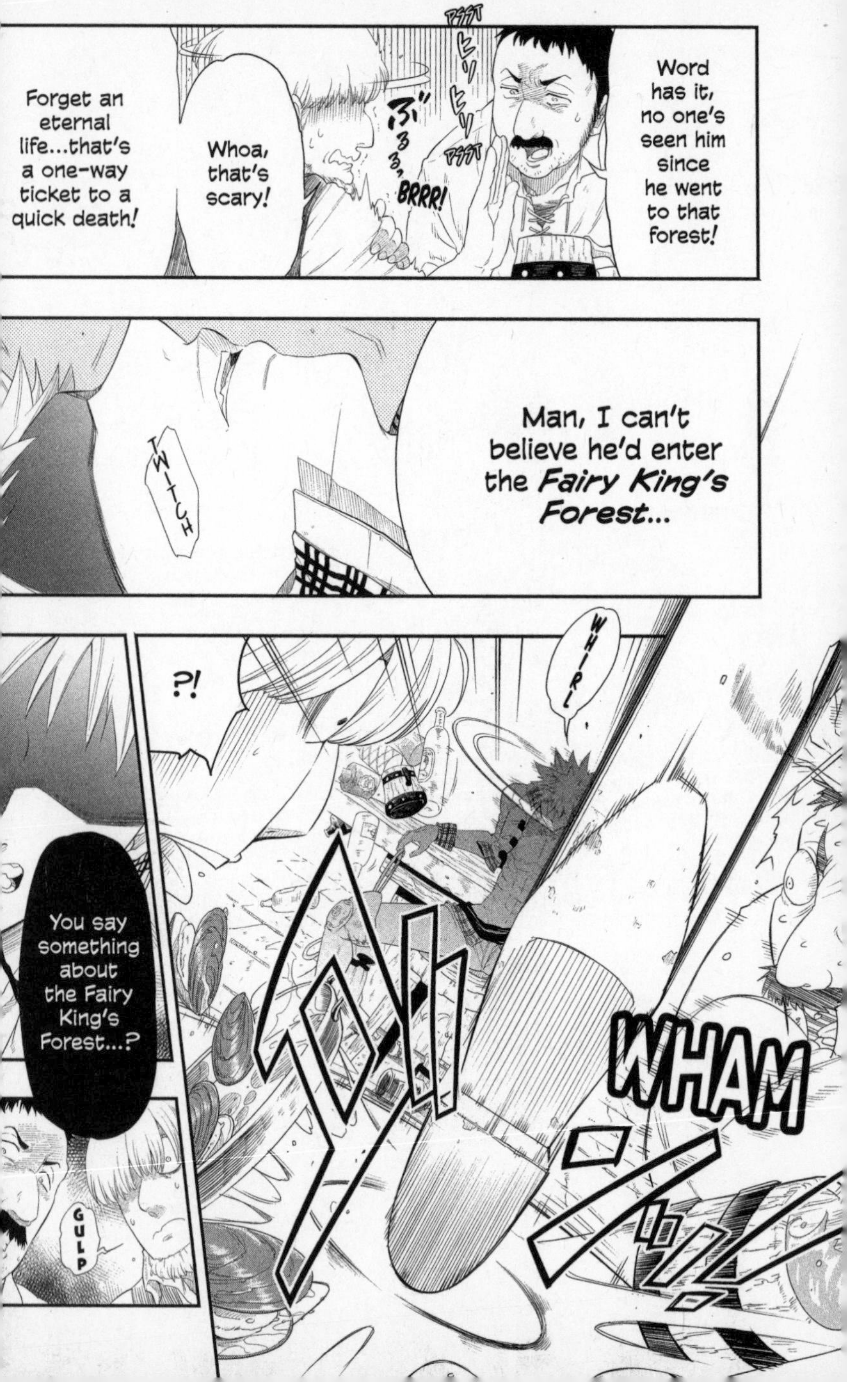
Word has it, no one's seen him since he went to that forest!
PSST
ヒソ
ヒソ
PSST
ぶるるっ
BRRR!
Whoa, that's scary!
Forget an eternal life...that's a one-way ticket to a quick death!
Man, I can't believe he'd enter the *Fairy King's Forest*...
TWITCH
WHIRL
?!
WHAM
You say something about the Fairy King's Forest...?
GULP

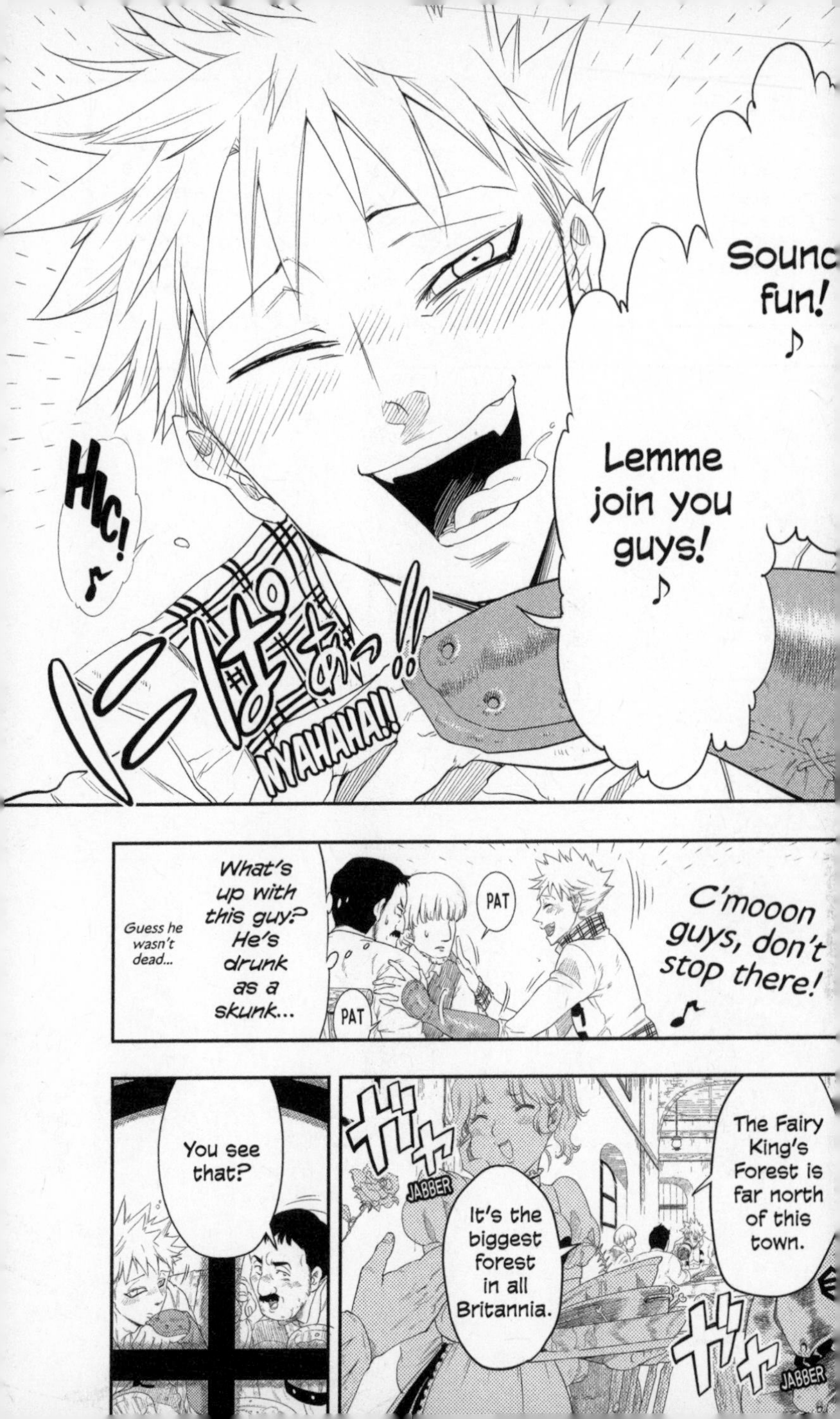
Sounc fun! ♪
Lemme join you guys! ♪
HIC! ♪
MYAHAHA!!
C'mooon guys, don't stop there! ♪
PAT
PAT
What's up with this guy? He's drunk as a skunk...
Guess he wasn't dead...
The Fairy King's Forest is far north of this town.
JABBER
It's the biggest forest in all Britannia.
JABBER
You see that?

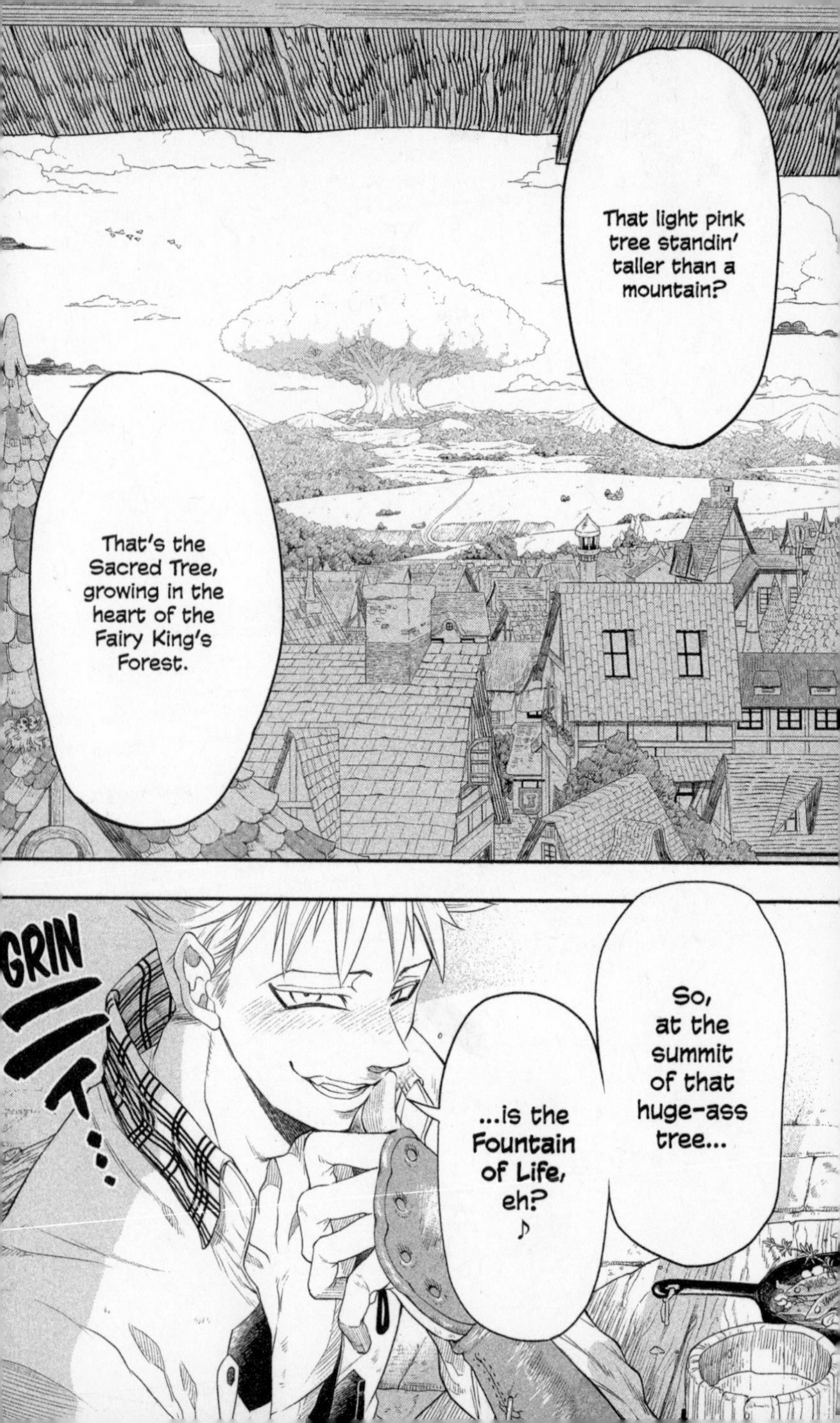
That light pink tree standin' taller than a mountain?
That's the Sacred Tree, growing in the heart of the Fairy King's Forest.
So, at the summit of that huge-ass tree...
...is the Fountain of Life, eh? ♪
GRIN...

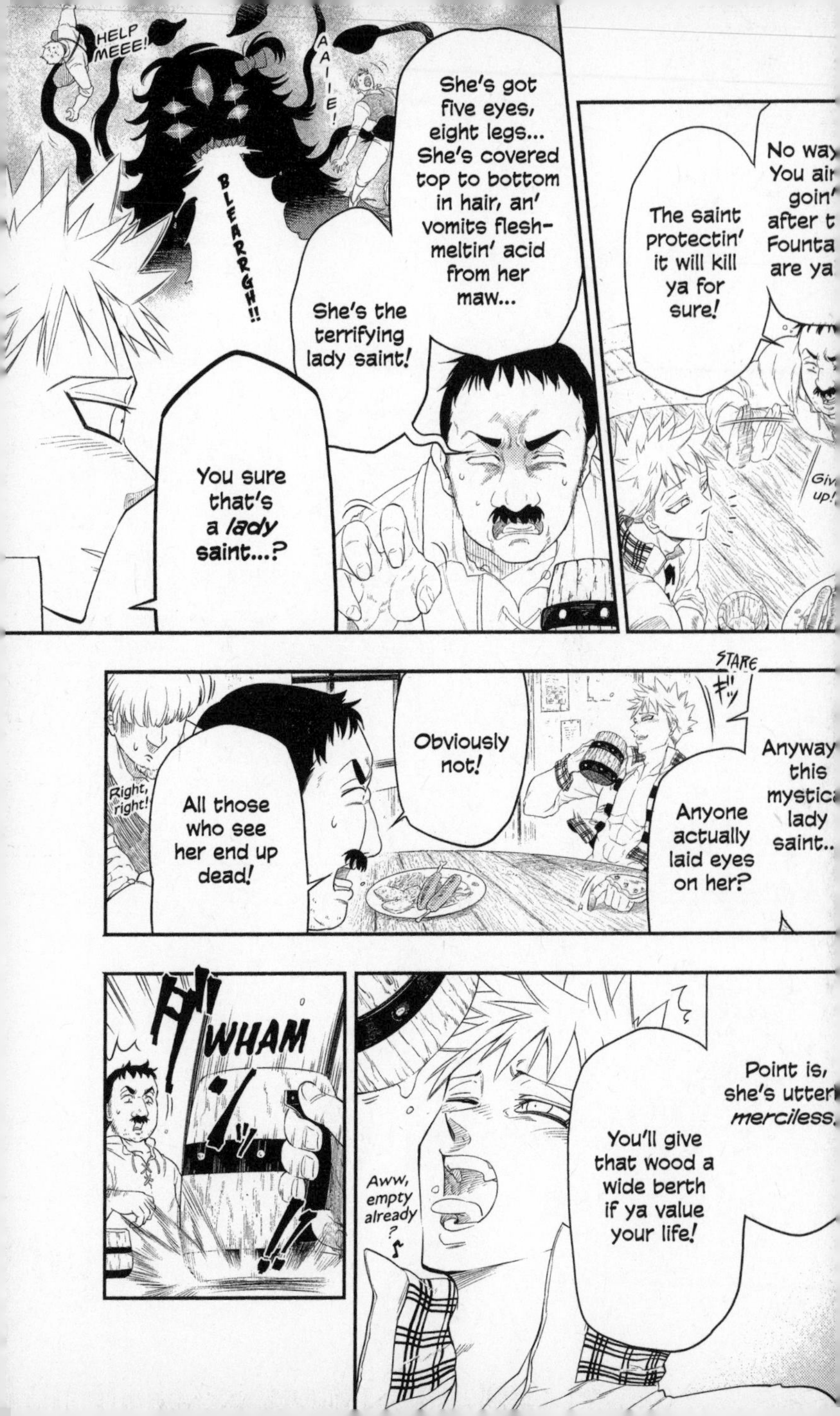
No way
You air
goin'
after t
Founta
are ya
The saint protectin' it will kill ya for sure!
Giv up!
She's got five eyes, eight legs... She's covered top to bottom in hair, an' vomits flesh-meltin' acid from her maw...
HELP MEEE!
AAIIE!
BLEARRGH!!
She's the terrifying lady saint!
You sure that's a *lady* saint...?
STARE
Anyway this mystic lady saint..
Anyone actually laid eyes on her?
Obviously not!
All those who see her end up dead!
Right, right!
Point is, she's utter *merciless*.
You'll give that wood a wide berth if ya value your life!
Aww, empty already?
WHAM

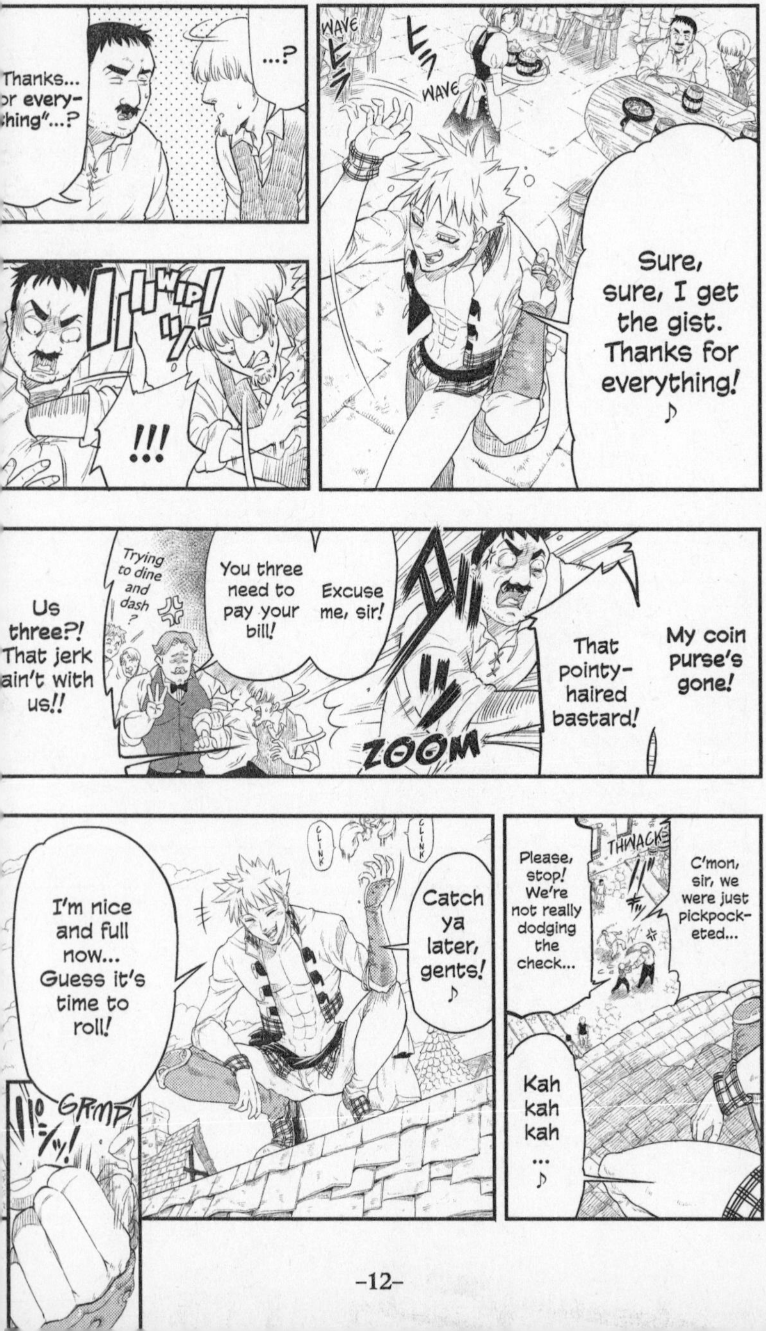
WAVE
WAVE
Sure, sure, I get the gist. Thanks for everything! ♪
Thanks... or every-hing"...?
...?
WIP!
!!!
My coin purse's gone!
That pointy-haired bastard!
ZOOM
Excuse me, sir!
You three need to pay your bill!
Trying to dine and dash?
Us three?! That jerk ain't with us!!
THWACK
C'mon, sir, we were just pickpocketed...
Please, stop! We're not really dodging the check...
Kah kah kah ... ♪
CLINK
CLINK
Catch ya later, gents! ♪
I'm nice and full now... Guess it's time to roll!
GRMP

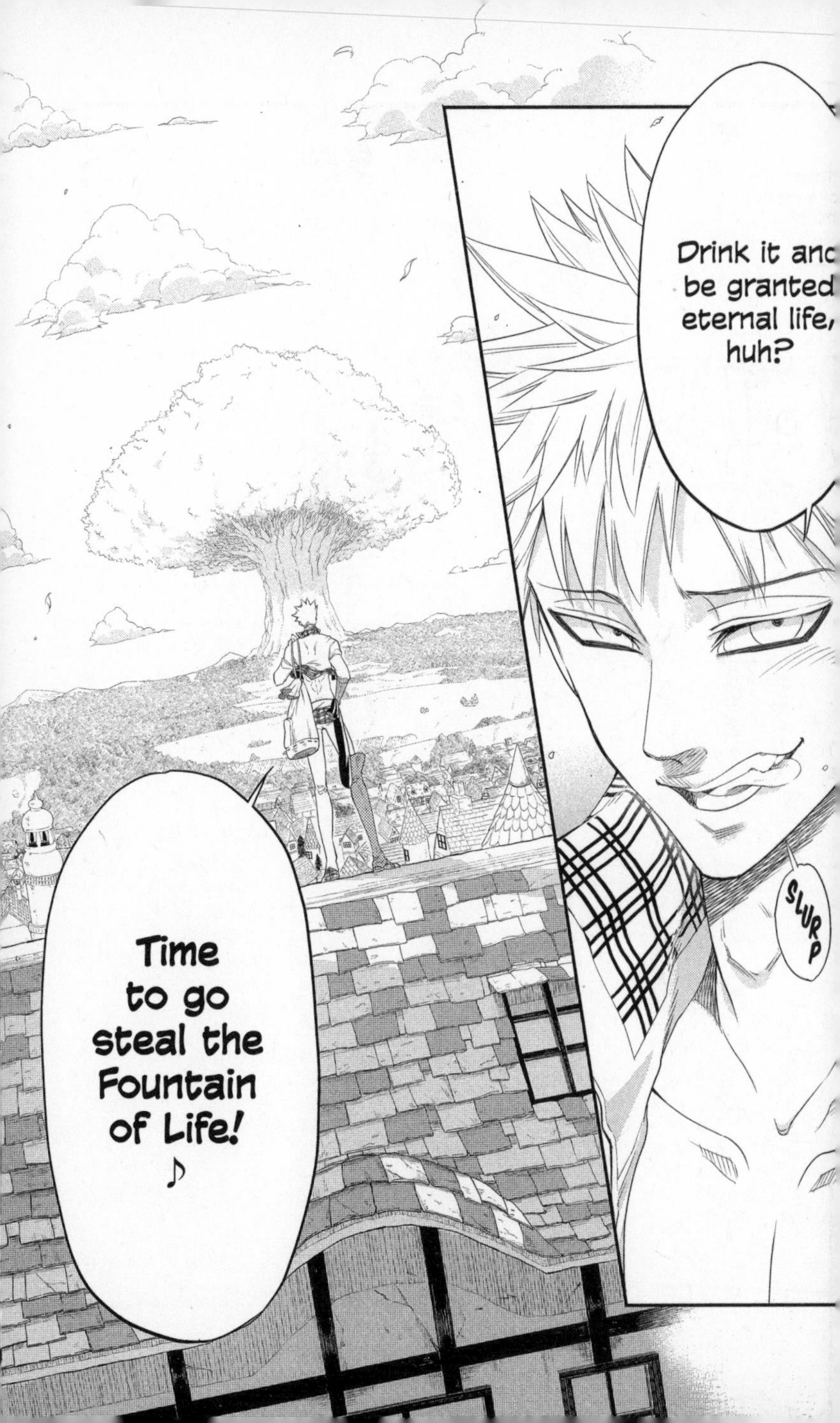
Drink it and be granted eternal life, huh?
SLURP
Time to go steal the Fountain of Life! ♪

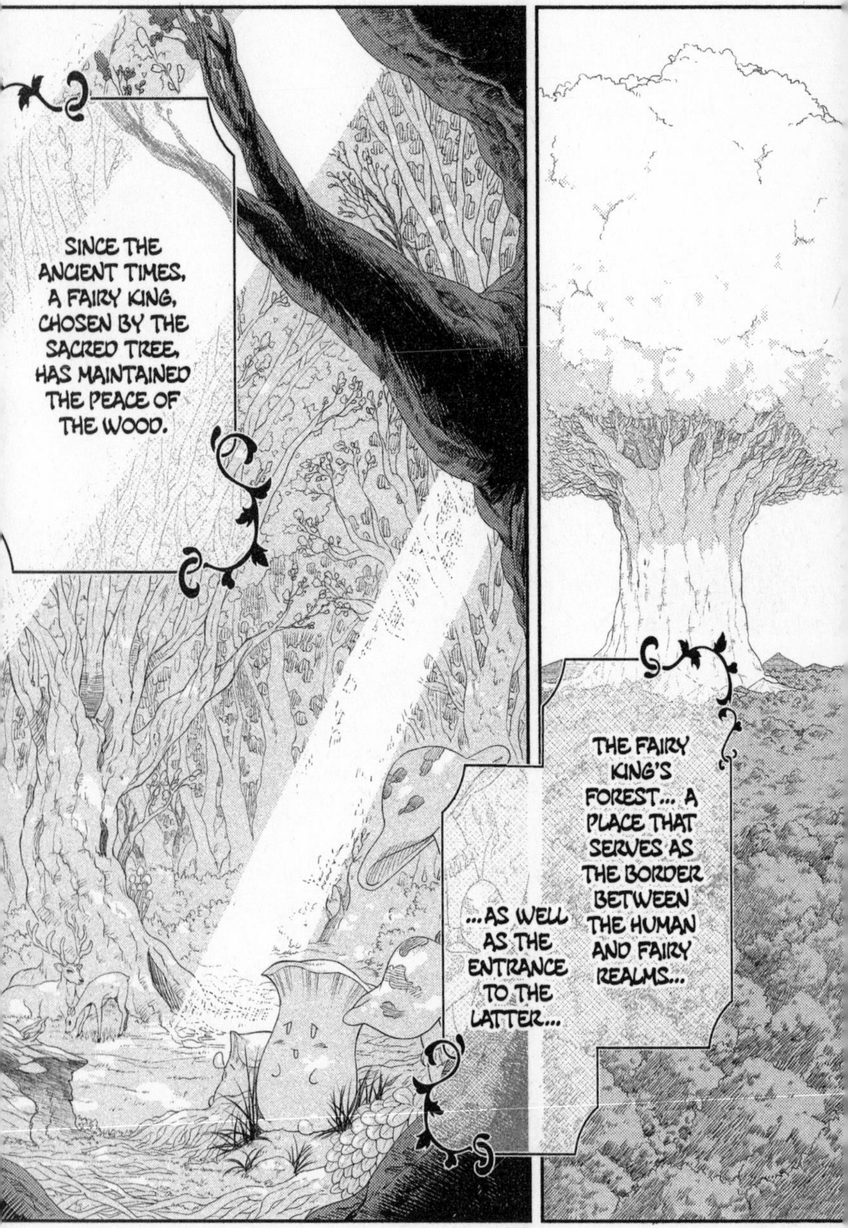
THE FAIRY KING'S FOREST... A PLACE THAT SERVES AS THE BORDER BETWEEN THE HUMAN AND FAIRY REALMS...
...AS WELL AS THE ENTRANCE TO THE LATTER...
SINCE THE ANCIENT TIMES, A FAIRY KING, CHOSEN BY THE SACRED TREE, HAS MAINTAINED THE PEACE OF THE WOOD.

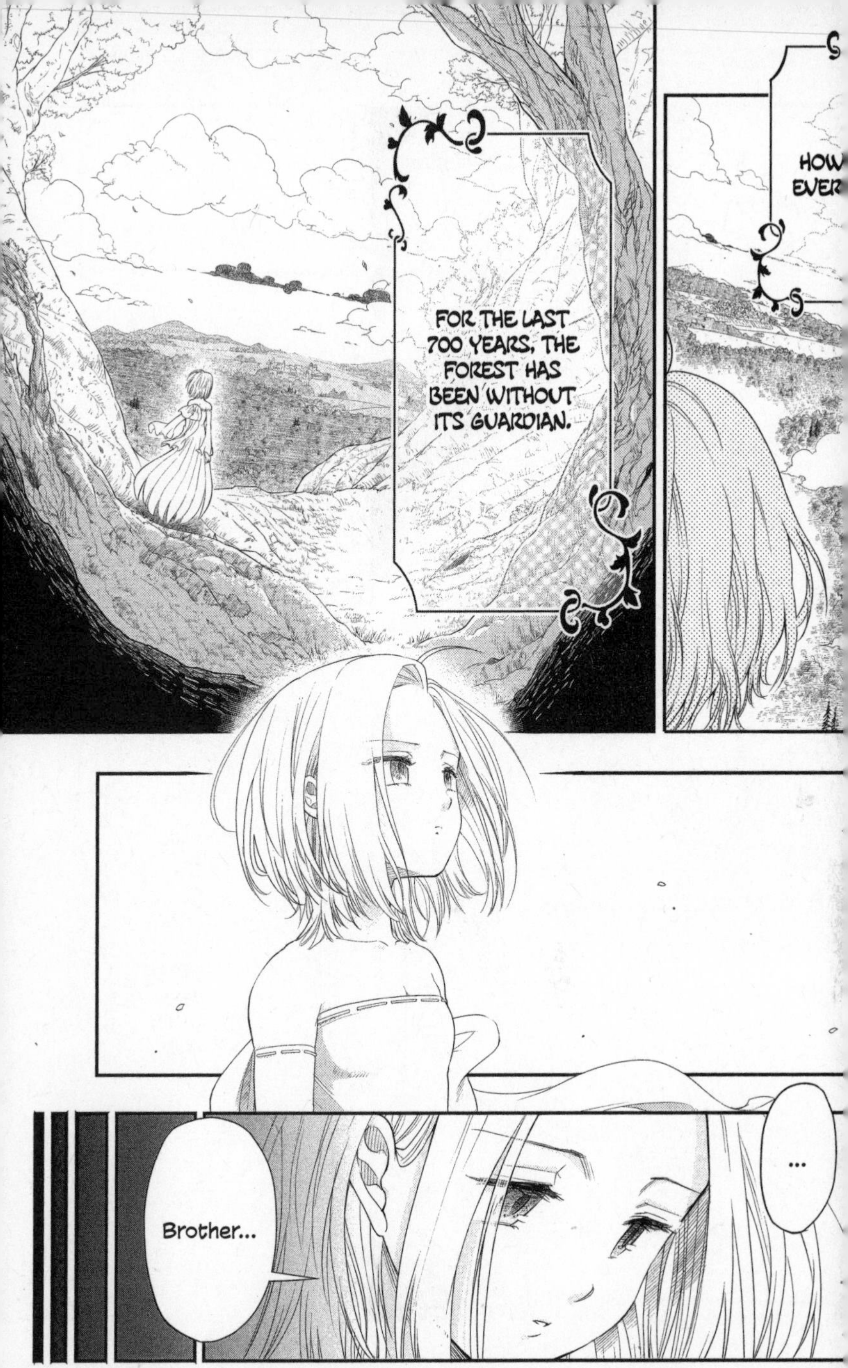
HOW EVER
FOR THE LAST 700 YEARS, THE FOREST HAS BEEN WITHOUT ITS GUARDIAN.
...
Brother...

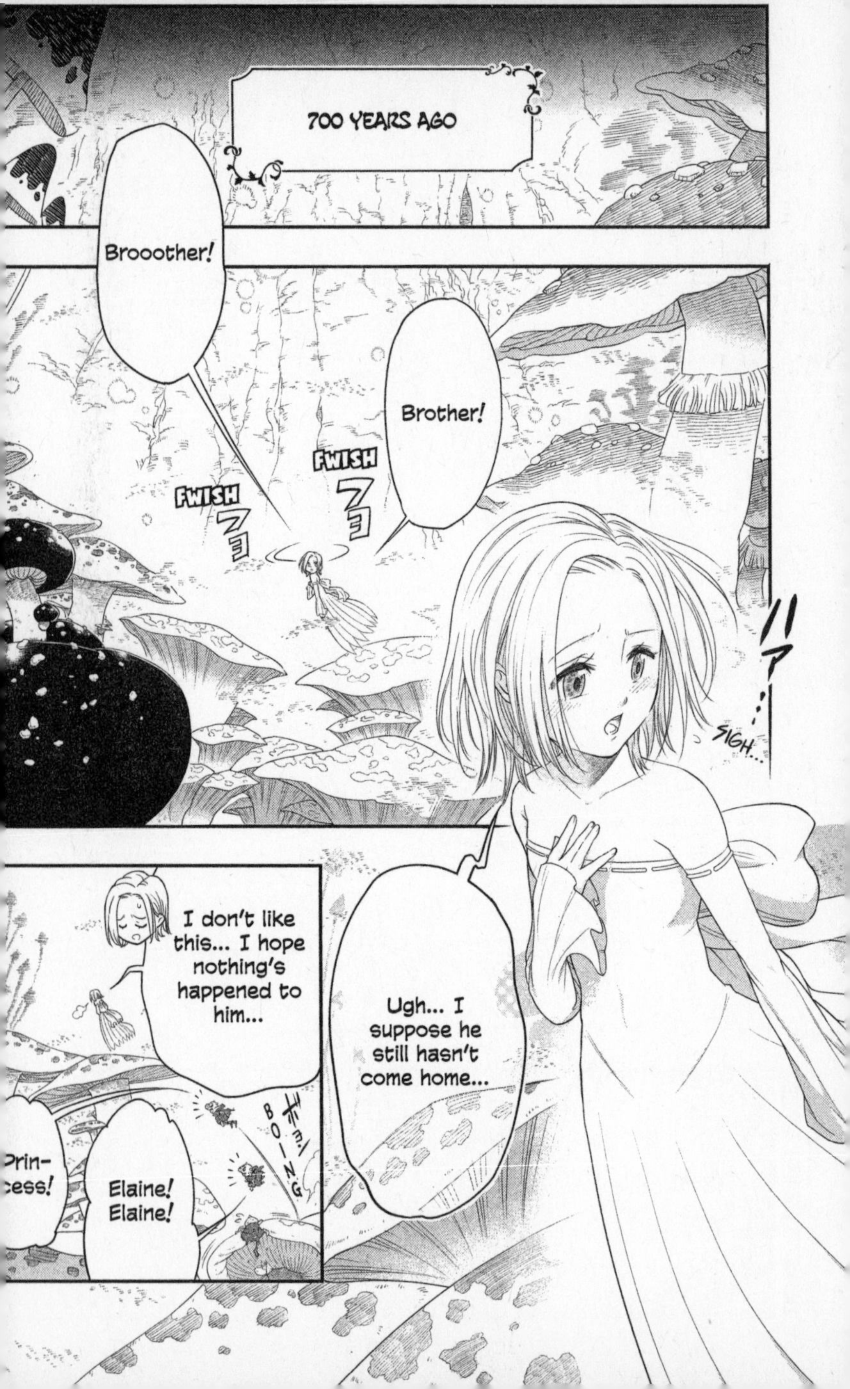
700 YEARS AGO
Brooother!
Brother!
FWISH フヨ
FWISH フヨ
ハア… SIGH...
Ugh... I suppose he still hasn't come home...
I don't like this... I hope nothing's happened to him...
Elaine! Elaine!
Prin-cess!
ボヨ BOING

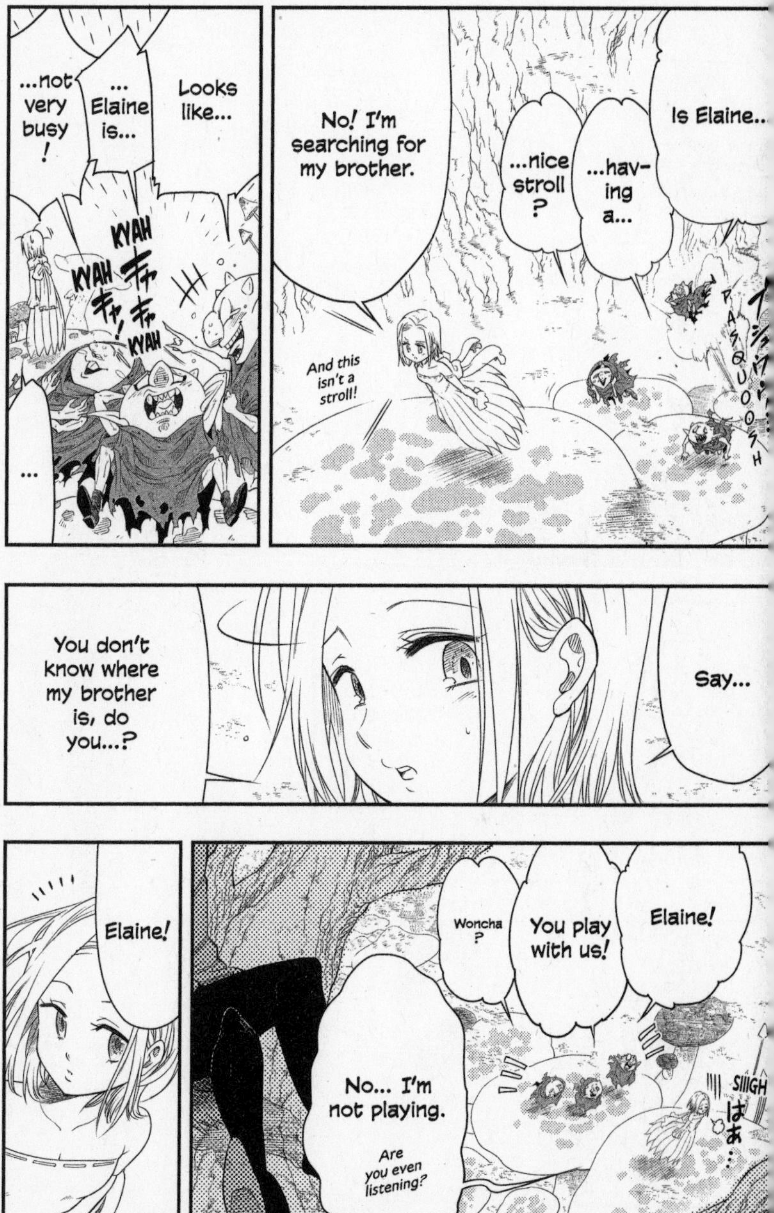

Is Elaine...
...hav-ing a...
...nice stroll?
PASQUOOOSH
No! I'm searching for my brother.
And this isn't a stroll!
Looks like...
...Elaine is...
...not very busy!
KYAH
KYAH
KYAH
...
Say...
You don't know where my brother is, do you...?
Elaine!
You play with us!
Woncha?
SIIGH
No... I'm not playing.
Are you even listening?
Elaine!

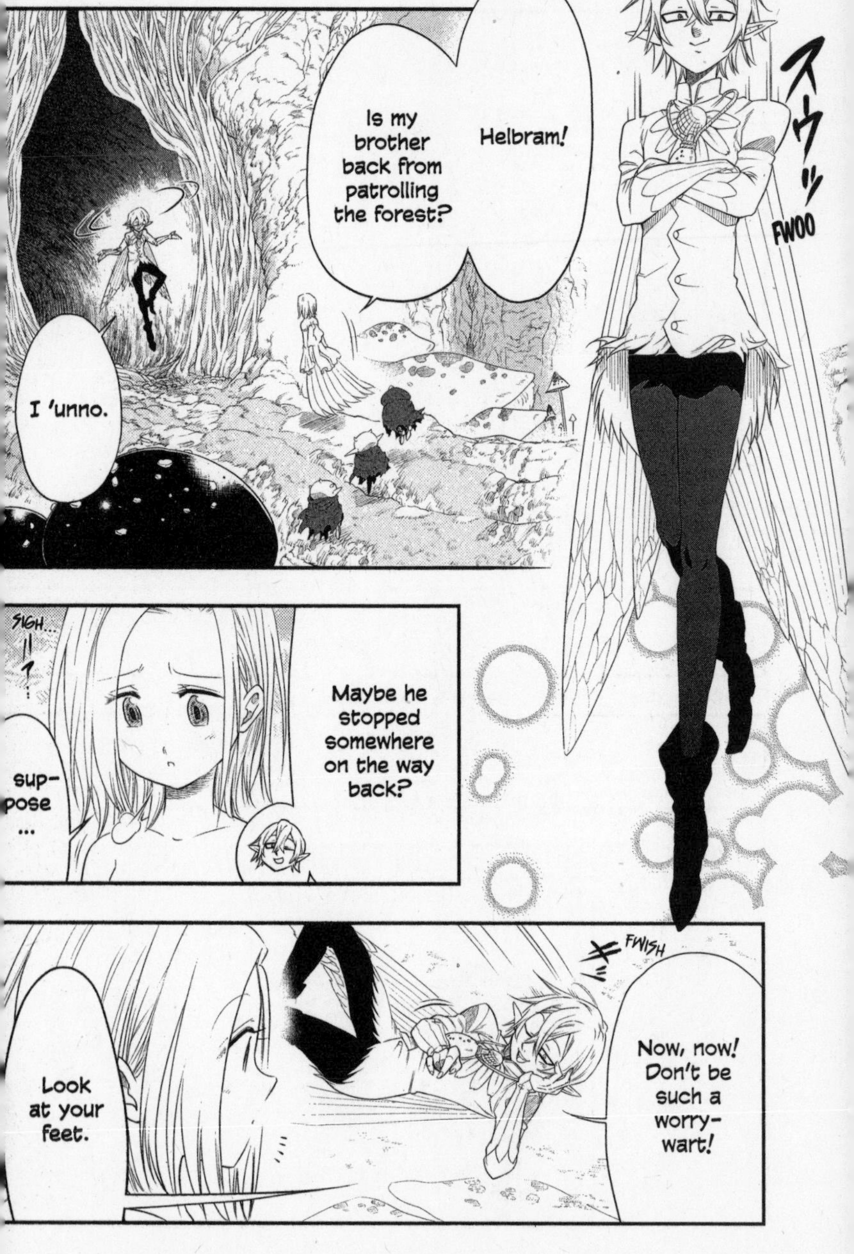
スーウッ
FWOO
Helbram!
Is my brother back from patrolling the forest?
I 'unno.
Maybe he stopped somewhere on the way back?
SIGH...
sup- pose ...
FWISH
Now, now! Don't be such a worry-wart!
Look at your feet.

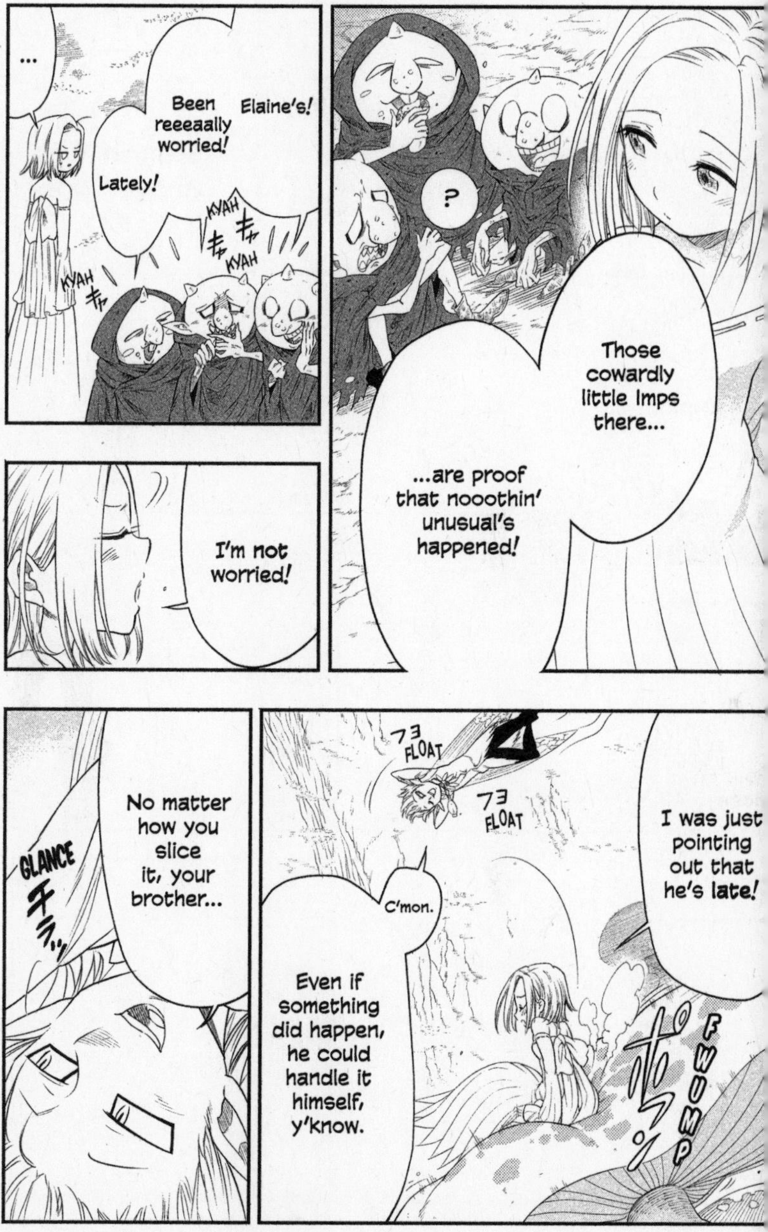
?
Those cowardly little Imps there...
...are proof that nooothin' unusual's happened!
...
Elaine's!
Been reeeaally worried!
Lately!
KYAH
KYAH
KYAH
I'm not worried!
I was just pointing out that he's late!
FLOAT
FLOAT
FWUMP
C'mon.
Even if something did happen, he could handle it himself, y'know.
GLANCE
No matter how you slice it, your brother...

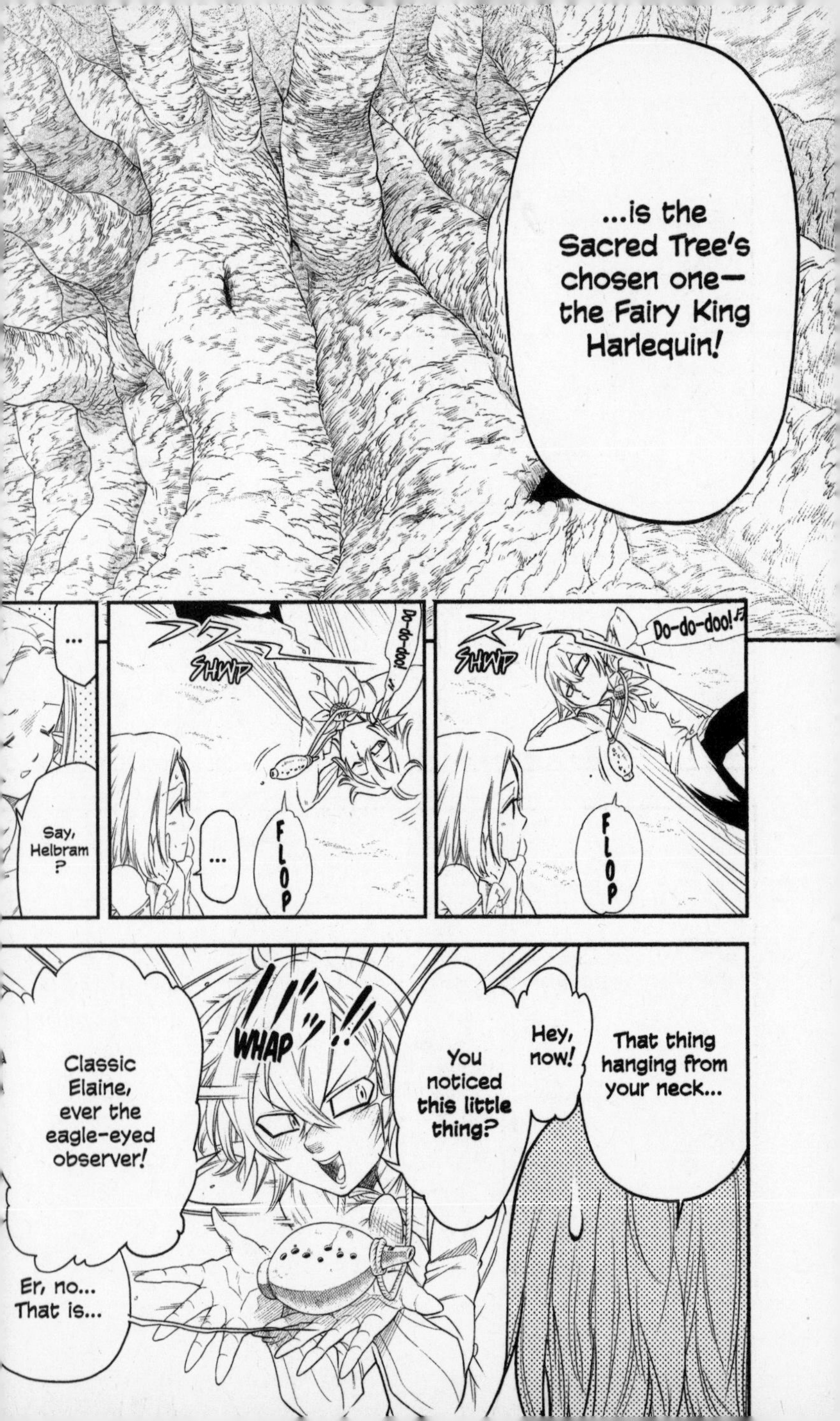
...is the Sacred Tree's chosen one— the Fairy King Harlequin!
Do-do-doo!
SHWP
FLOP
Do-do-doo!
SHWP
...
FLOP
...
Say, Helbram?
That thing hanging from your neck...
Hey, now!
You noticed this little thing?
WHAP
Classic Elaine, ever the eagle-eyed observer!
Er, no... That is...

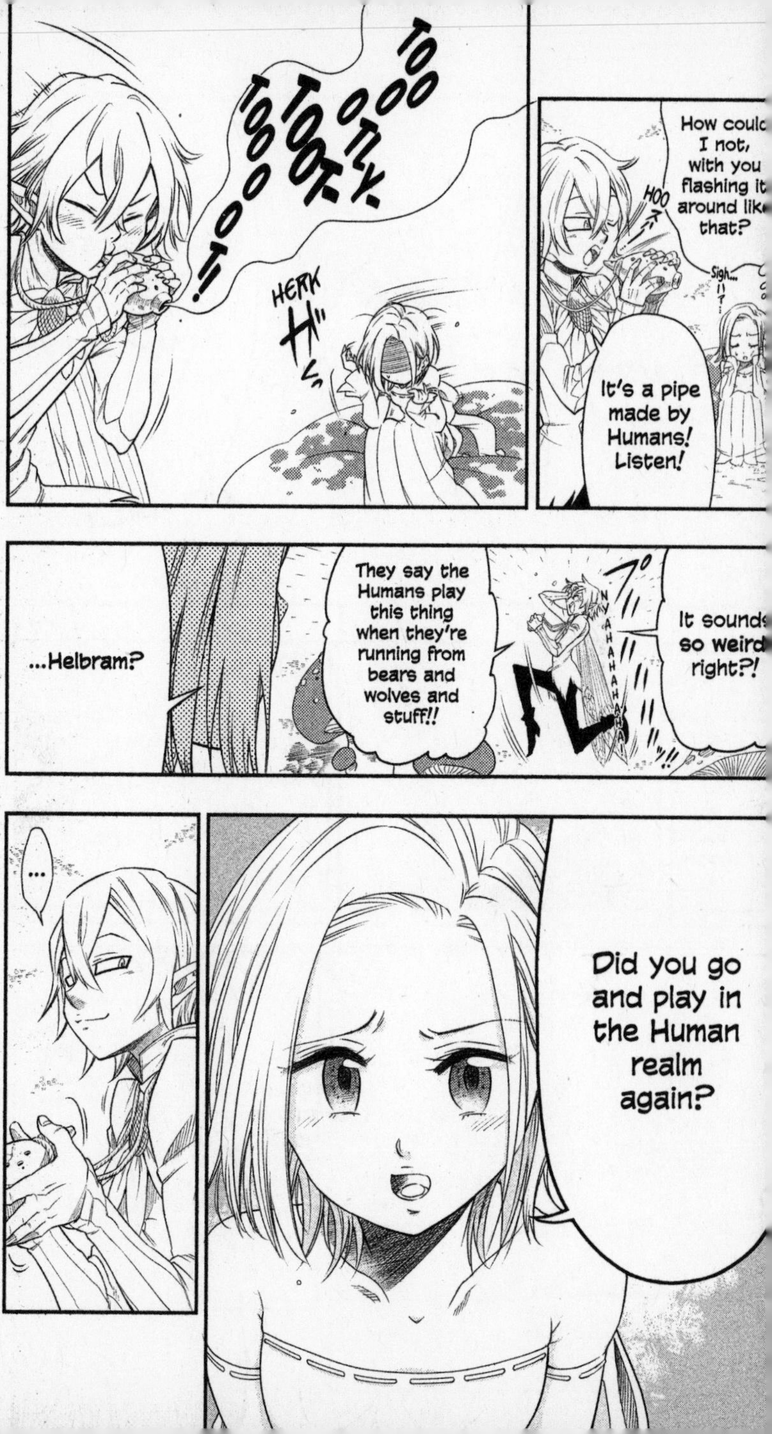

How could I not, with you flashing it around like that?
HOO
Sigh...
It's a pipe made by Humans! Listen!
TOOOOTLY
TOOOT
TOOOOT!!
HERK
They say the Humans play this thing when they're running from bears and wolves and stuff!!
It sounds so weird right?!
...Helbram?
...
Did you go and play in the Human realm again?

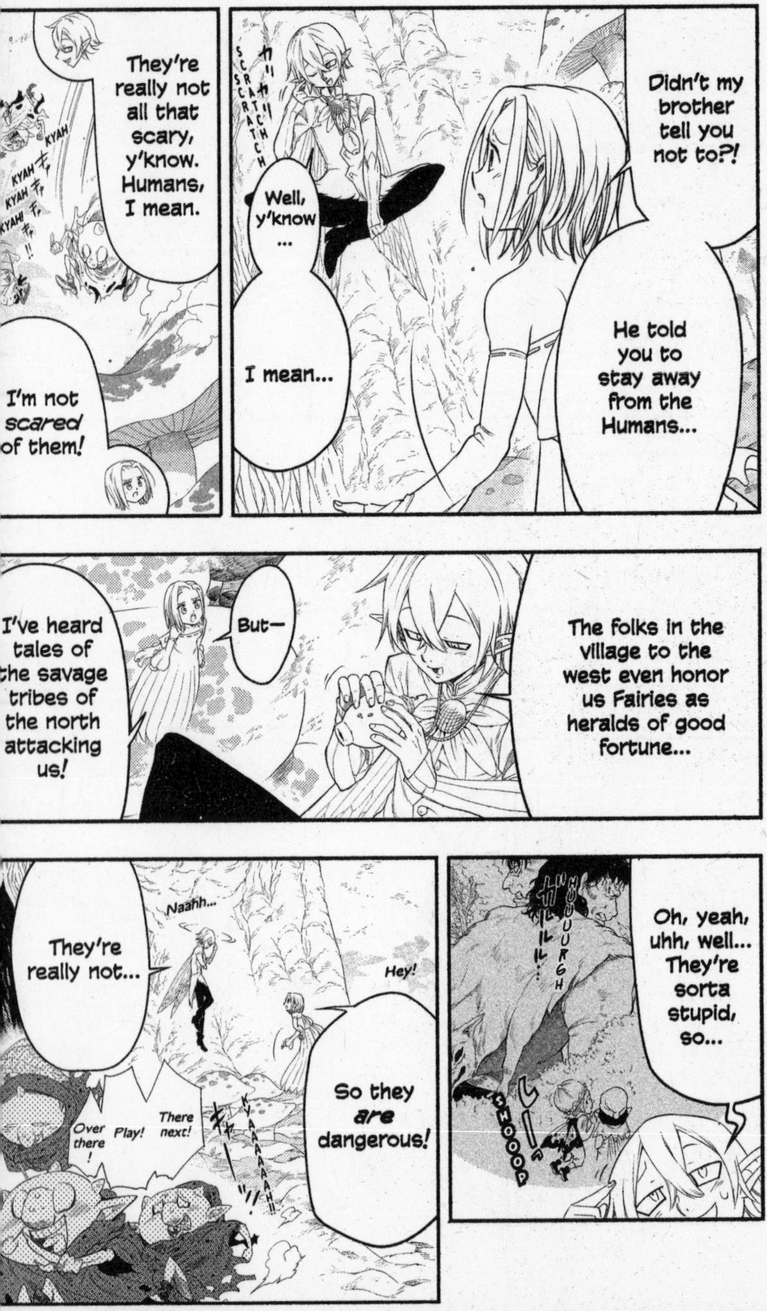
Didn't my brother tell you not to?!
SCRATCH SCRATCH
Well, y'know...
He told you to stay away from the Humans...
I mean...
They're really not all that scary, y'know. Humans, I mean.
KYAH
KYAH KYAH KYAH!
I'm not *scared* of them!
The folks in the village to the west even honor us Fairies as heralds of good fortune...
But—
I've heard tales of the savage tribes of the north attacking us!
Oh, yeah, uhh, well... They're sorta stupid, so...
HUUURGH
SHOOOOP
Hey!
So they *are* dangerous!
Naahh...
They're really not...
KYAAAAAAAH!!
There next!
Play!
Over there!

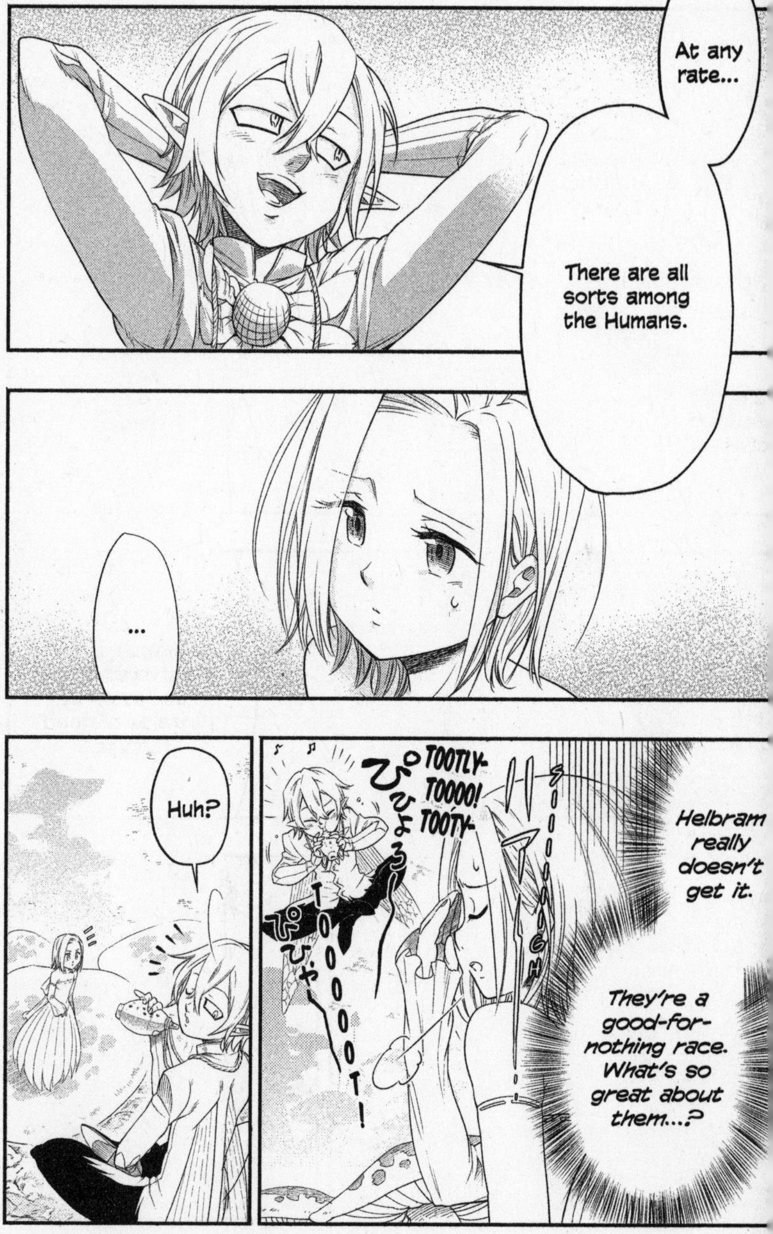
At any rate...
There are all sorts among the Humans.
...
Helbram really doesn't get it.
They're a good-for-nothing race. What's so great about them...?
SIIIIIIIGH
TOOTLY-TOOOO! TOOTY-
TOOOOOOOT!
ぴひょろ～
ぷひゃ～
Huh?

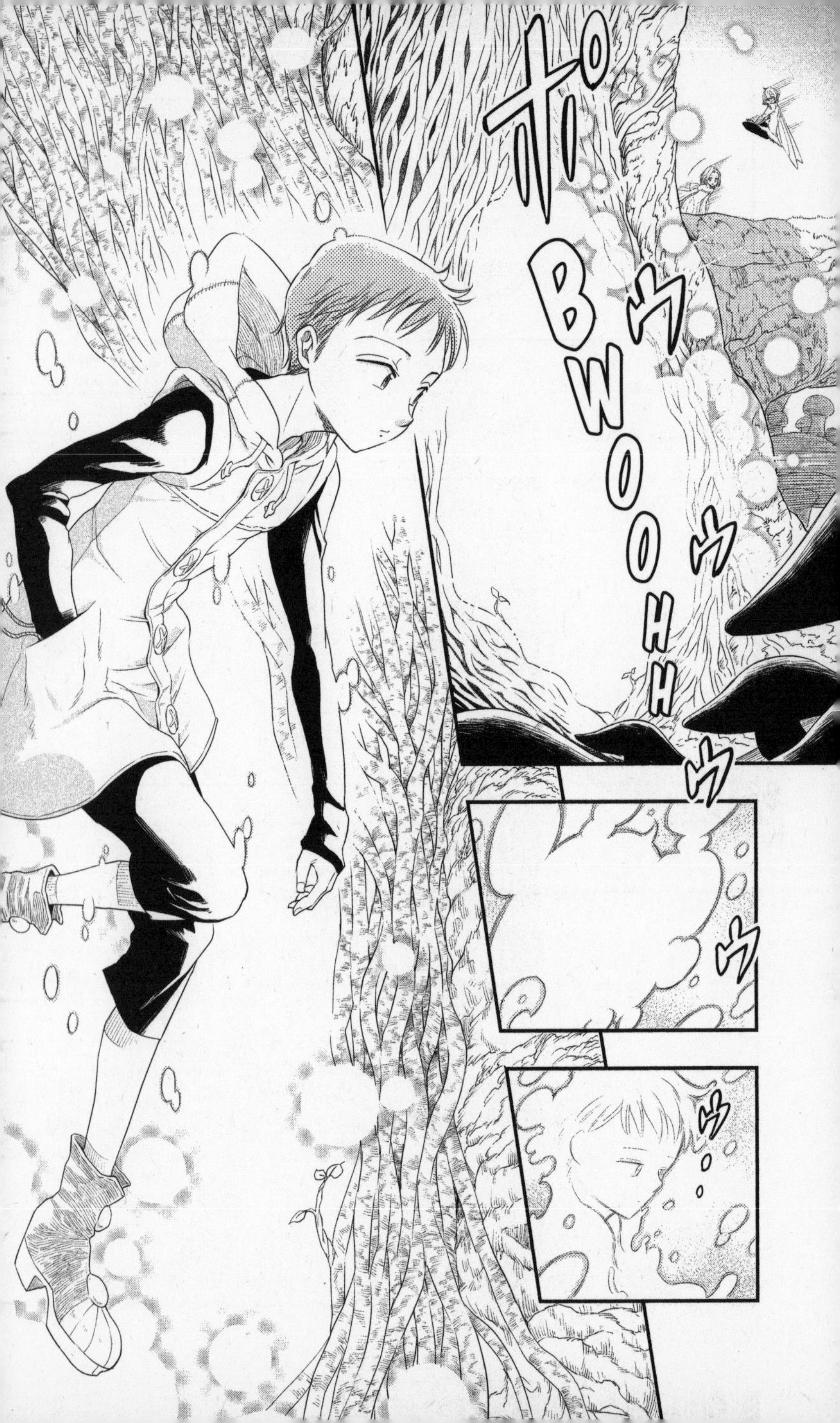
ポ
BWOOHH
ウウウウウ

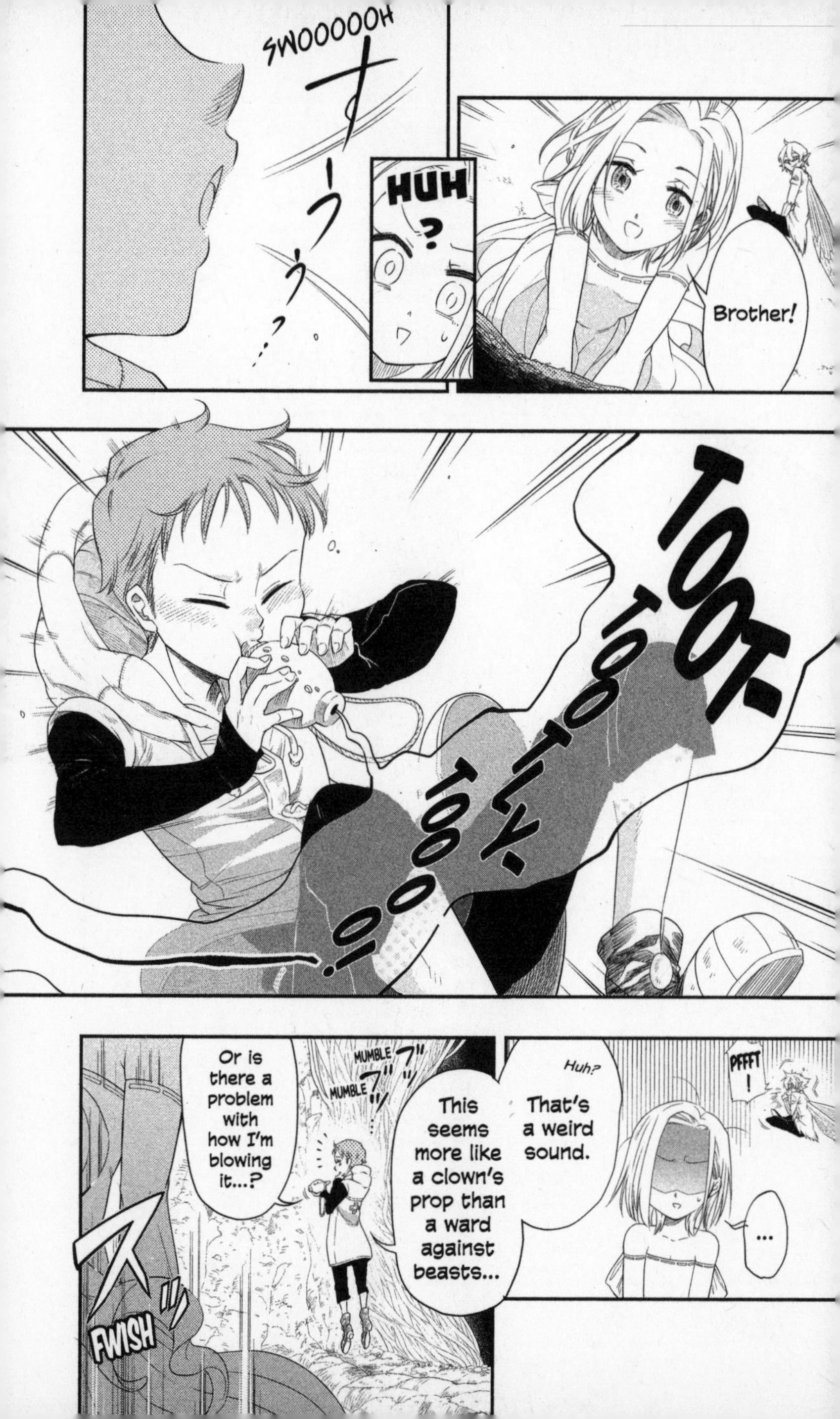
Brother!
HUH
?
SWOOOOOH
TOOT-
TOOTLY
TOOOOO!
PFFFT
!
Huh?
That's a weird sound.
...
This seems more like a clown's prop than a ward against beasts...
MUMBLE
MUMBLE
Or is there a problem with how I'm blowing it...?
FWISH

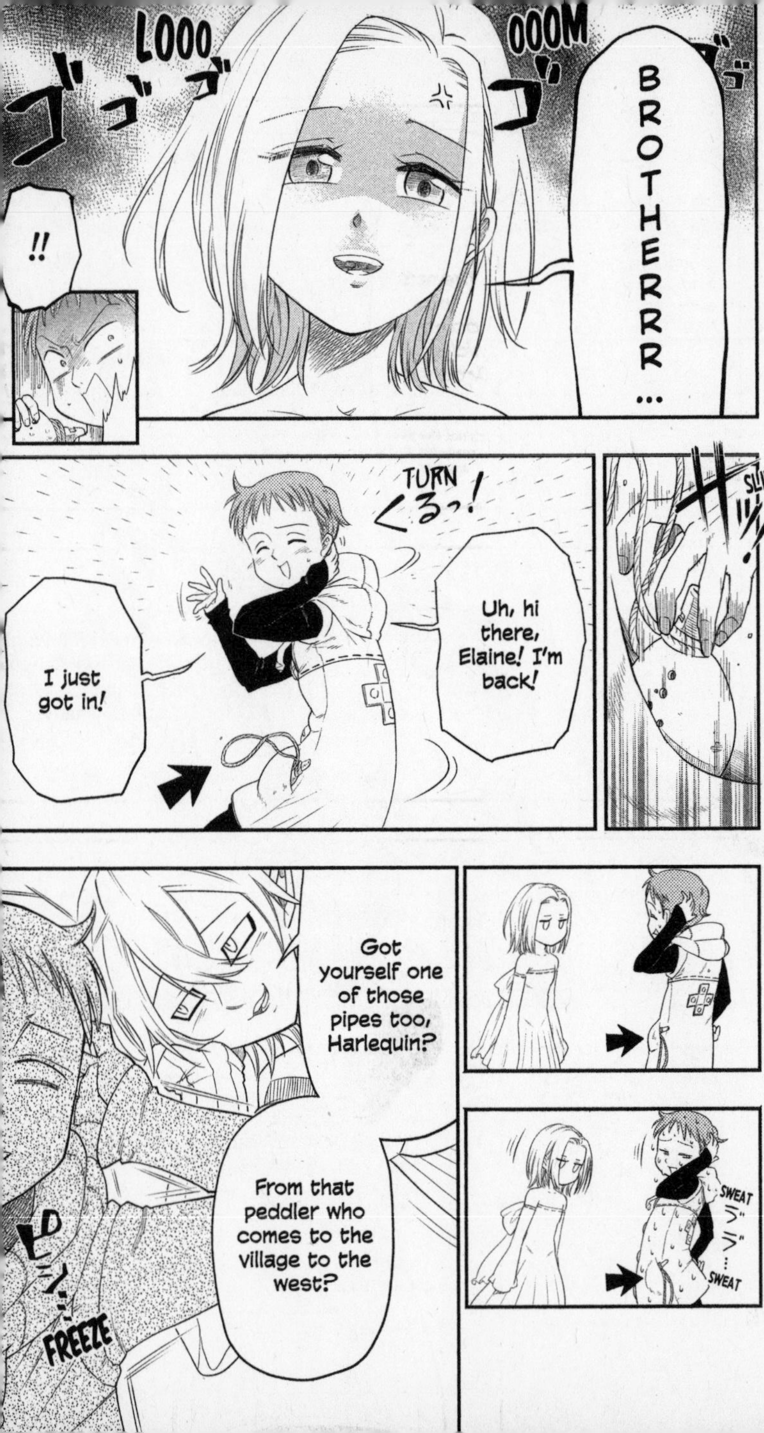
OOOM
ゴゴ
BROTHERRR...
LOOO
ゴゴゴ
!!
SLIP
TURN
くるっ!
Uh, hi there, Elaine! I'm back!
I just got in!
SWEAT
SWEAT
Got yourself one of those pipes too, Harlequin?
From that peddler who comes to the village to the west?
FREEZE

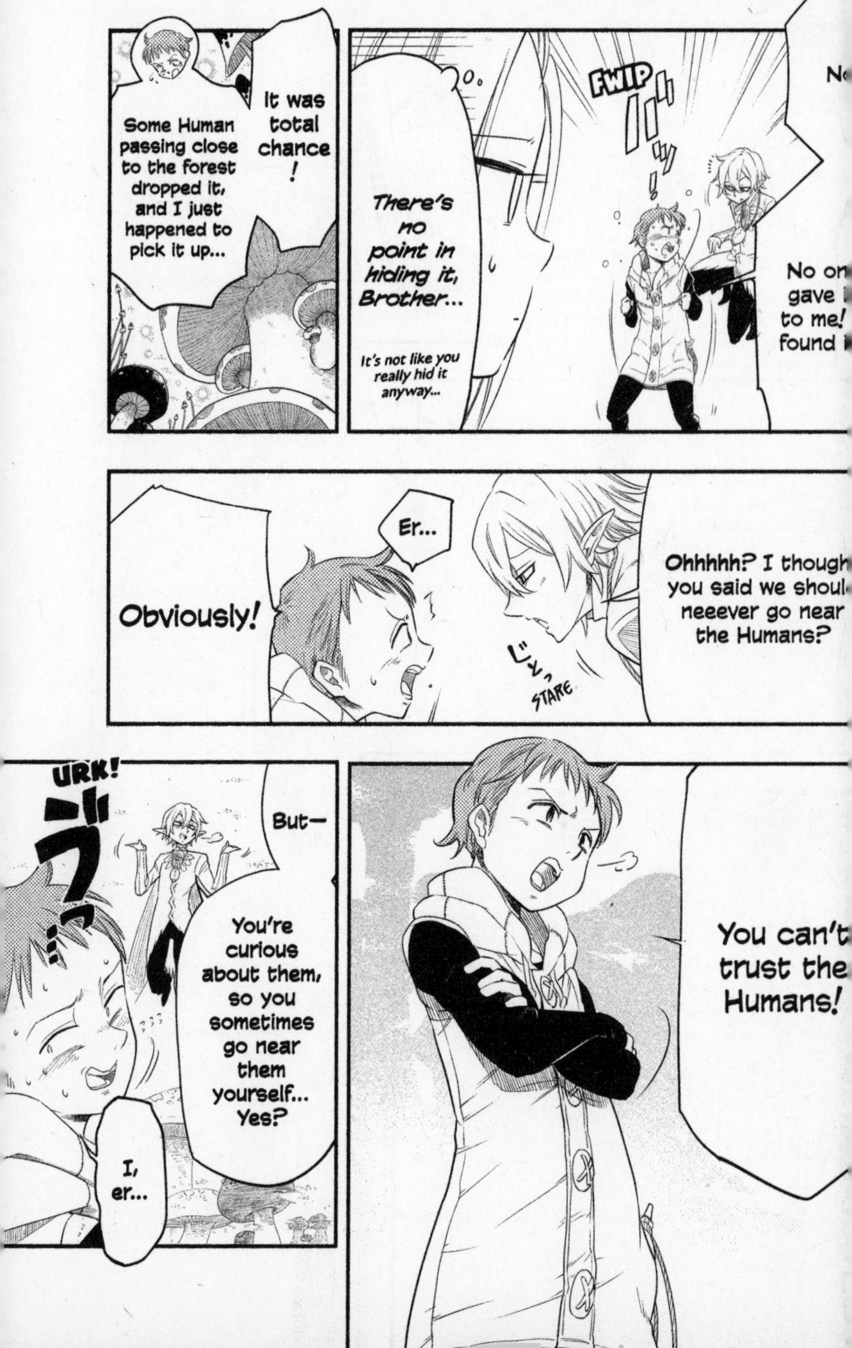
gave
to me!
found
FWIP
There's no point in hiding it, Brother...
It's not like you really hid it anyway...
It was total chance!
Some Human passing close to the forest dropped it, and I just happened to pick it up...
Ohhhhh? I though
you said we shoul
neeever go near the Humans?
STARE
Er...
Obviously!
You can't trust the Humans!
URK!
But—
You're curious about them, so you sometimes go near them yourself... Yes?
I, er...

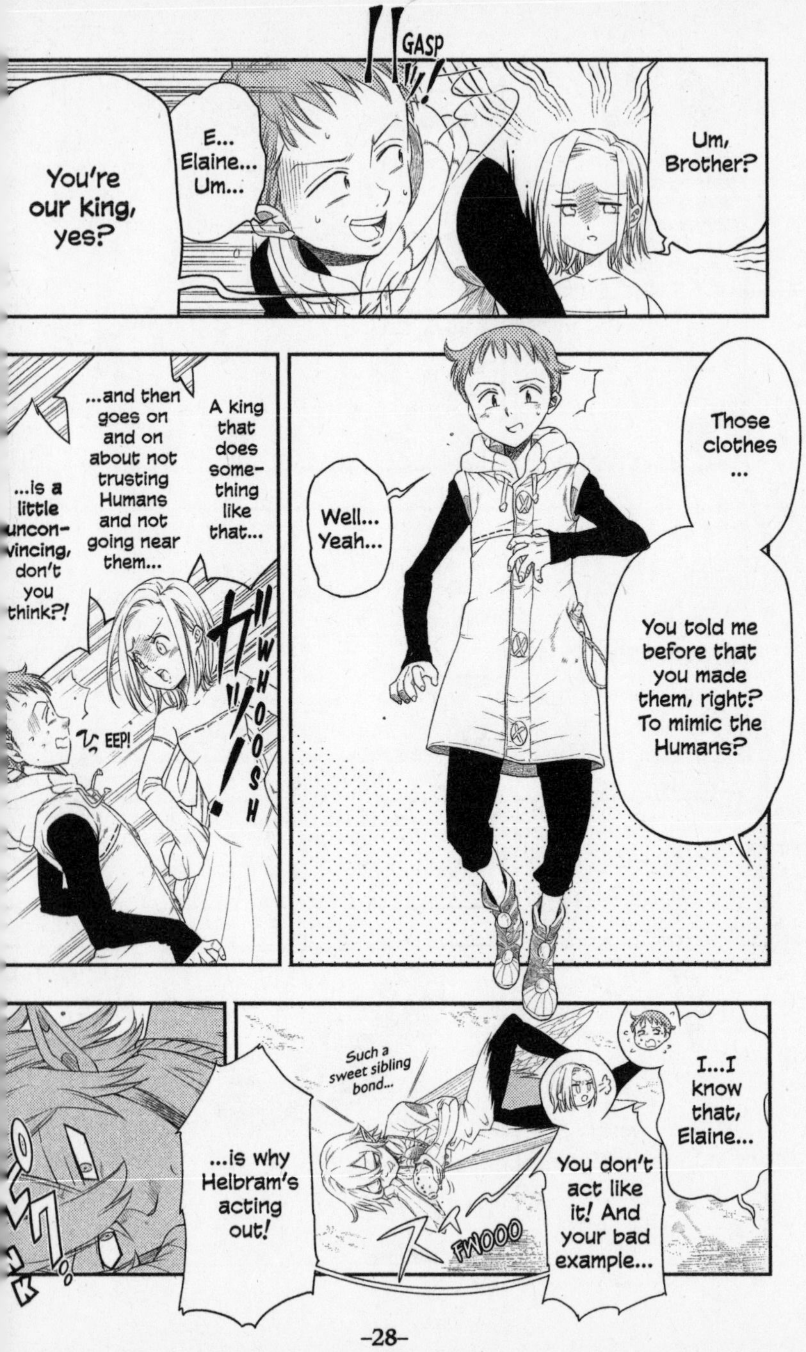

Um, Brother?
GASP
E... Elaine... Um...
You're our king, yes?
Those clothes ...
You told me before that you made them, right? To mimic the Humans?
Well... Yeah...
A king that does something like that...
...and then goes on and on about not trusting Humans and not going near them...
...is a little uncon-vincing, don't you think?!
WHOOSH
EEP!
I...I know that, Elaine...
You don't act like it! And your bad example...
Such a sweet sibling bond...
FWOOO
...is why Helbram's acting out!

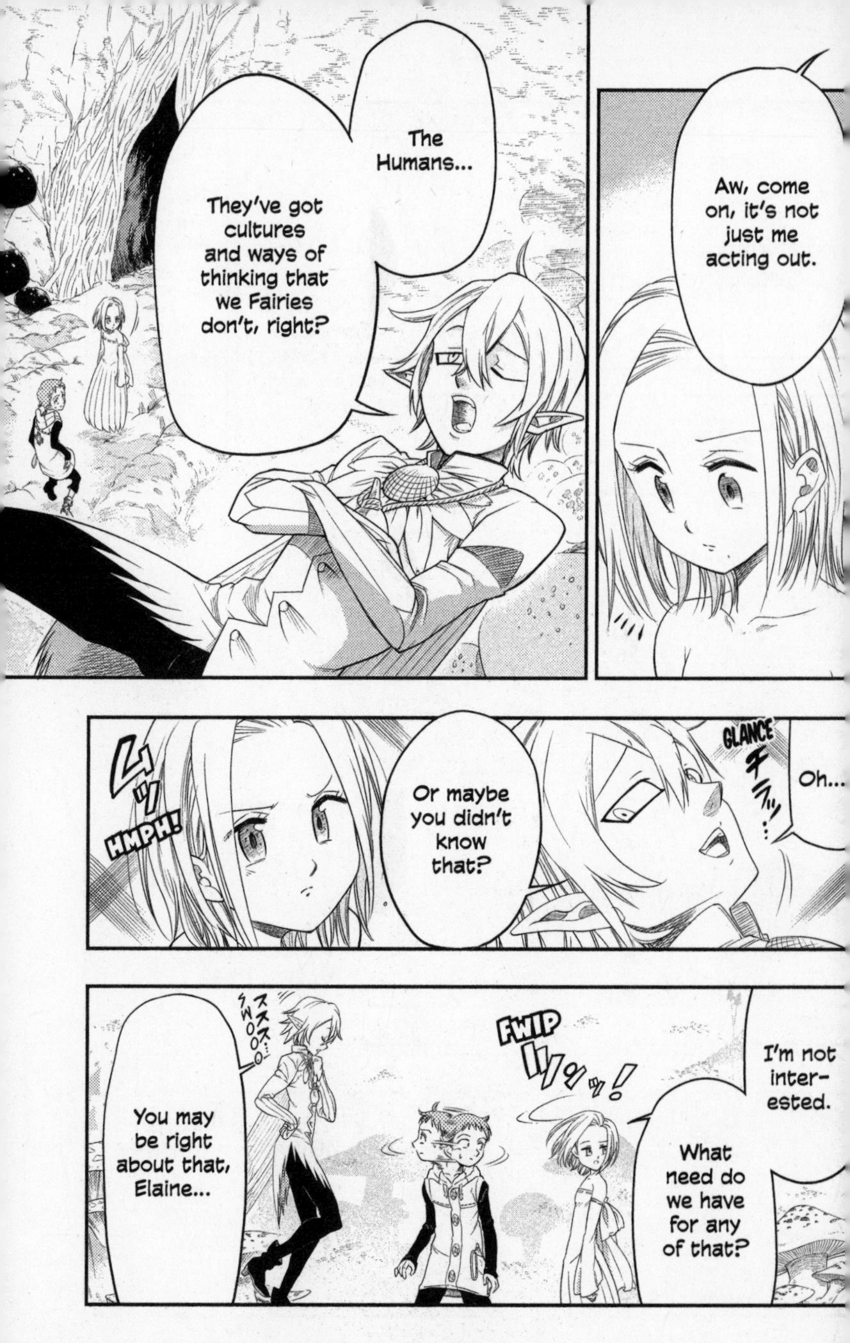
Aw, come on, it's not just me acting out.
The Humans...
They've got cultures and ways of thinking that we Fairies don't, right?
GLANCE
Oh...
Or maybe you didn't know that?
HMPH!
I'm not inter-ested.
What need do we have for any of that?
FWIP
You may be right about that, Elaine...
SWOOO

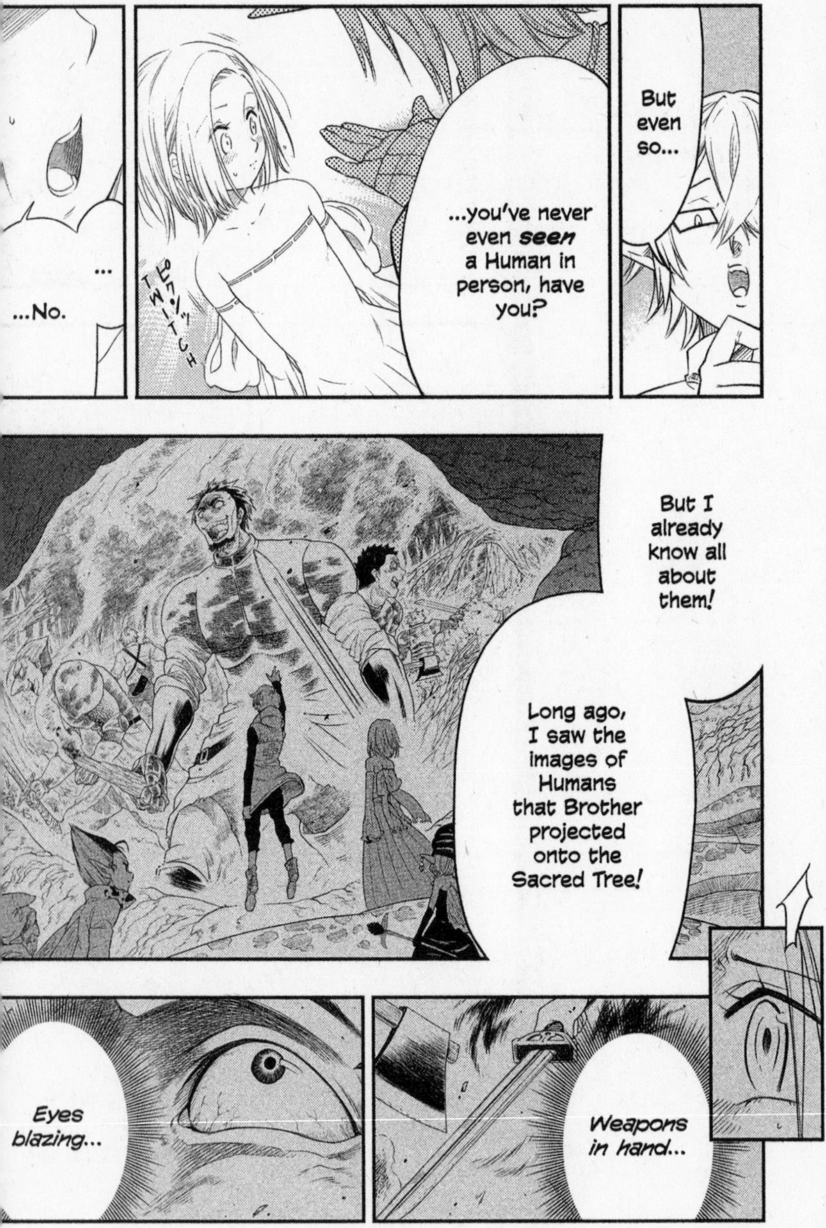

But even so...
...you've never even *seen* a Human in person, have you?
TWITCH
...
...No.
But I already know all about them!
Long ago, I saw the images of Humans that Brother projected onto the Sacred Tree!
Weapons in hand...
Eyes blazing...

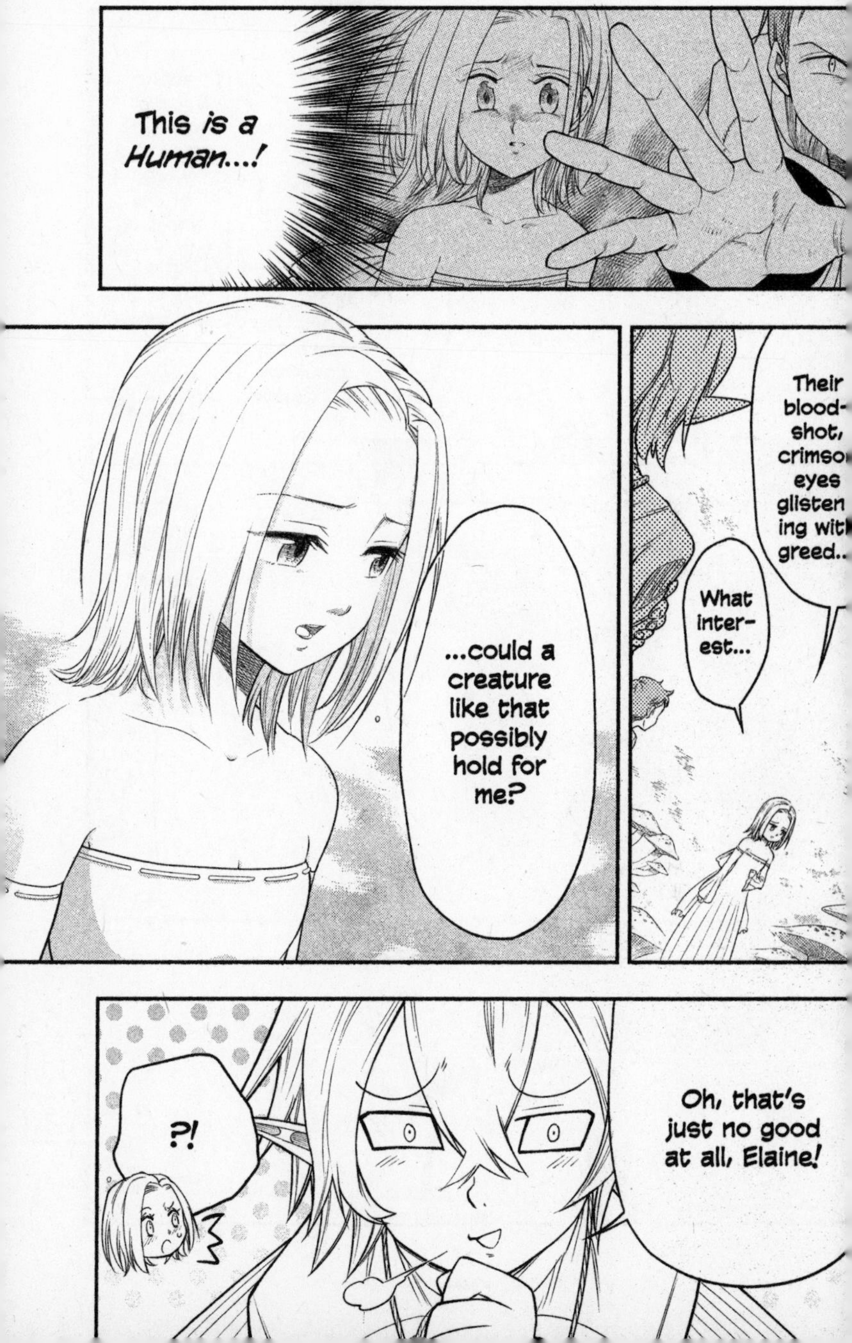
This is a Human...!
Their blood-shot, crimso eyes glisten ing wit greed..
What inter-est...
...could a creature like that possibly hold for me?
Oh, that's just no good at all, Elaine!
?!

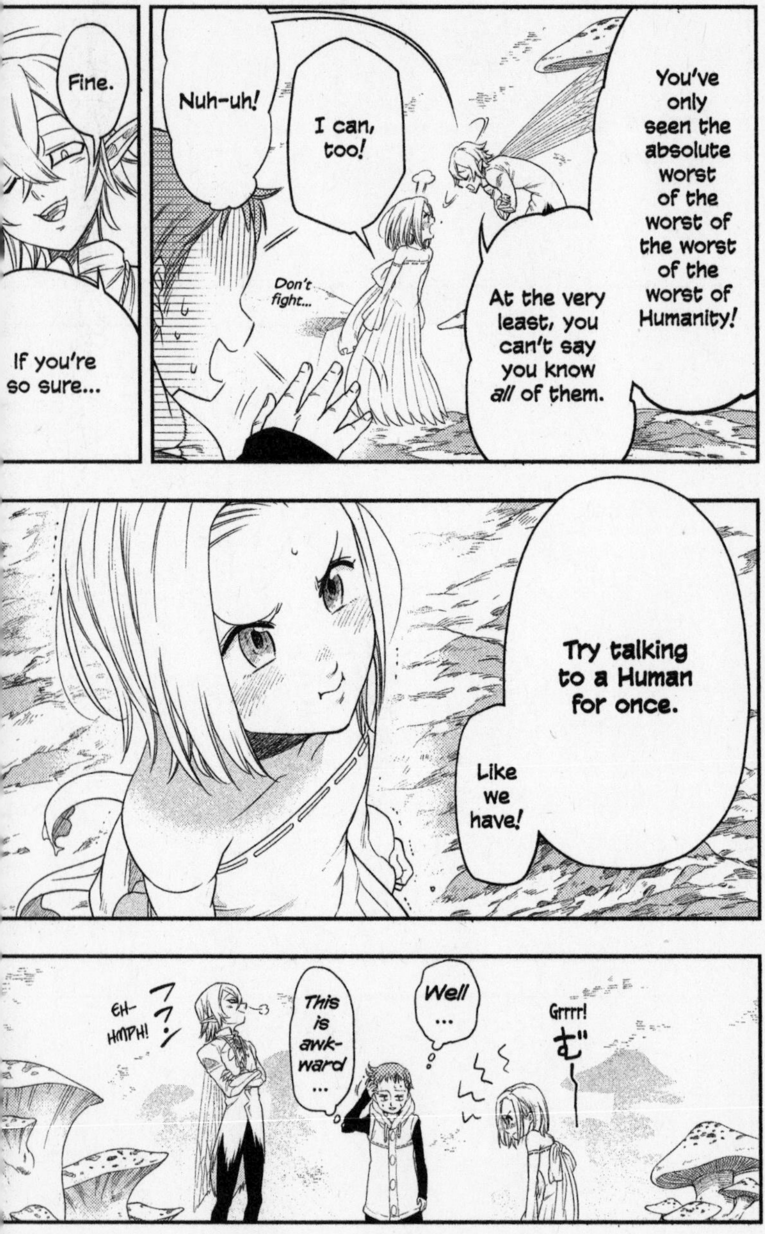
You've only seen the absolute worst of the worst of the worst of the worst of Humanity!
At the very least, you can't say you know *all* of them.
I can, too!
Nuh-uh!
Don't fight...
Fine.
If you're so sure...
Try talking to a Human for once.
Like we have!
Grrrr!
Well ...
This is awkward ...
EH-HMPH!

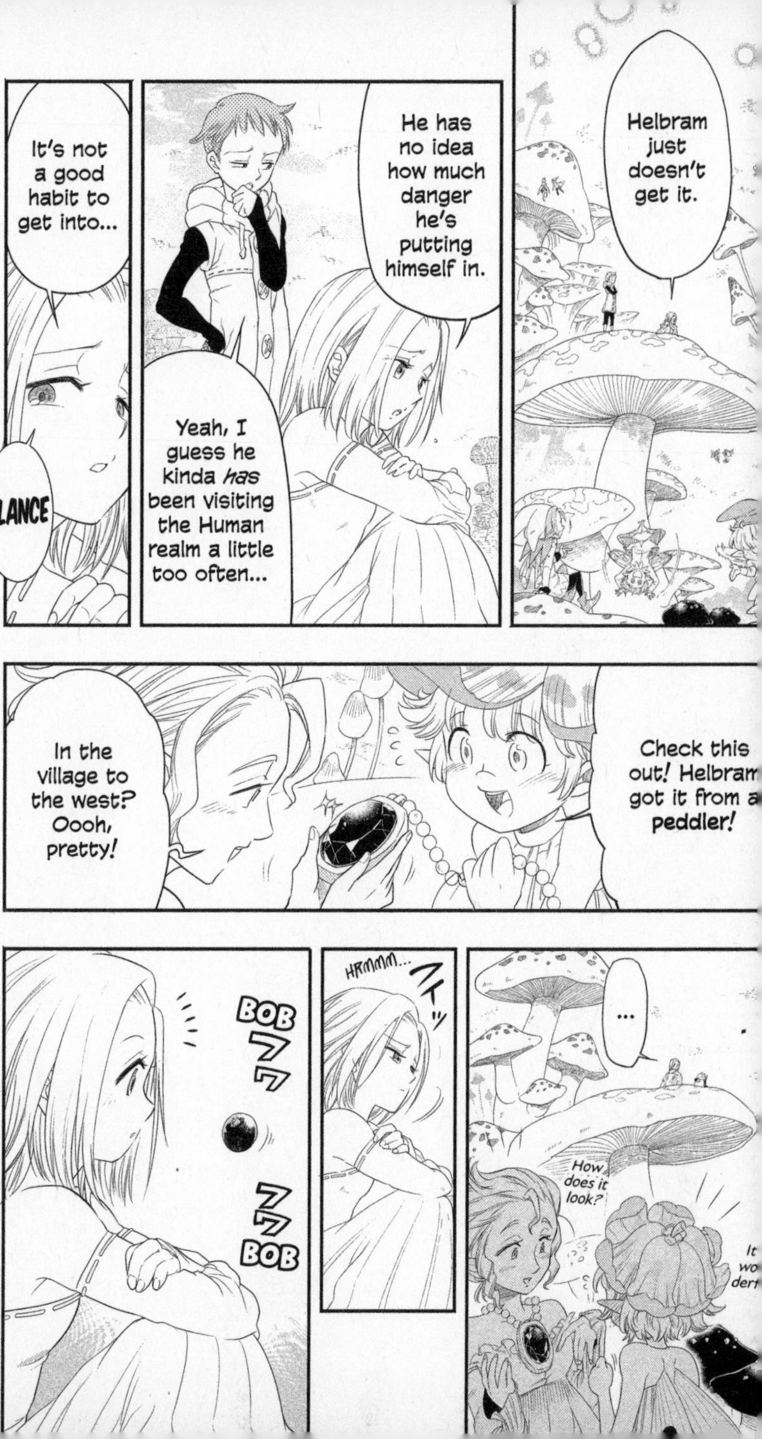
Helbram just doesn't get it.
He has no idea how much danger he's putting himself in.
Yeah, I guess he kinda *has* been visiting the Human realm a little too often...
It's not a good habit to get into...
GLANCE
Check this out! Helbram got it from a peddler!
In the village to the west? Oooh, pretty!
...
How does it look?
HRMMM...
BOB
BOB

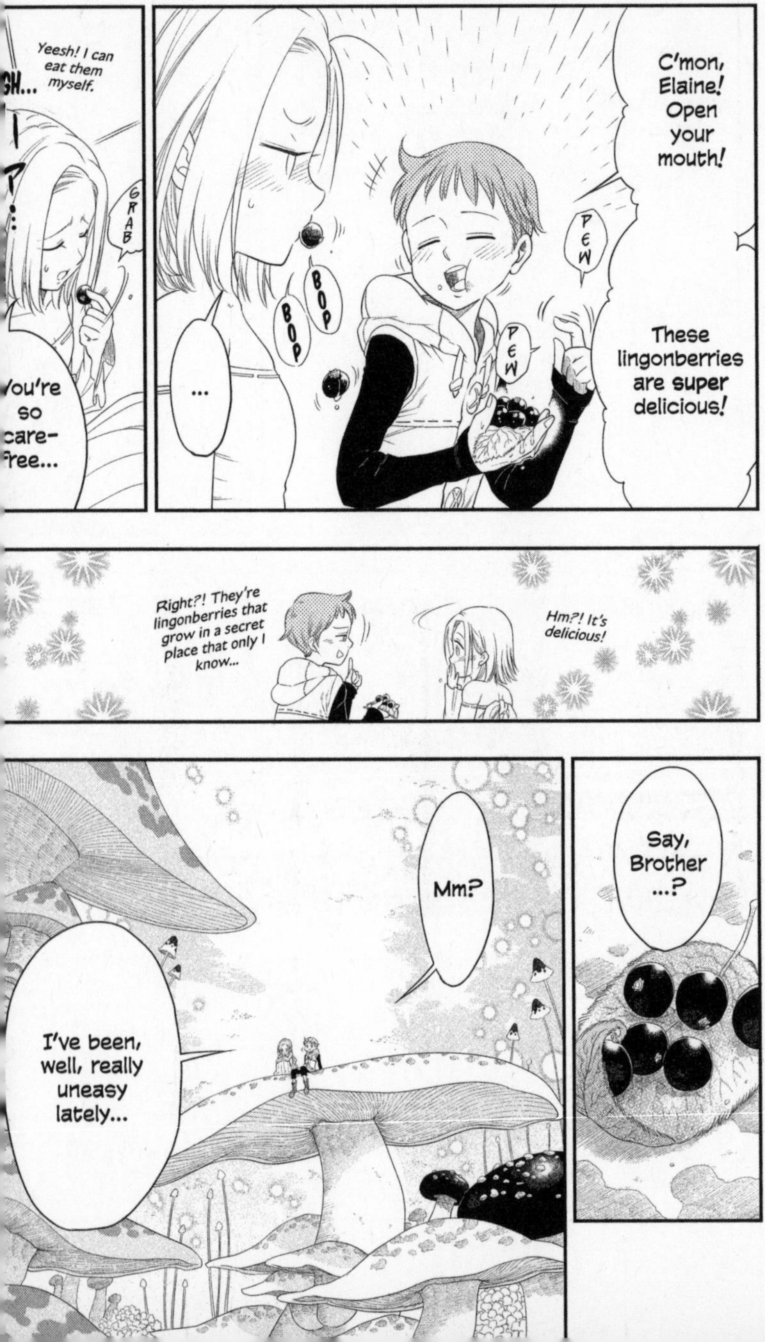
C'mon, Elaine! Open your mouth!
PEW
PEW
These lingonberries are super delicious!
BOP
BOP
...
Yeesh! I can eat them myself.
GRAB
ou're so care-free...
Hm?! It's delicious!
Right?! They're lingonberries that grow in a secret place that only I know...
Say, Brother...?
Mm?
I've been, well, really uneasy lately...

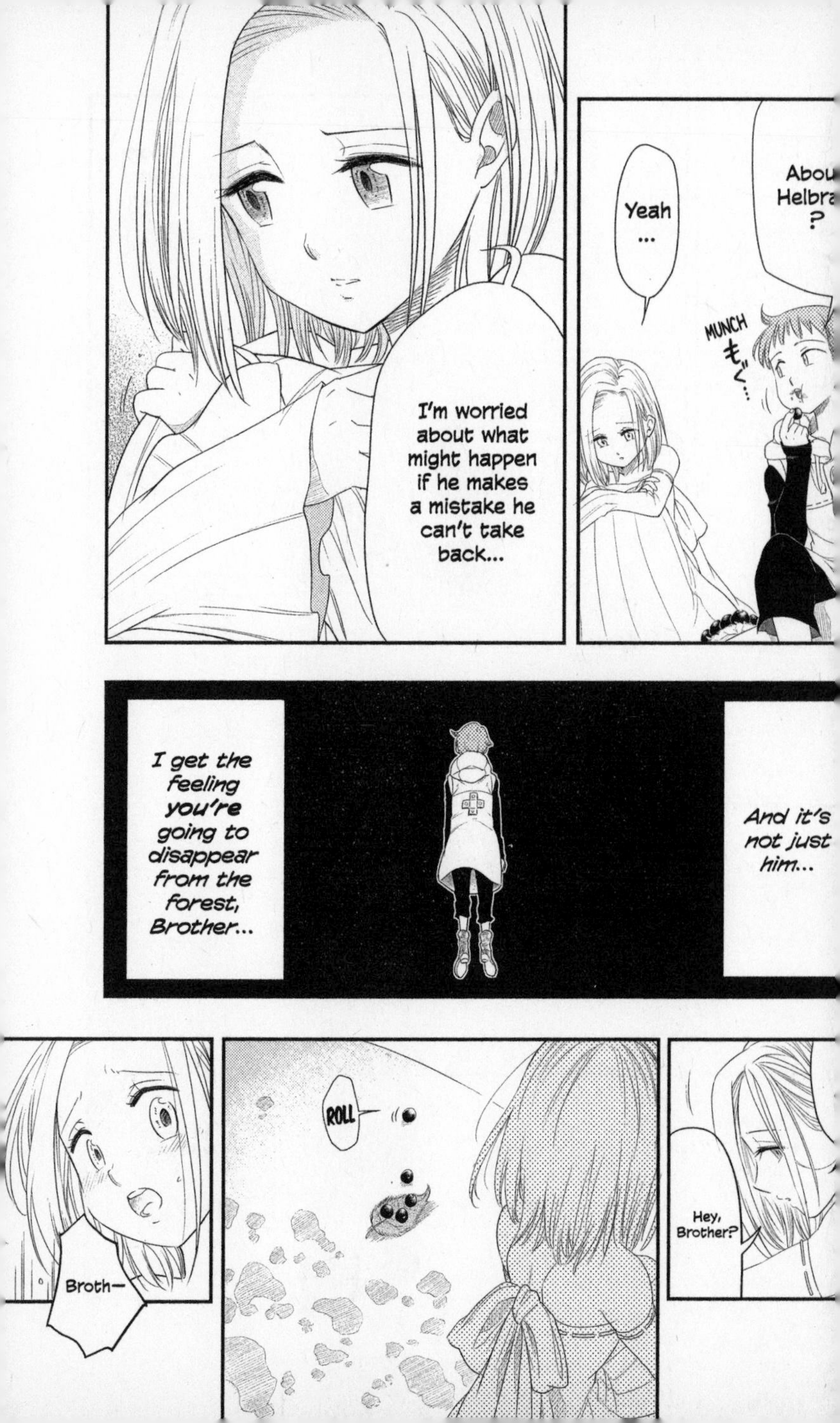
Abou Helbra ?
MUNCH
もぐ…
Yeah …
I'm worried about what might happen if he makes a mistake he can't take back...
And it's not just him...
I get the feeling you're going to disappear from the forest, Brother...
Hey, Brother?
ROLL
Broth—

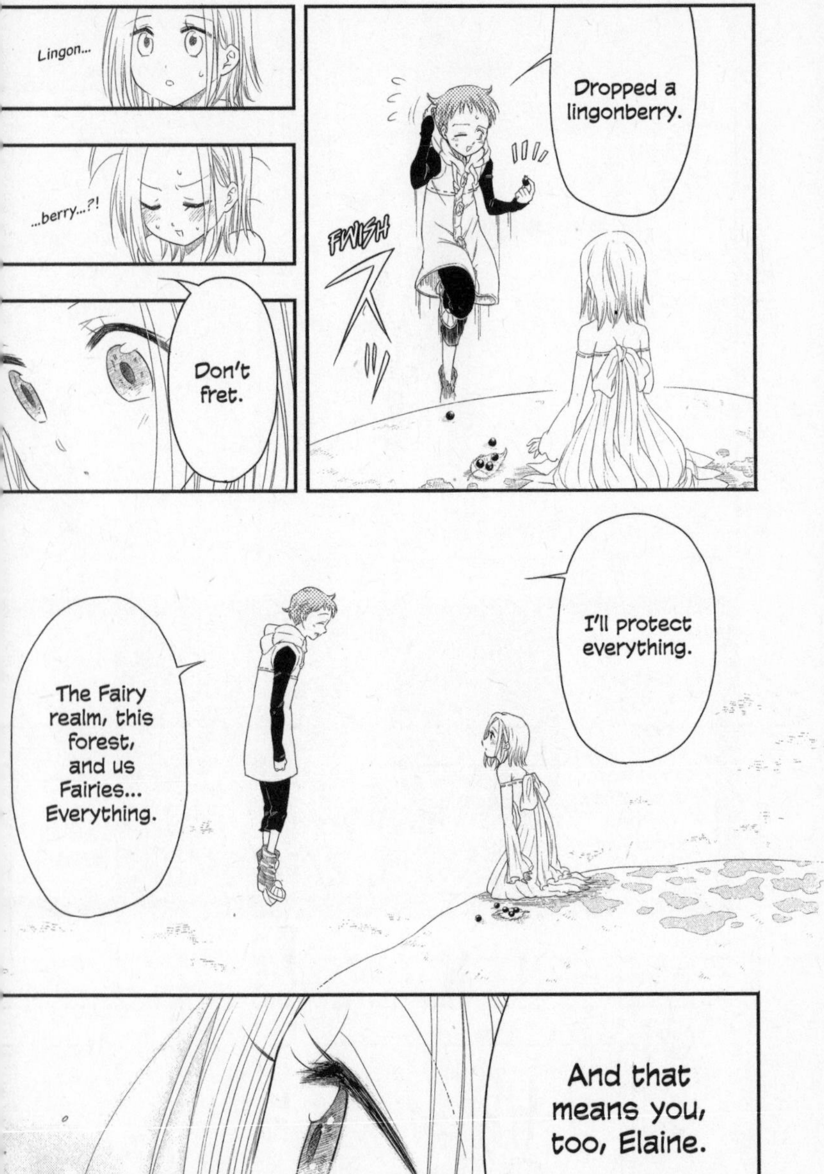
Dropped a lingonberry.
FWISH
Lingon...
...berry...?!
Don't fret.
I'll protect everything.
The Fairy realm, this forest, and us Fairies... Everything.
And that means you, too, Elaine.

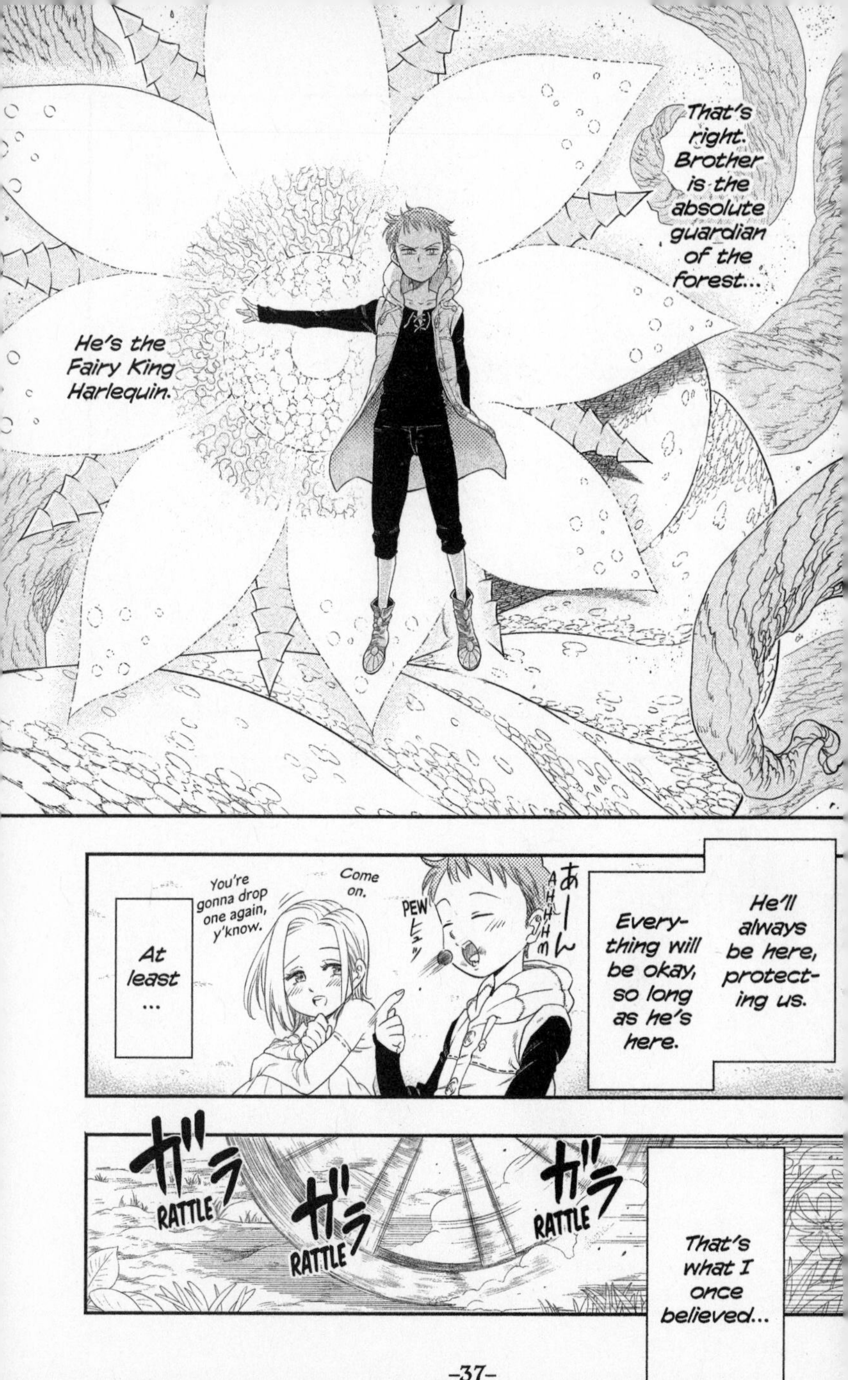
That's right. Brother is the absolute guardian of the forest...
He's the Fairy King Harlequin.
He'll always be here, protecting us.
Every-thing will be okay, so long as he's here.
あーん
AHHHM
PEW
ヒュッ
Come on.
You're gonna drop one again, y'know.
At least ...
That's what I once believed...
ガラ
RATTLE
ガラ
RATTLE
ガラ
RATTLE

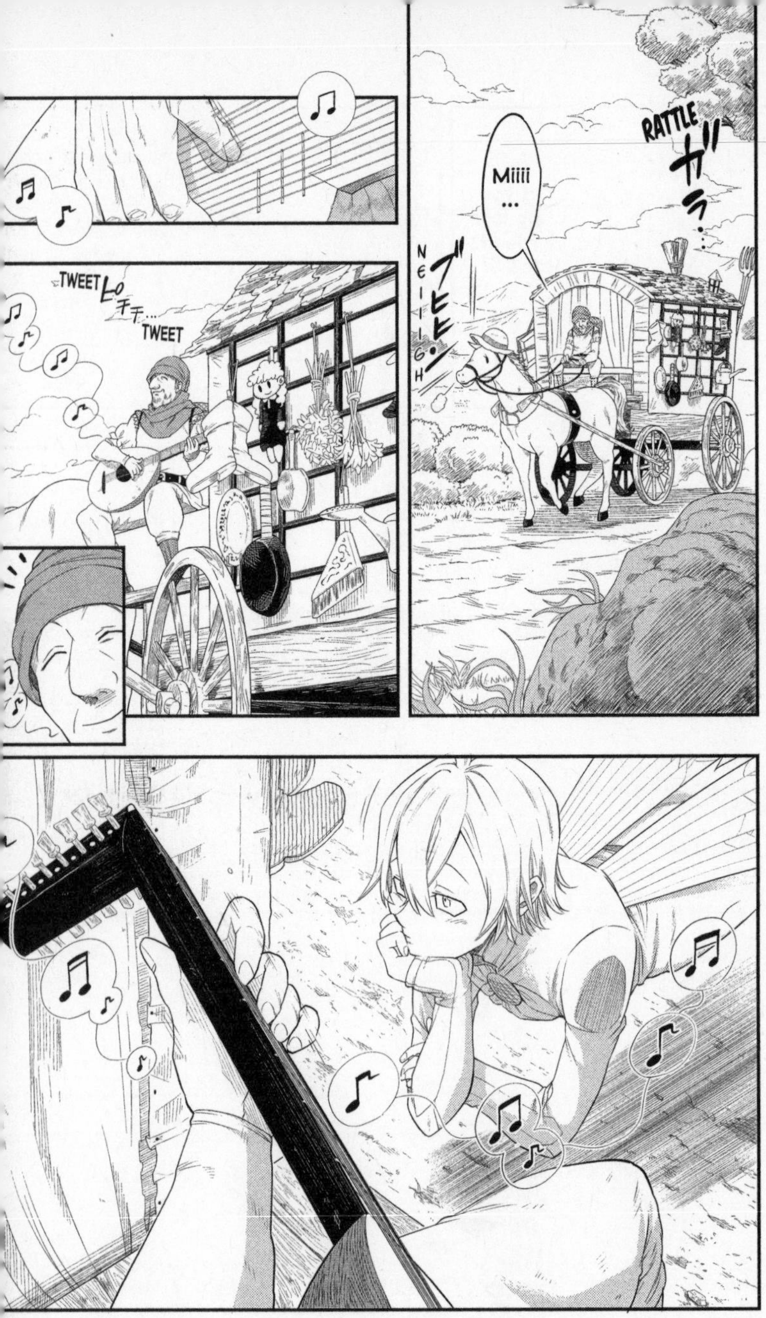

RATTLE
ガラ…
Miiii
...
NEIIIGH
ブヒヒン
TWEET
ピチチ…
TWEET

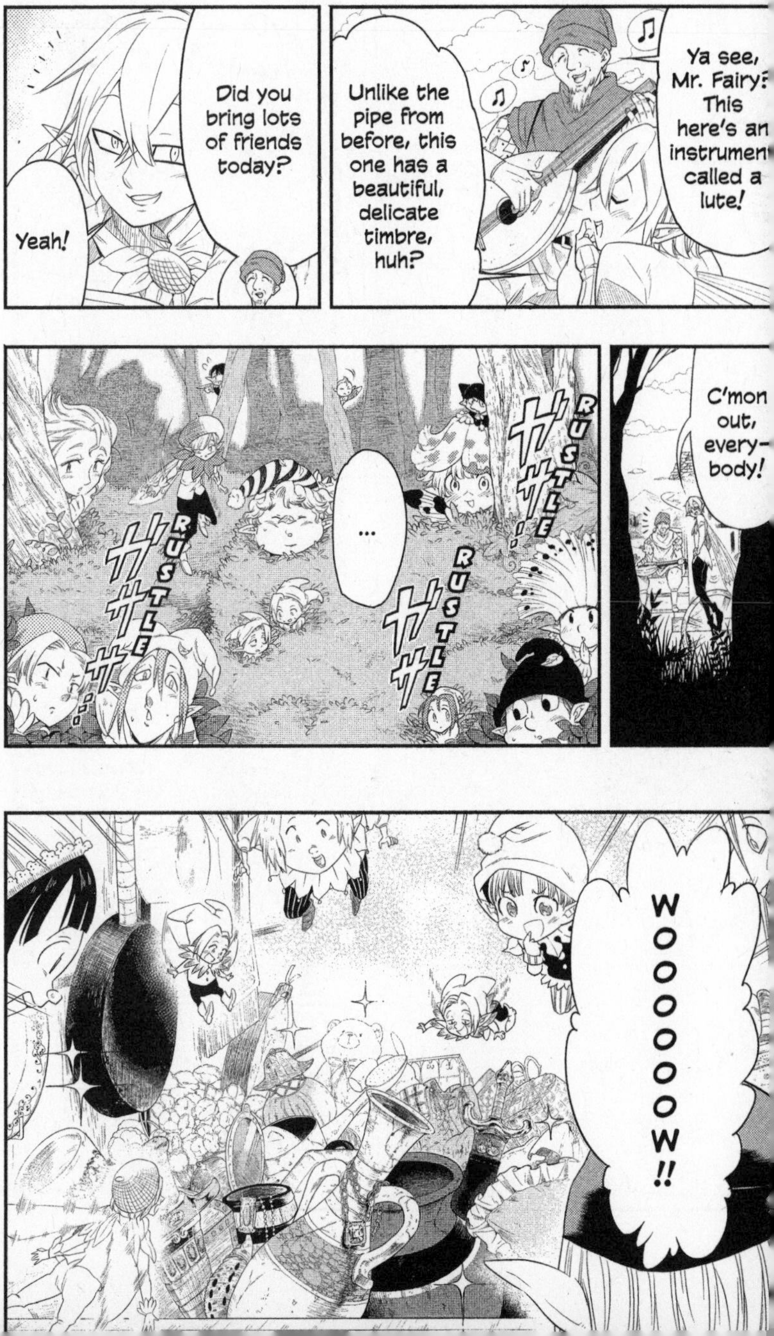
Ya see, Mr. Fairy? This here's an instrumen called a lute!
Unlike the pipe from before, this one has a beautiful, delicate timbre, huh?
Did you bring lots of friends today?
Yeah!
C'mon out, everybody!
RUSTLE
RUSTLE
...
RUSTLE
WOOOOOOOW!!

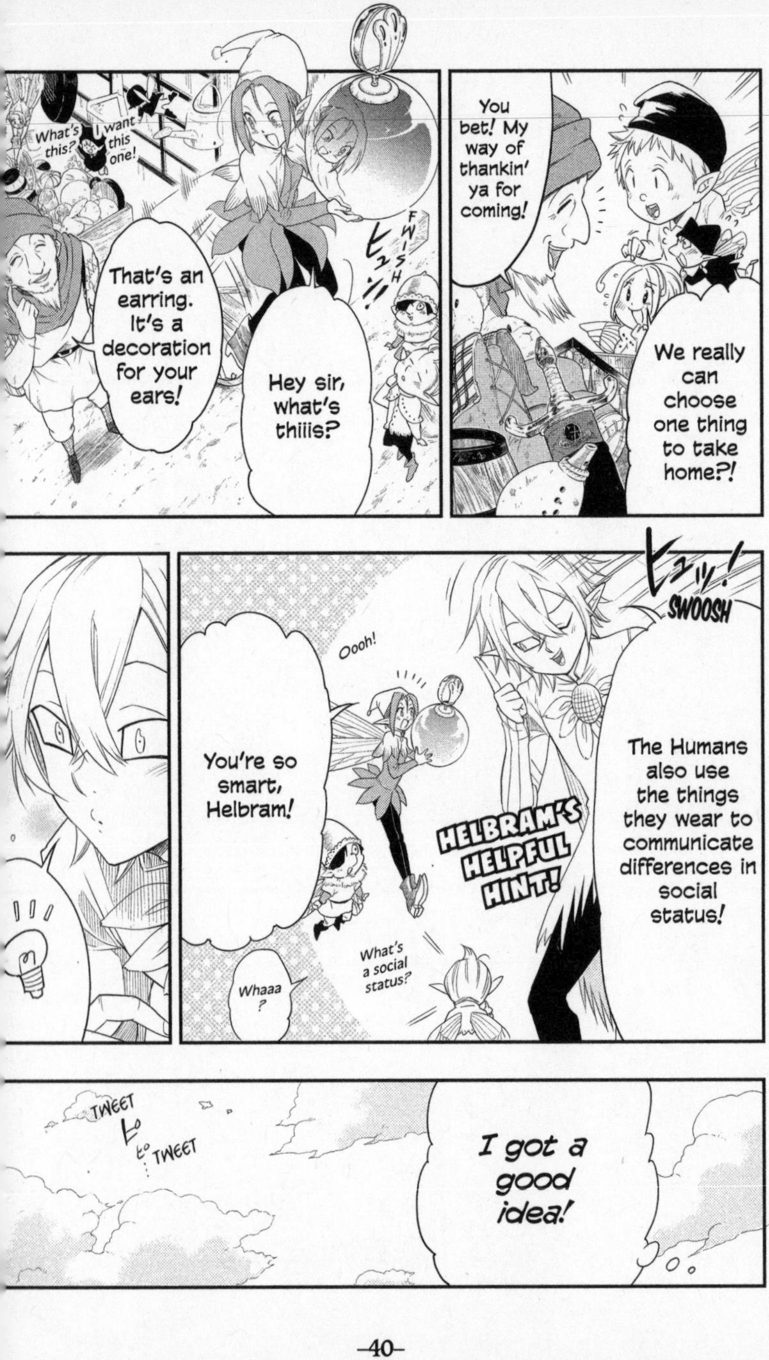

We really can choose one thing to take home?!
You bet! My way of thankin' ya for coming!
ヒュ
FWISH
Hey sir, what's thiiis?
That's an earring. It's a decoration for your ears!
What's this?
I want this one!
ヒュッ!
SWOOSH
The Humans also use the things they wear to communicate differences in social status!
HELBRAM'S HELPFUL HINT!
Oooh!
You're so smart, Helbram!
What's a social status?
Whaaa?
I got a good idea!
TWEET
ピ
ぴ
TWEET

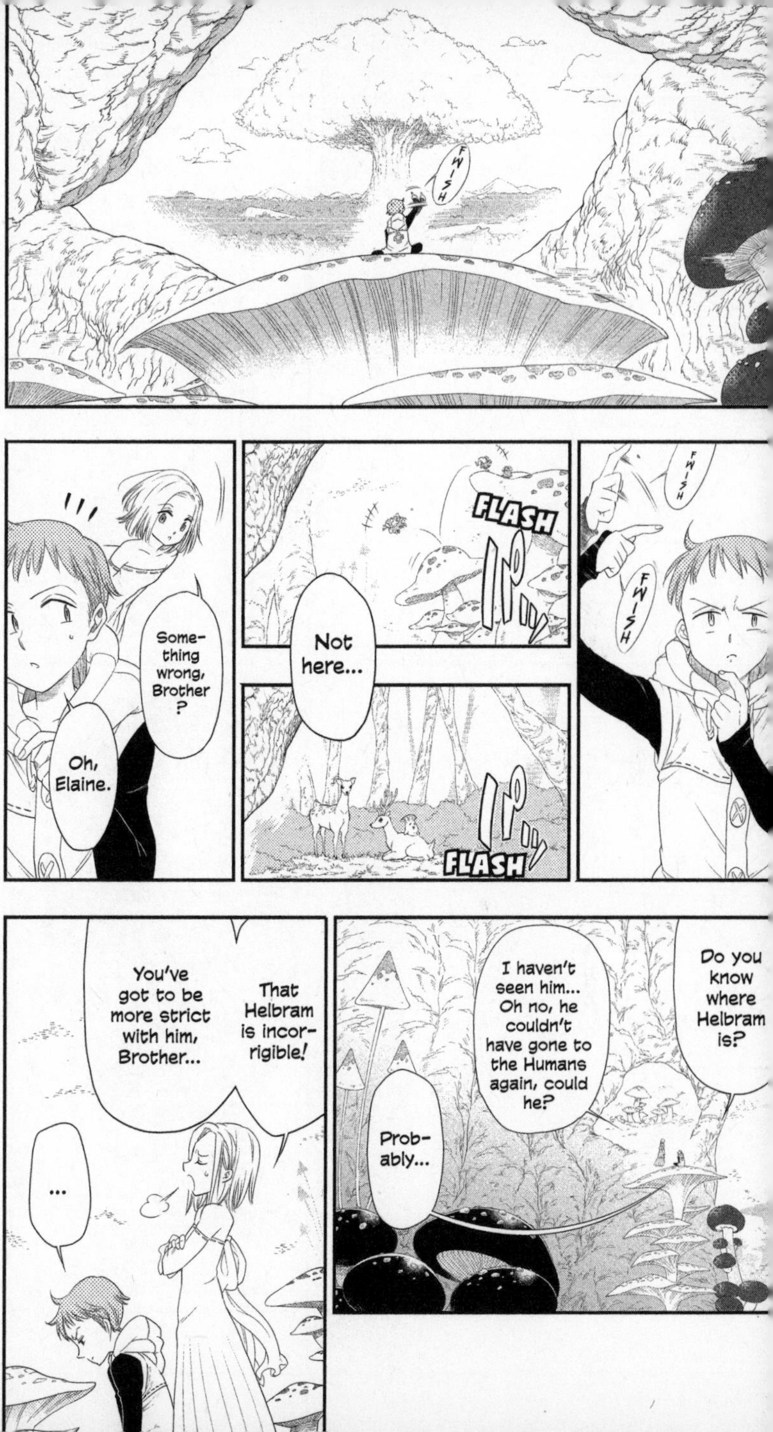
FWISH
FWISH
FWISH
FLASH
Not here...
FLASH
Something wrong, Brother?
Oh, Elaine.
Do you know where Helbram is?
I haven't seen him... Oh no, he couldn't have gone to the Humans again, could he?
Probably...
That Helbram is incorrigible!
You've got to be more strict with him, Brother...
...

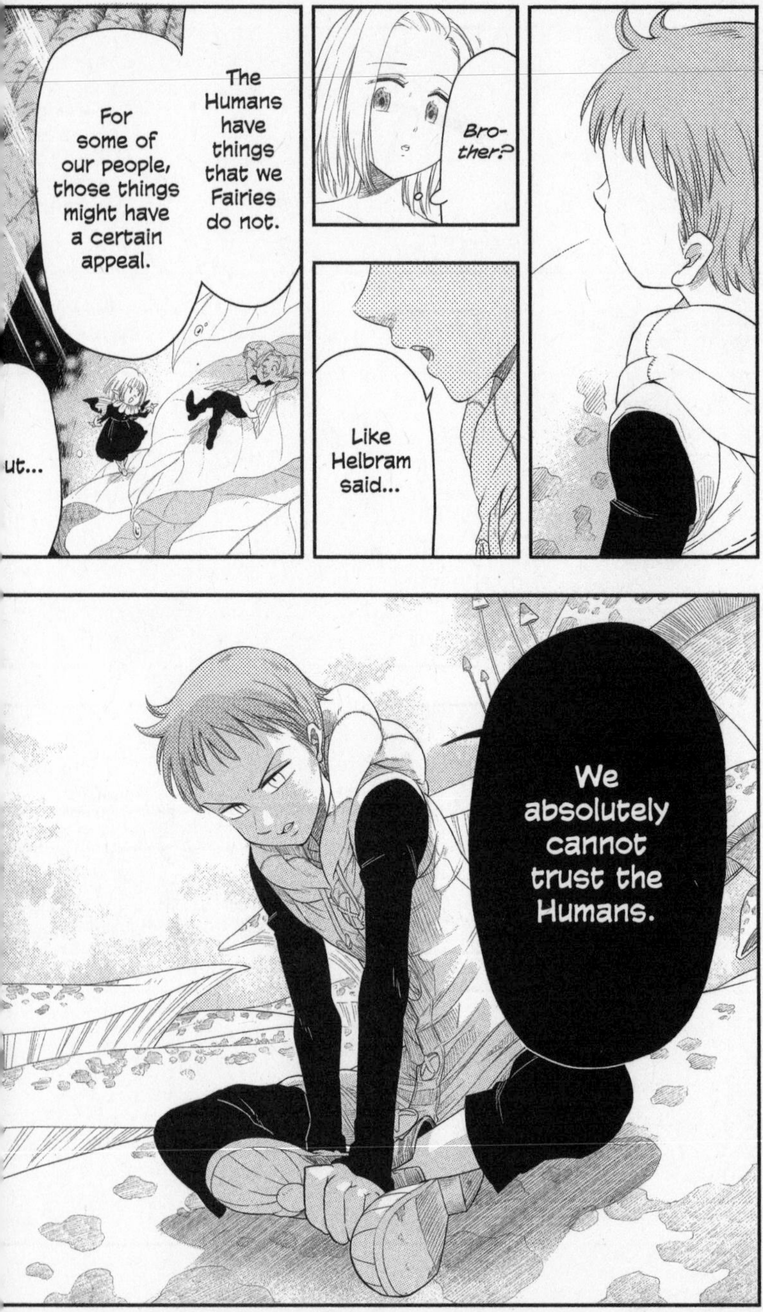
Bro- ther?
Like Helbram said...
The Humans have things that we Fairies do not.
For some of our people, those things might have a certain appeal.
ut...
We absolutely cannot trust the Humans.

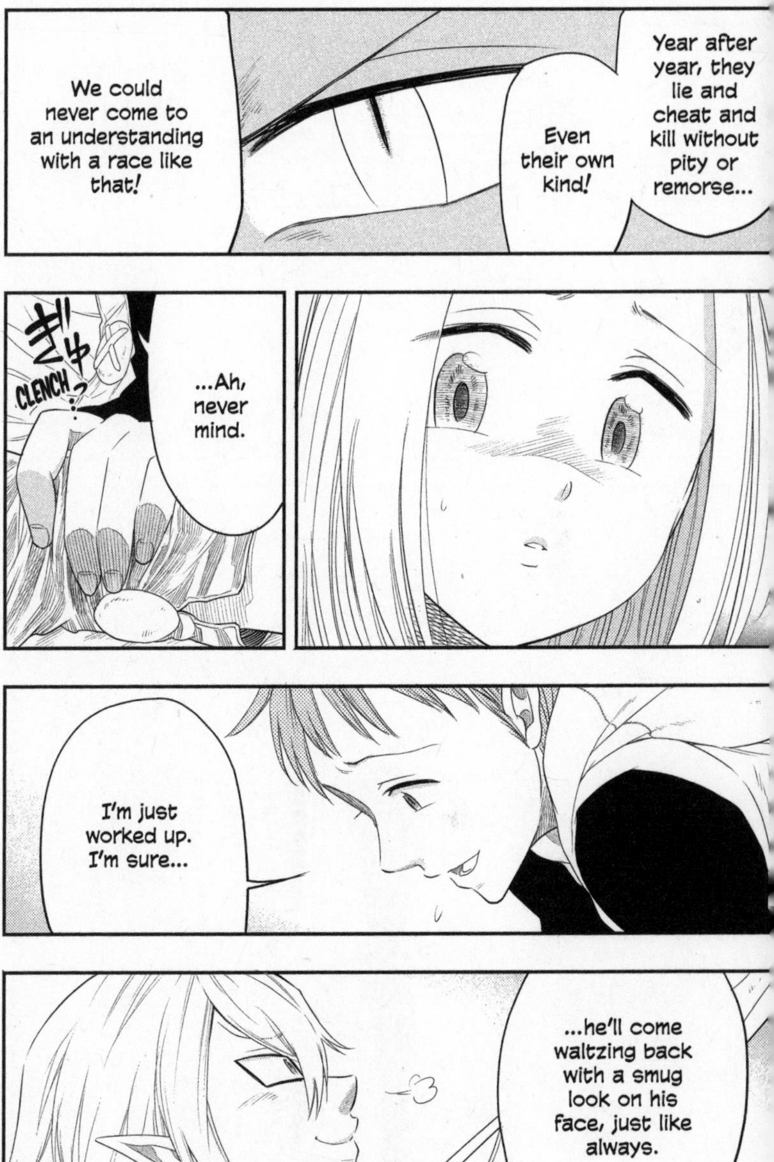
Year after year, they lie and cheat and kill without pity or remorse...
Even their own kind!
We could never come to an understanding with a race like that!
...Ah, never mind.
ぎゅ
CLENCH
I'm just worked up. I'm sure...
...he'll come waltzing back with a smug look on his face, just like always.

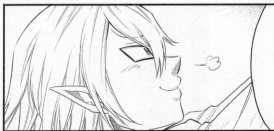

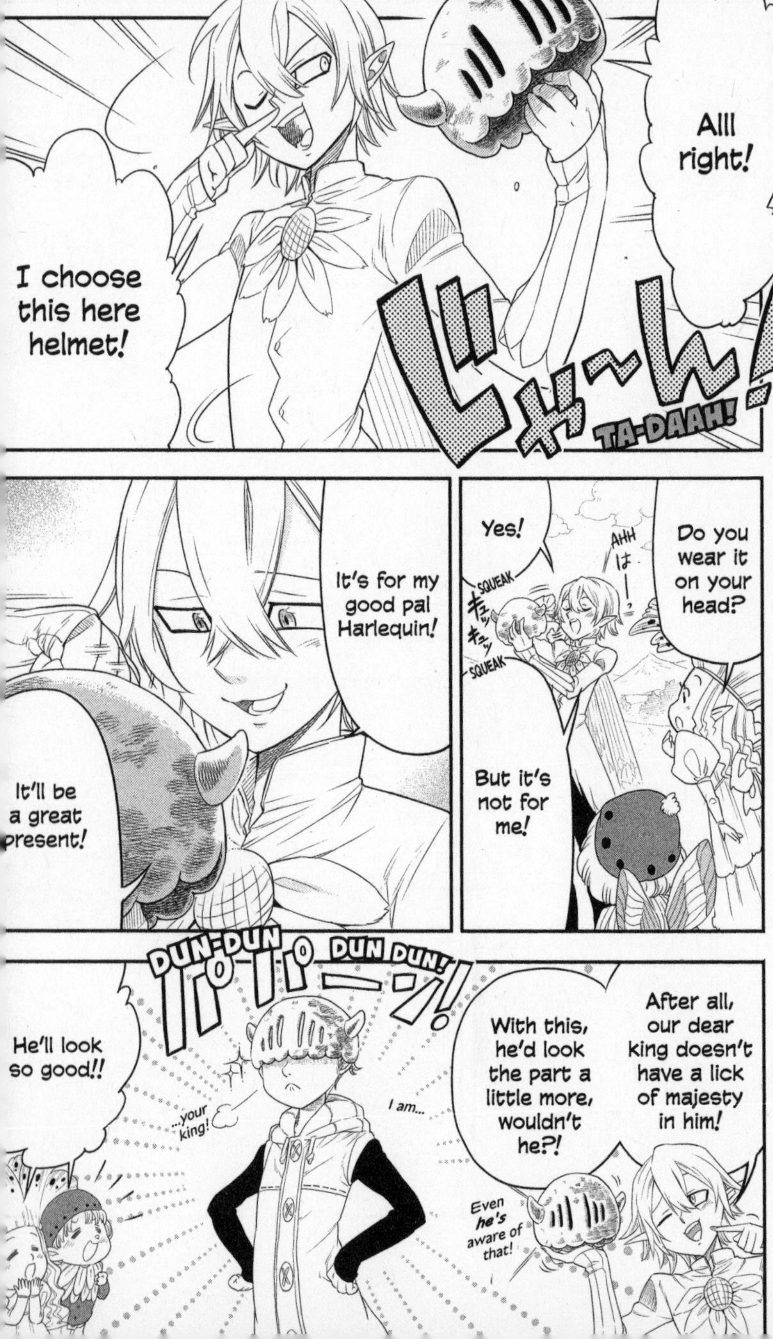
Alll right!
I choose this here helmet!
じゃ～ん!
TA-DAAH!
Do you wear it on your head?
Yes!
AHH
はー…?
SQUEAK
キュッ キュッ
SQUEAK
But it's not for me!
It's for my good pal Harlequin!
It'll be a great present!
After all, our dear king doesn't have a lick of majesty in him!
With this, he'd look the part a little more, wouldn't he?!
Even he's aware of that!
I am...
...your king!
DUN-DUN
パパーッ!
DUN DUN!
He'll look so good!!

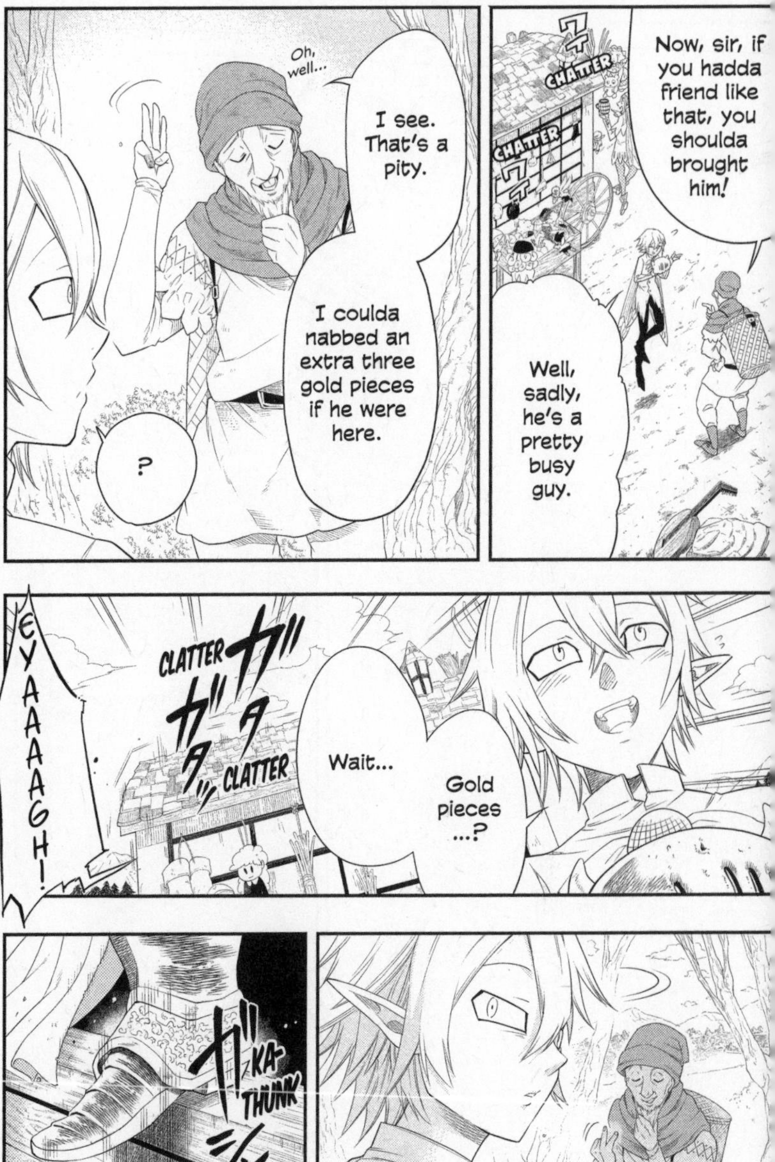
Now, sir, if you hadda friend like that, you shoulda brought him!
CHATTER
CHATTER
Well, sadly, he's a pretty busy guy.
Oh, well...
I see. That's a pity.
I coulda nabbed an extra three gold pieces if he were here.
?
Wait...
Gold pieces ...?
CLATTER
CLATTER
EYAAAAAGH!
KA-THUNK

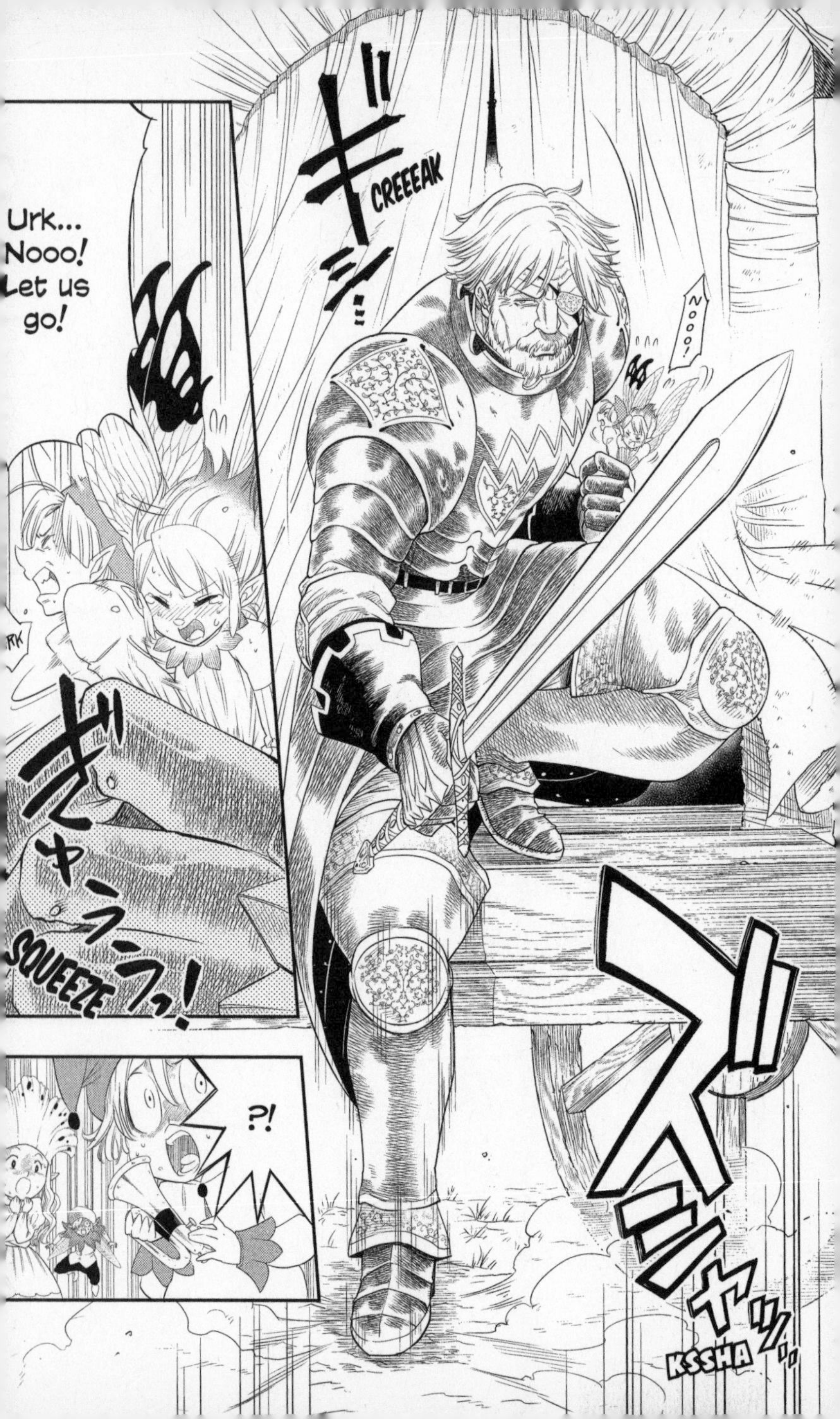
CREEEAK
NOOO!
Urk... Nooo! Let us go!
RK
SQUEEZE
?!
KSSHA

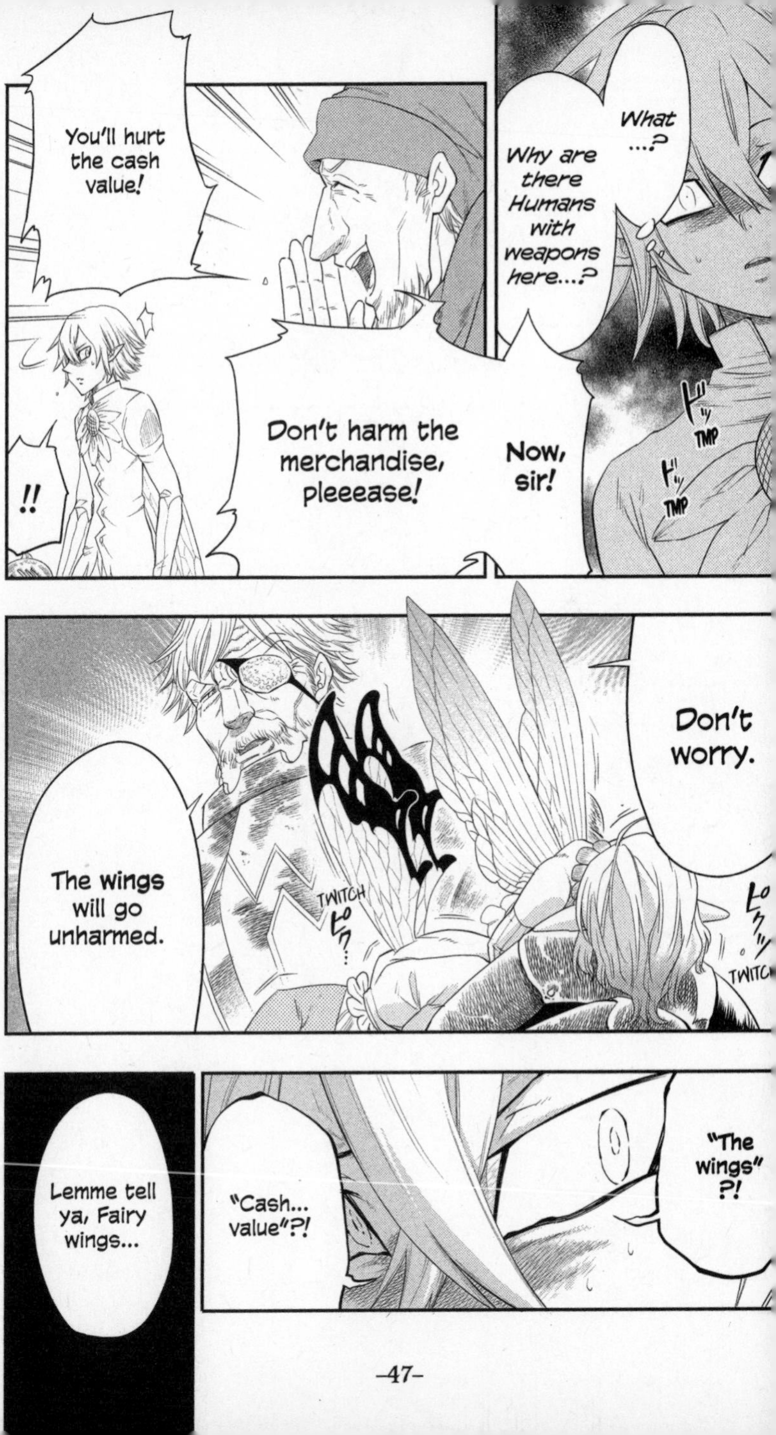

What ...?
Why are there Humans with weapons here...?
Now, sir!
TMP
TMP
You'll hurt the cash value!
Don't harm the merchandise, pleeease!
!!
Don't worry.
The wings will go unharmed.
TWITCH
TWITCH
"The wings"?!
"Cash... value"?!
Lemme tell ya, Fairy wings...

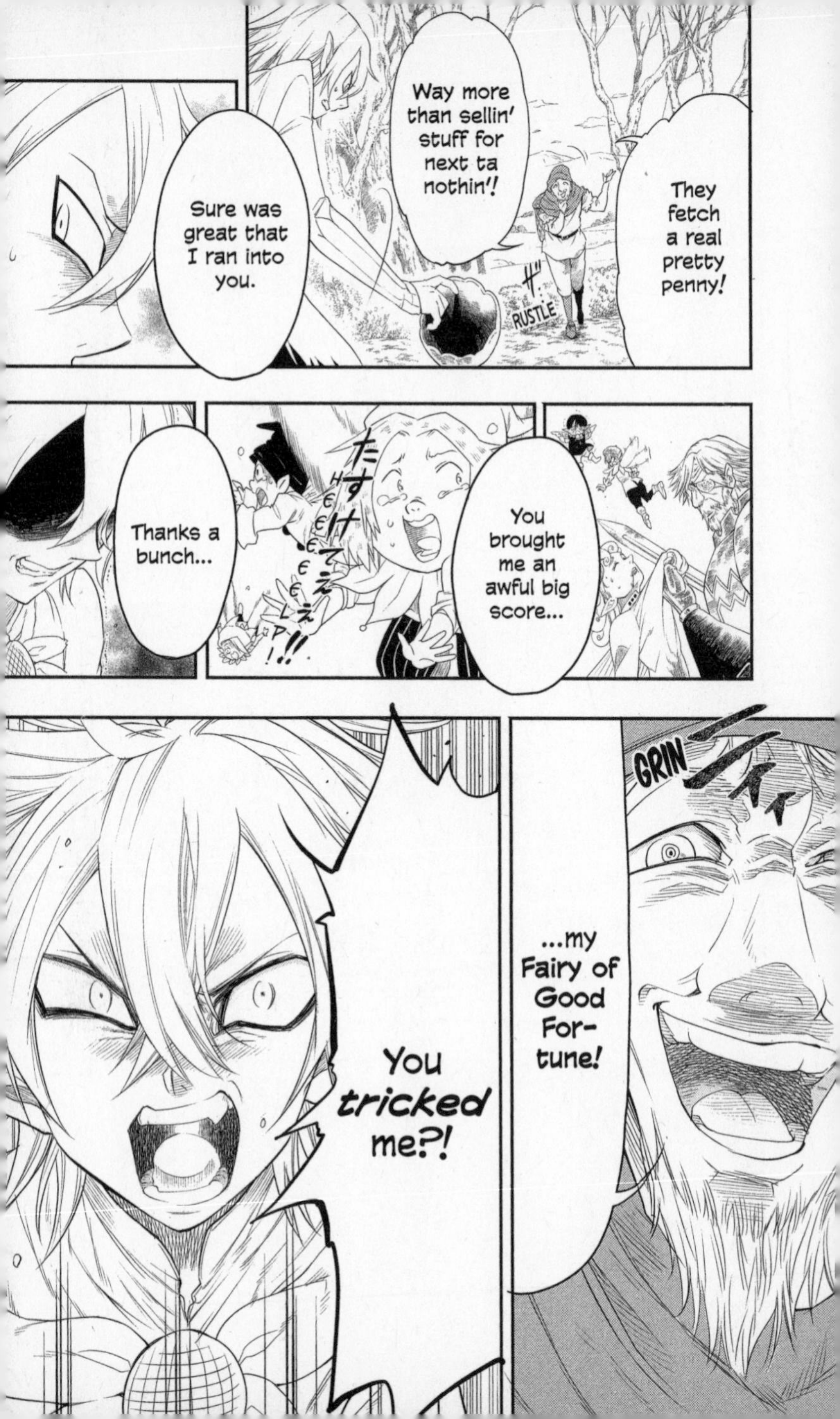
They fetch a real pretty penny!
Way more than sellin' stuff for next ta nothin'!
ザ
RUSTLE
Sure was great that I ran into you.
You brought me an awful big score...
たすけてぇぇ!!
HEEEEELP!!
Thanks a bunch...
GRIN
...my Fairy of Good Fortune!
You tricked me?!

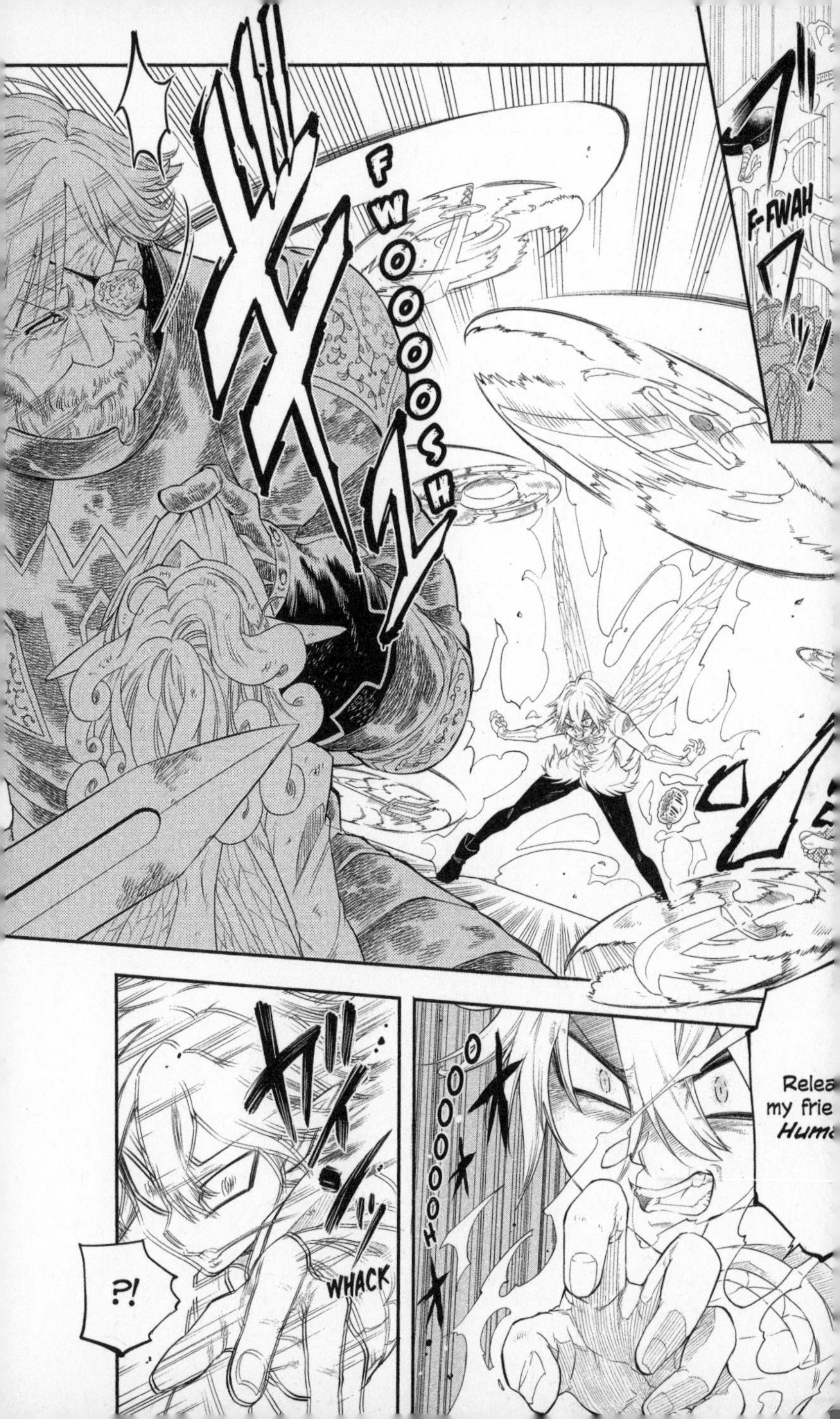
F-FWAH
FWOOOOOOSH
Relea
my frie
Huma
OOOOOOOH
WHACK
?!

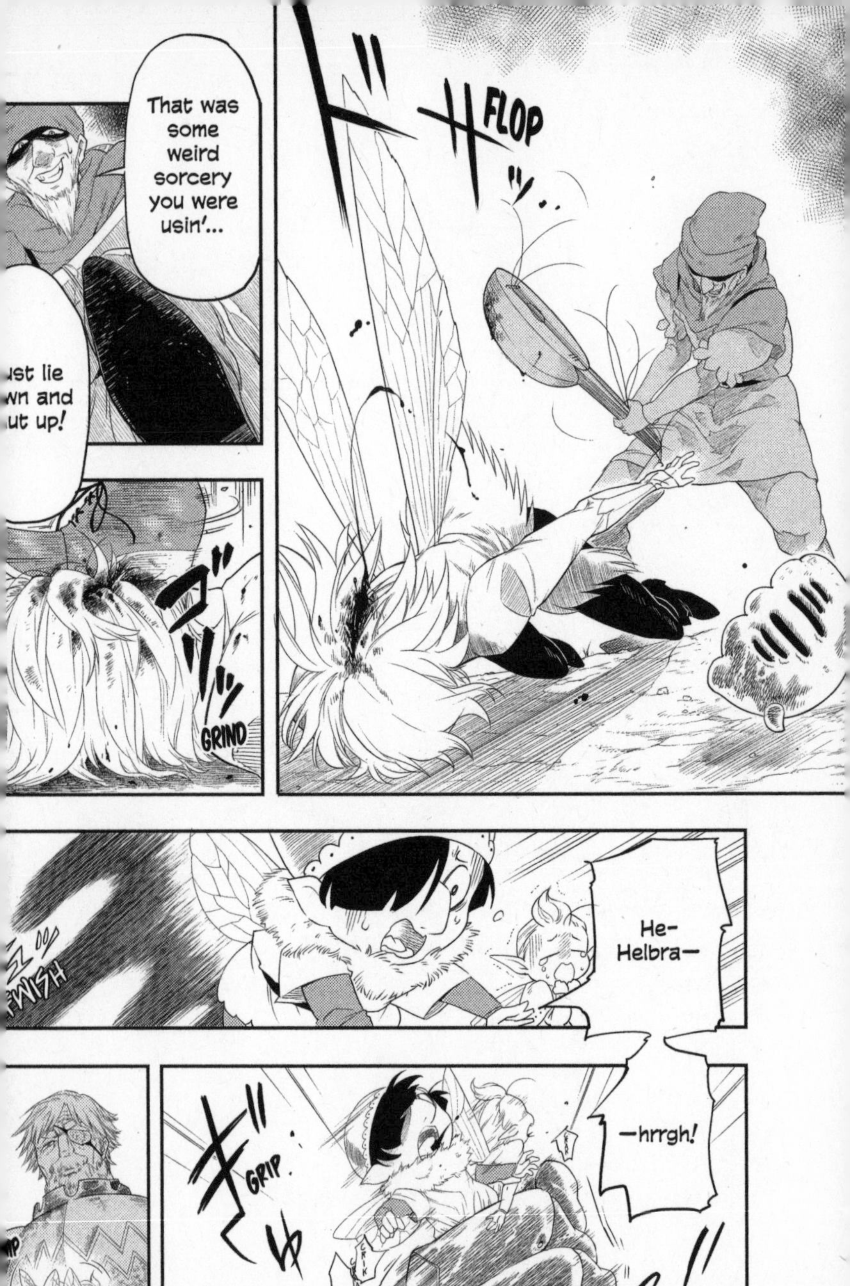
FLOP
That was some weird sorcery you were usin'...
ust lie wn and ut up!
GRIND
He- Helbra—
WISH
—hrrgh!
GRIP
CRIK CRAAK

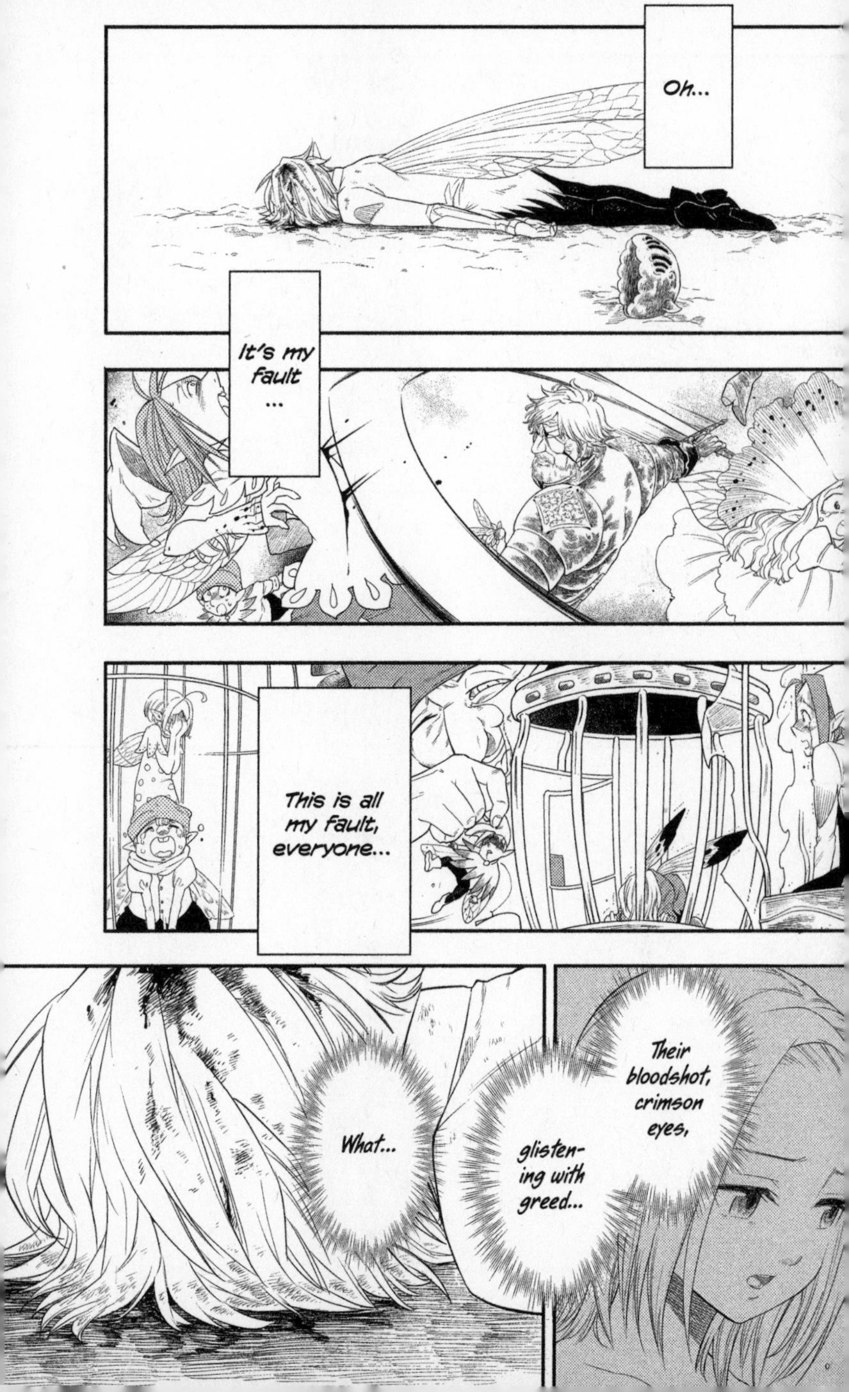
Oh...
It's my fault ...
This is all my fault, everyone...
Their bloodshot, crimson eyes,
glisten-ing with greed...
What...

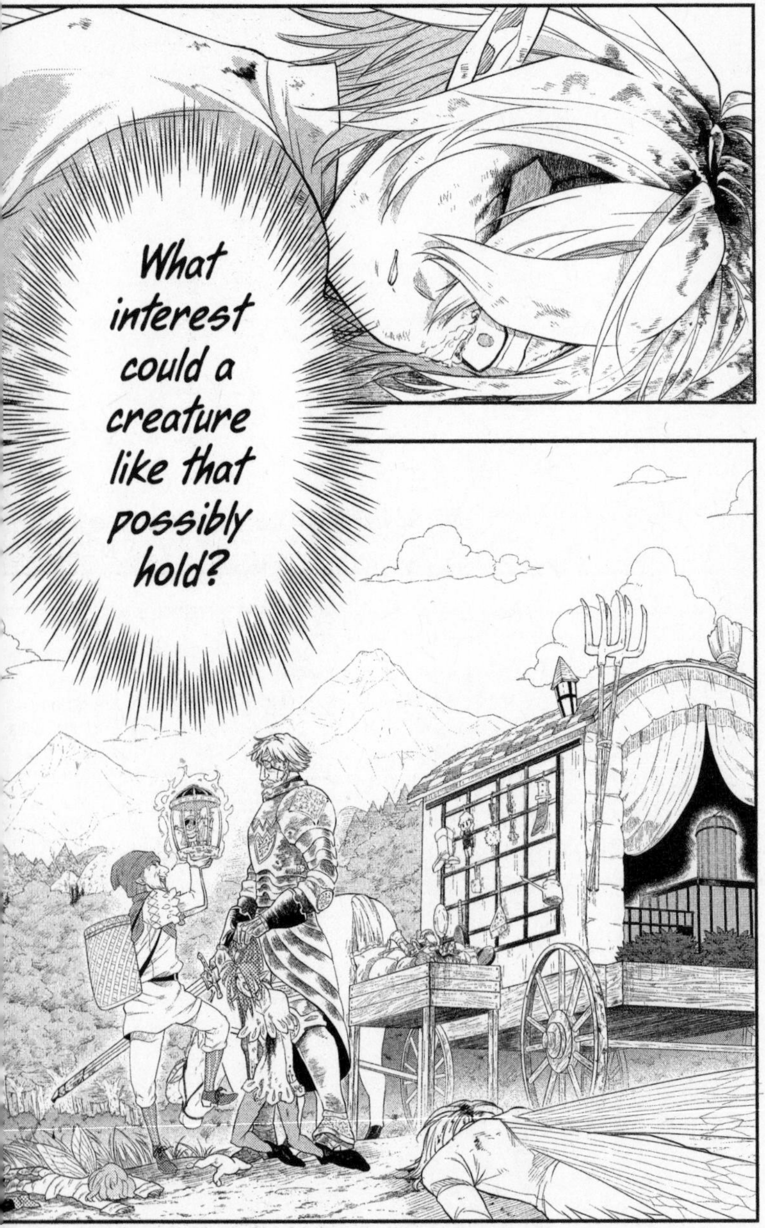
What interest could a creature like that possibly hold?

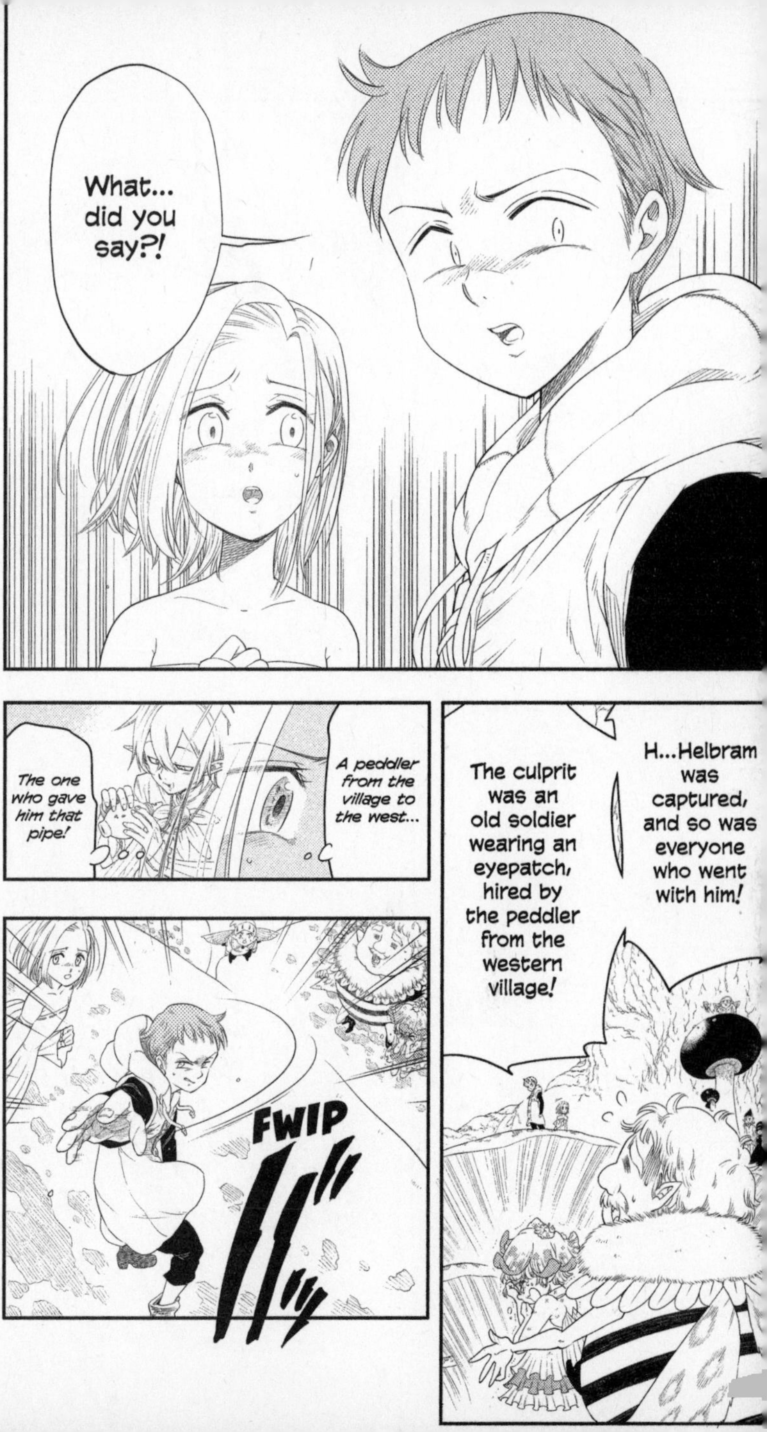
What... did you say?!
H...Helbram was captured, and so was everyone who went with him!
The culprit was an old soldier wearing an eyepatch, hired by the peddler from the western village!
A peddler from the village to the west...
The one who gave him that pipe!
FWIP

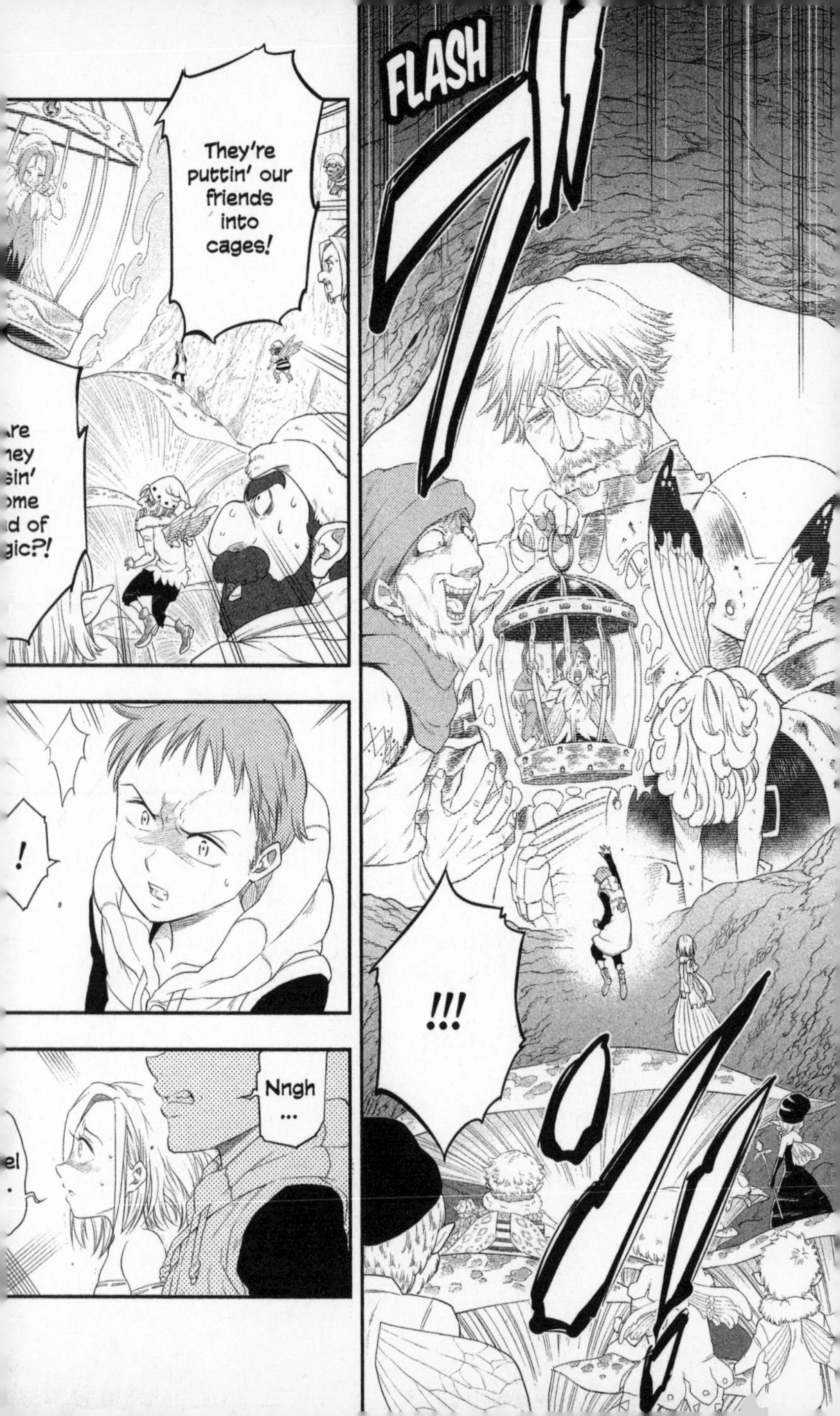
FLASH
!!!
They're puttin' our friends into cages!
!
Nngh ...

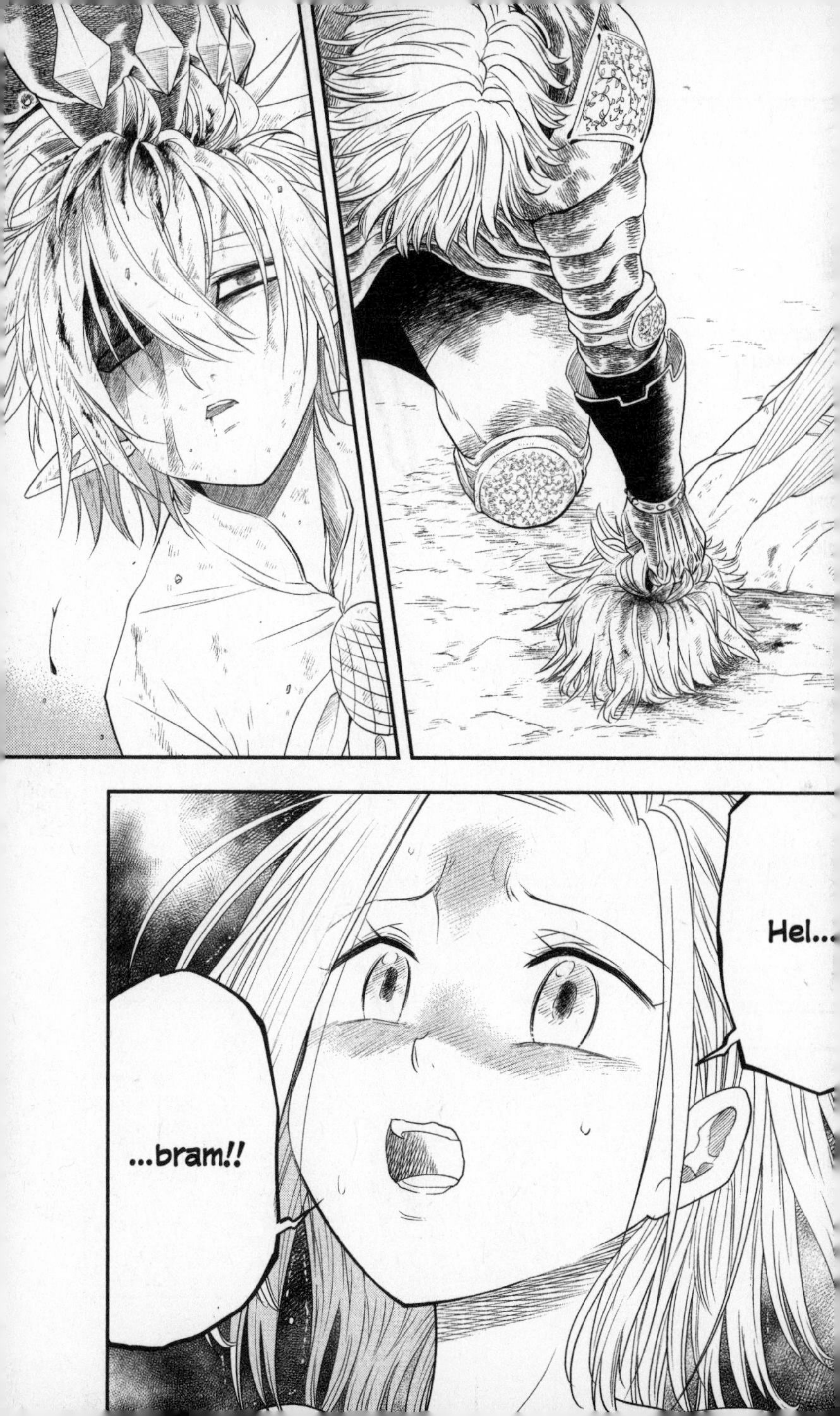
Hel...
...bram!!

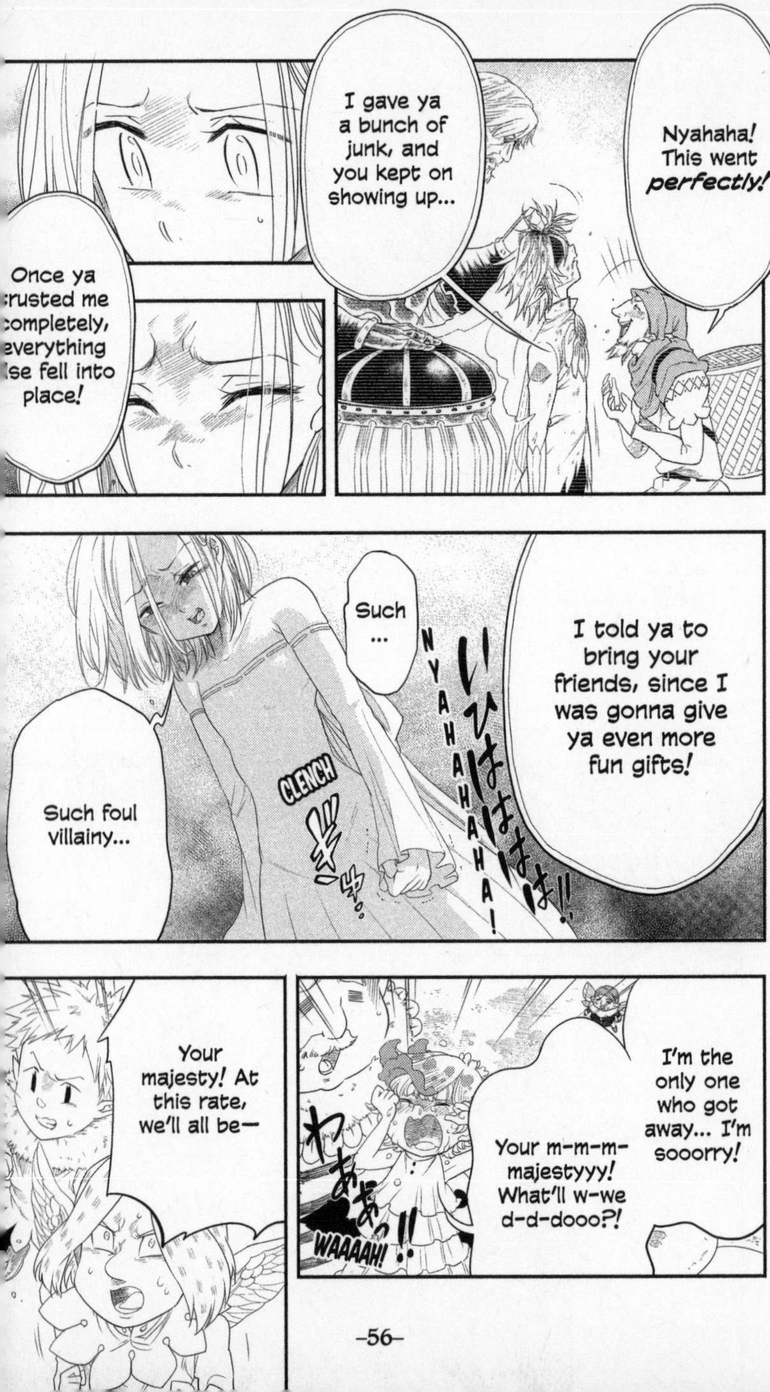
Nyahaha! This went *perfectly!*
I gave ya a bunch of junk, and you kept on showing up...
Once ya rusted me completely, everything se fell into place!
I told ya to bring your friends, since I was gonna give ya even more fun gifts!
NYAHAHAHAHA!
いひははは!!
Such ...
CLENCH
ぎゅっ
Such foul villainy...
I'm the only one who got away... I'm sooorry!
Your m-m-m-majestyyy! What'll w-we d-d-dooo?!
WAAAAH!
わあぁっ!!
Your majesty! At this rate, we'll all be—

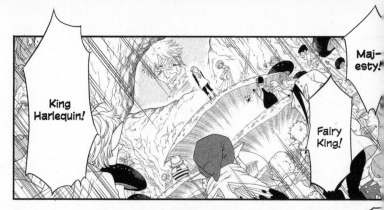

King Harlequin!

Maj- esty!

Fairy King!

Brother ...

Your maj- esty!!

My king!

Bro... ther ...?

FWOOM

!!

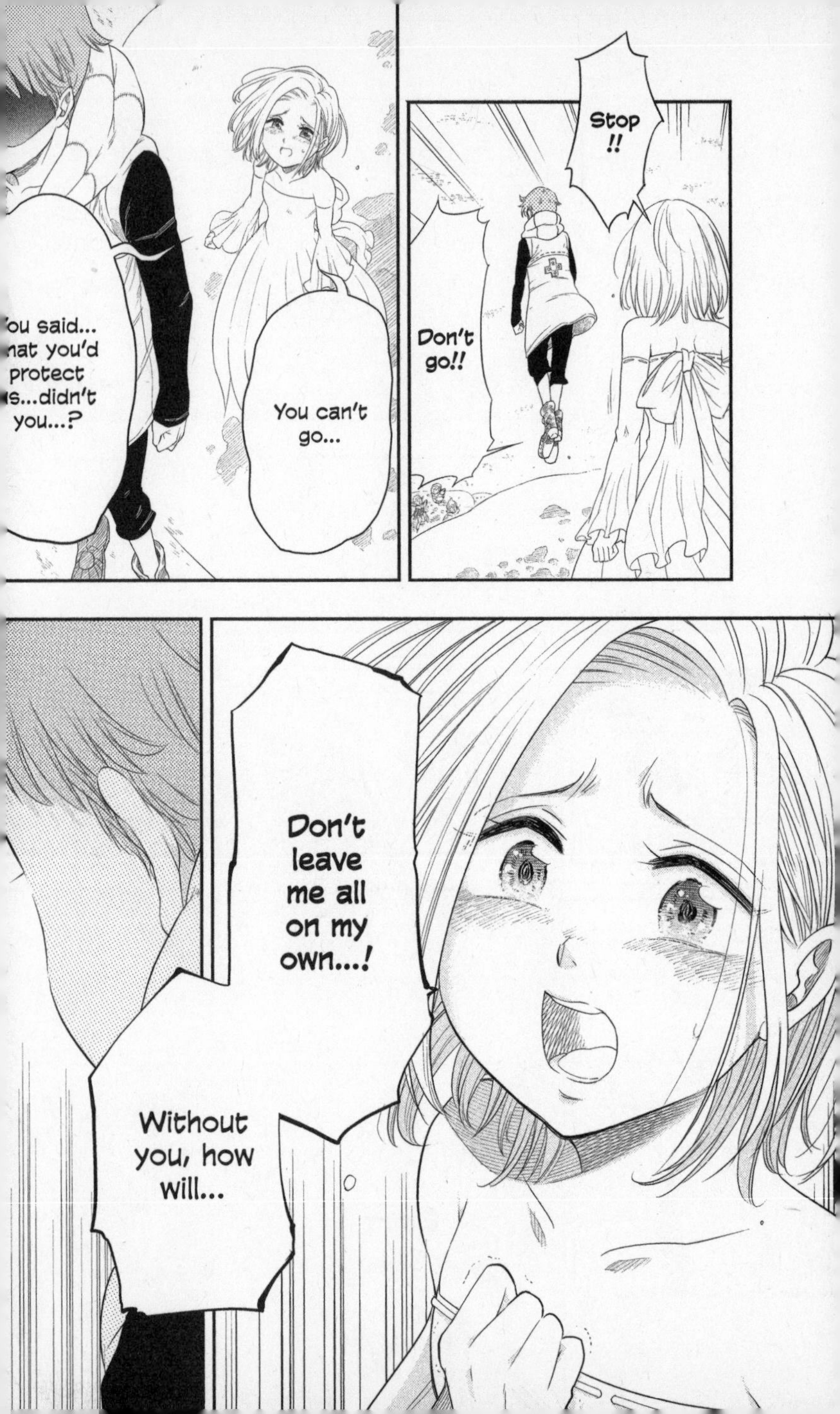
Stop!!
Don't go!!
You can't go...
ou said... nat you'd protect s...didn't you...?
Don't leave me all on my own...!
Without you, how will...

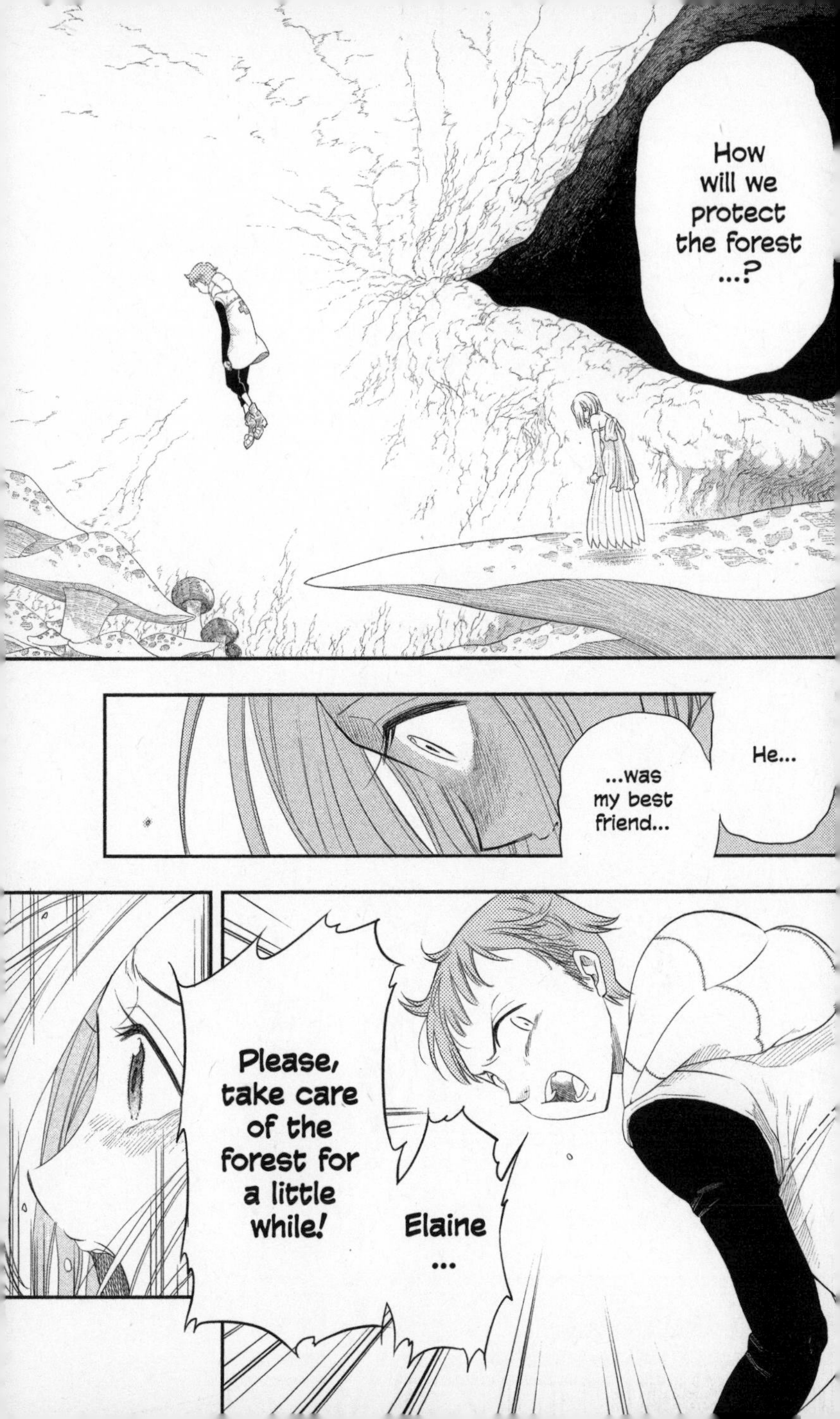
How will we protect the forest ...?
He...
...was my best friend...
Please, take care of the forest for a little while!
Elaine ...

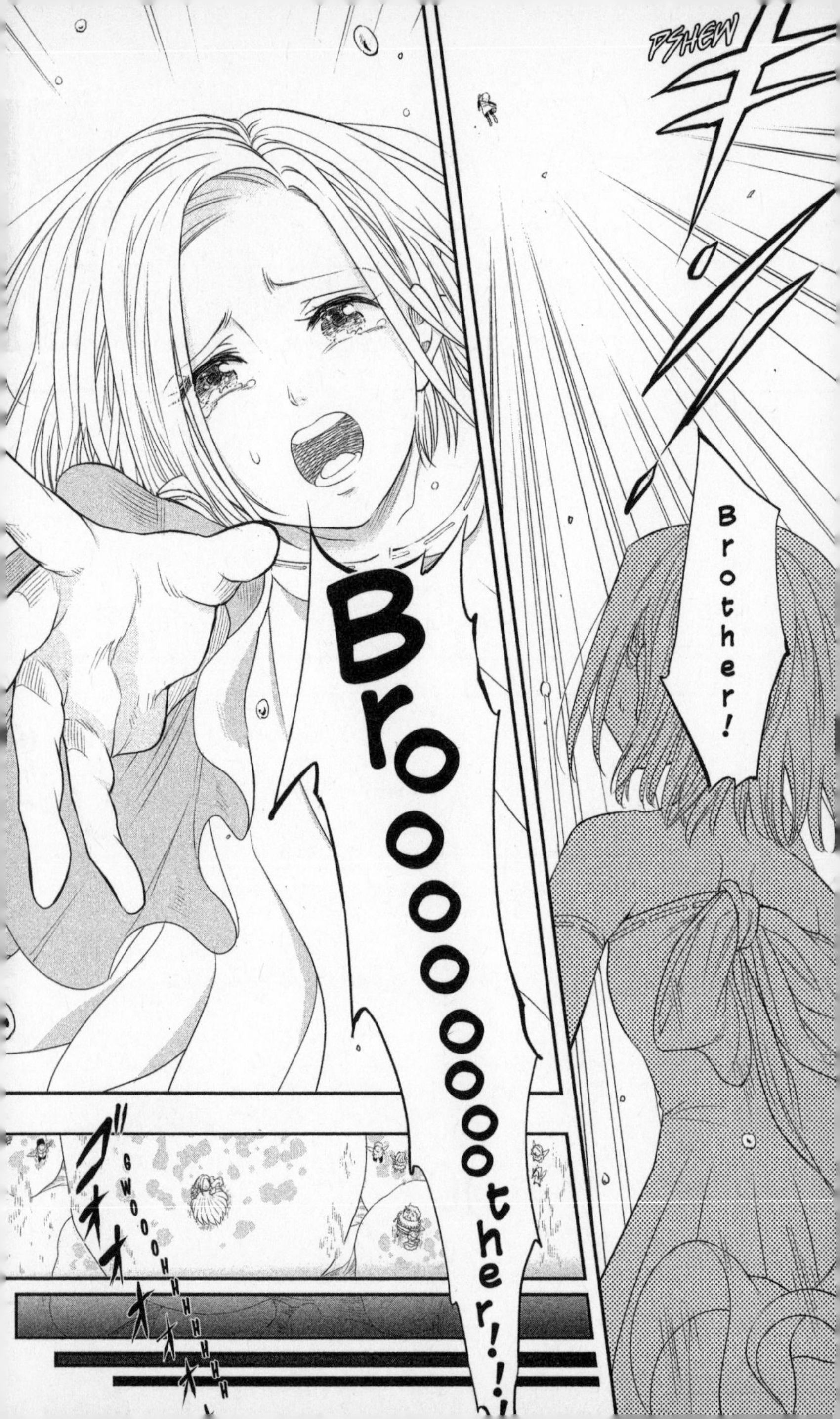

PSHEW
Brother!
Broooooother!!!
GWOOOHHHHHHH

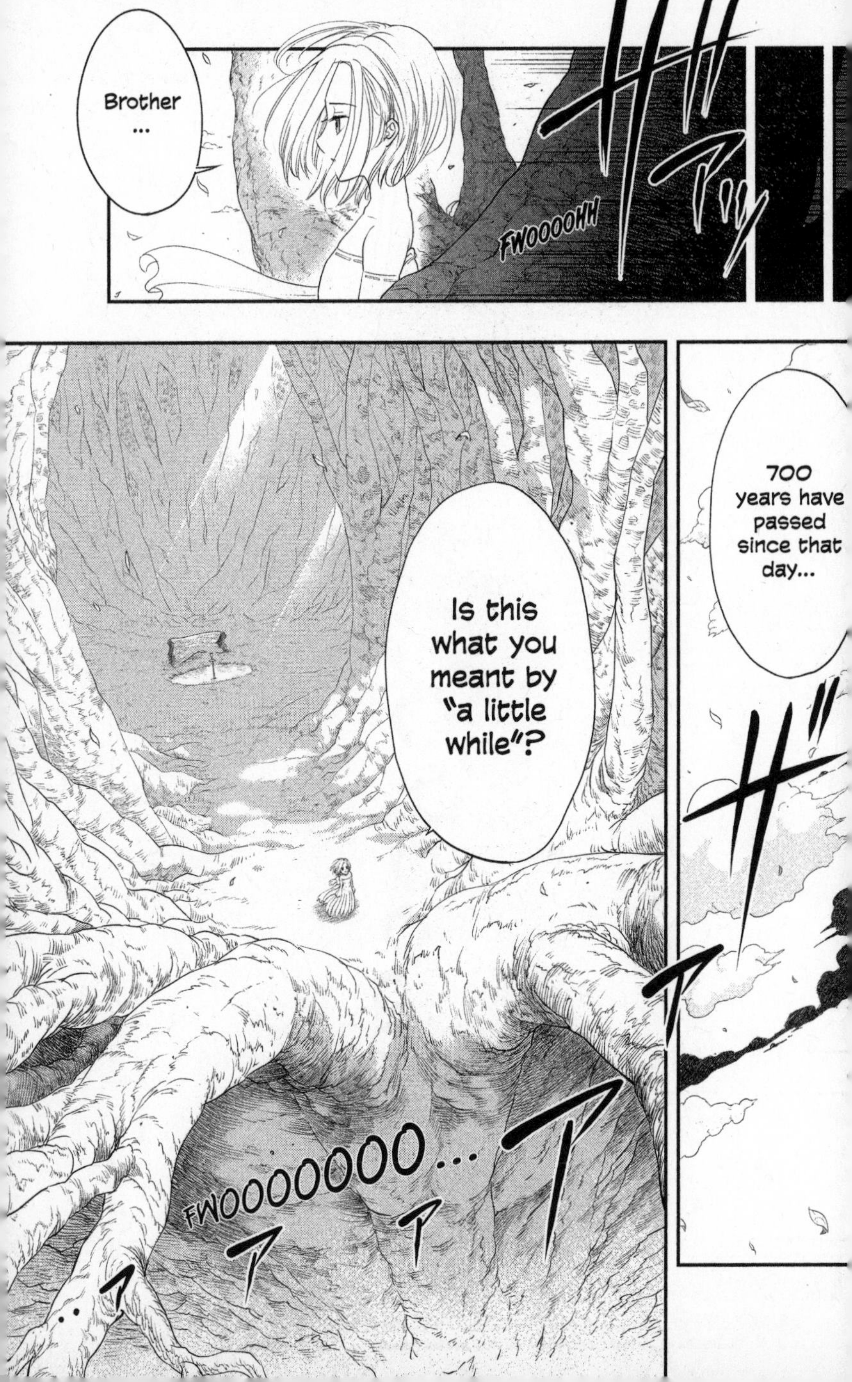
FWOOOOHH
Brother ...
700 years have passed since that day...
Is this what you meant by "a little while"?
FWOOOOOOO...

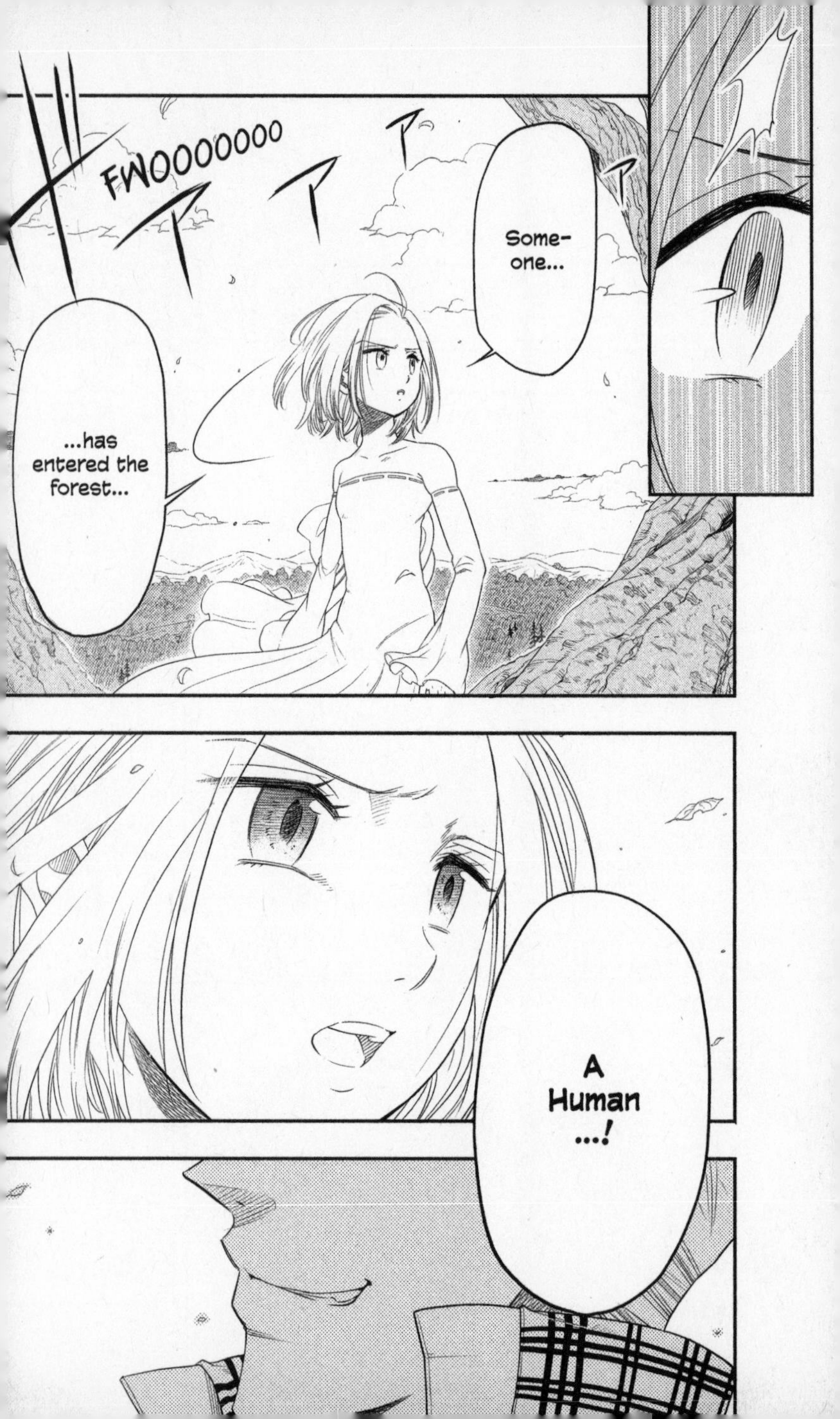

Some-one...
FWOOOOOOO
...has entered the forest...
A Human ...!

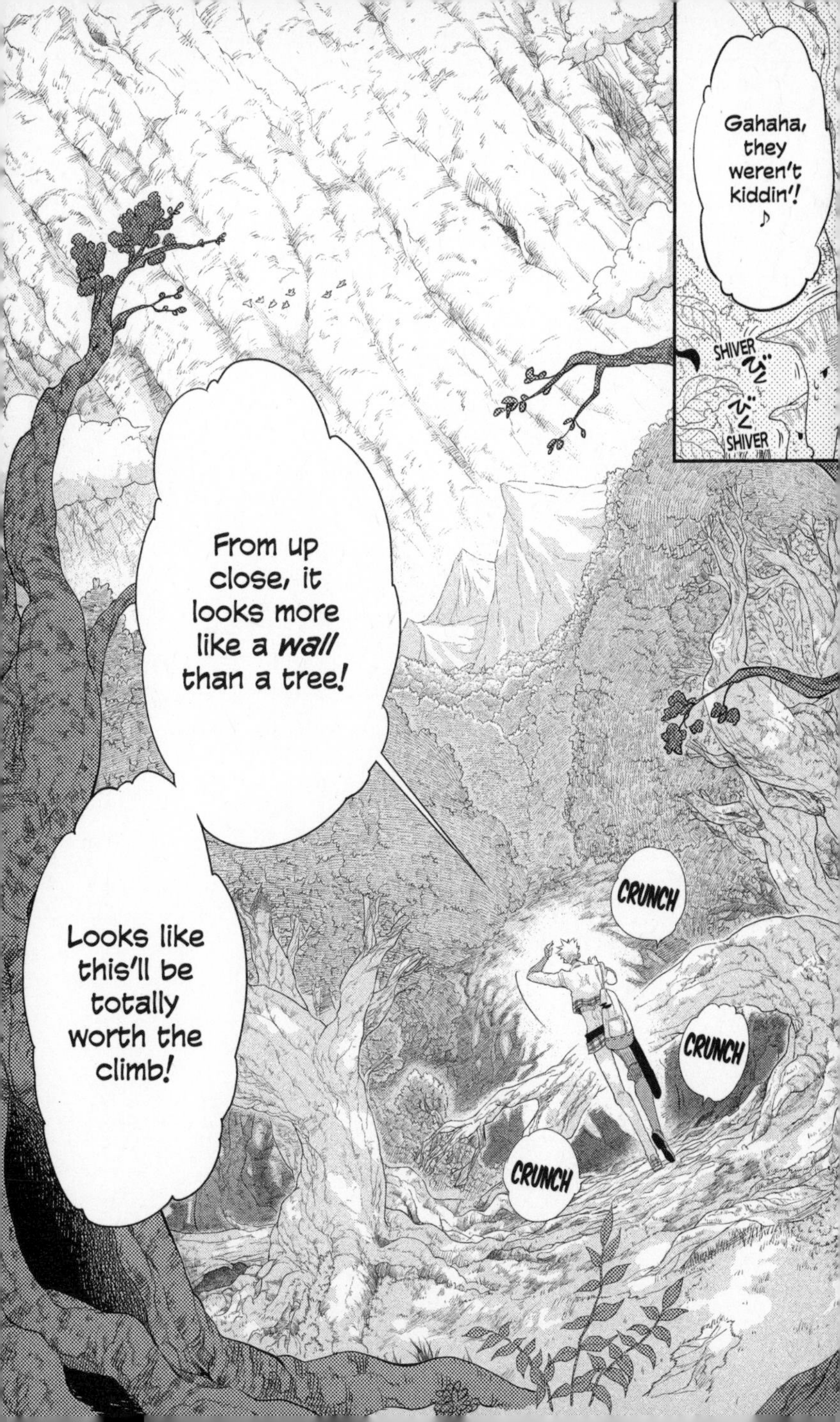
Gahaha, they weren't kiddin'! ♪
SHIVER
SHIVER
From up close, it looks more like a *wall* than a tree!
Looks like this'll be totally worth the climb!
CRUNCH
CRUNCH
CRUNCH

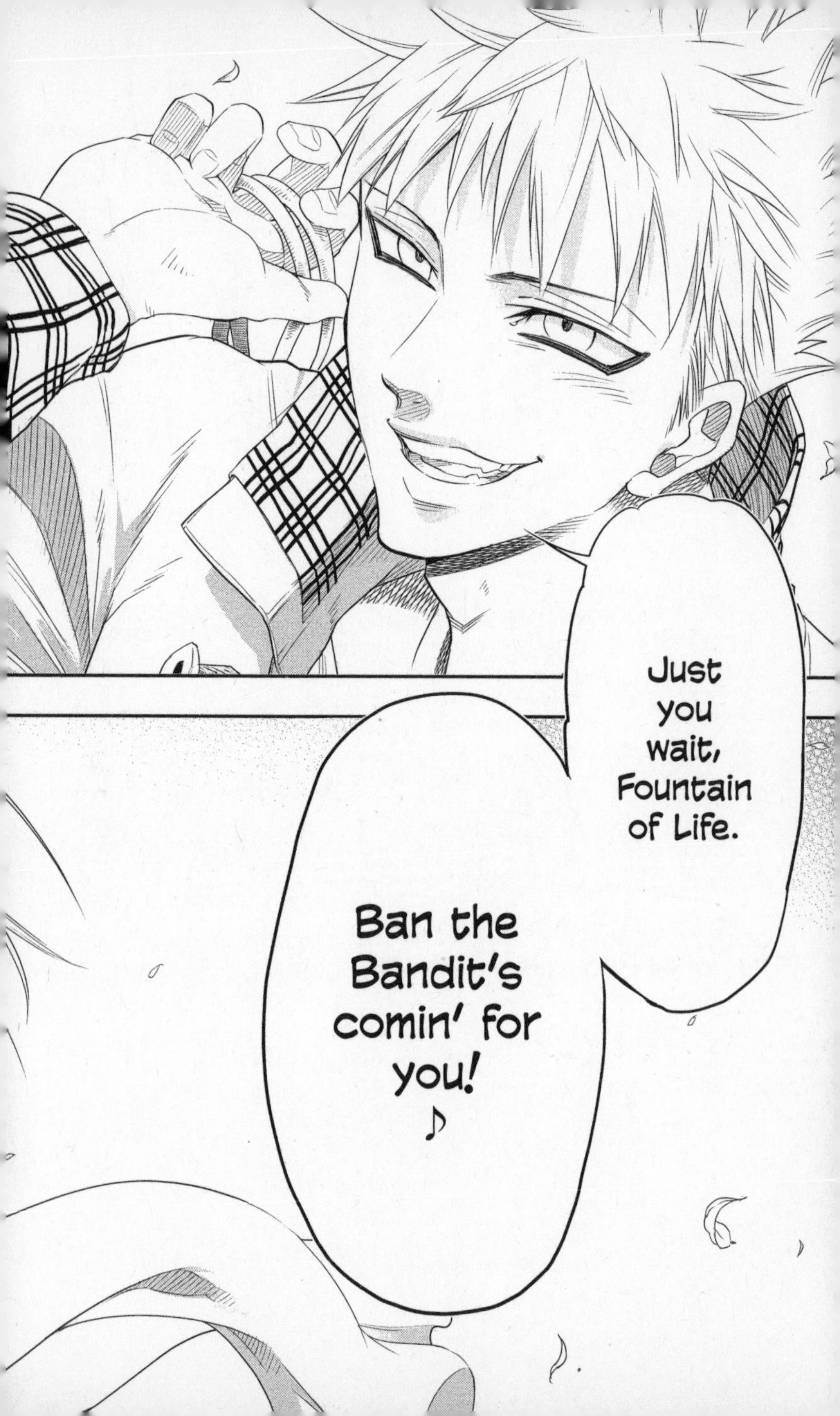
Just you wait, Fountain of Life.
Ban the Bandit's comin' for you! ♪

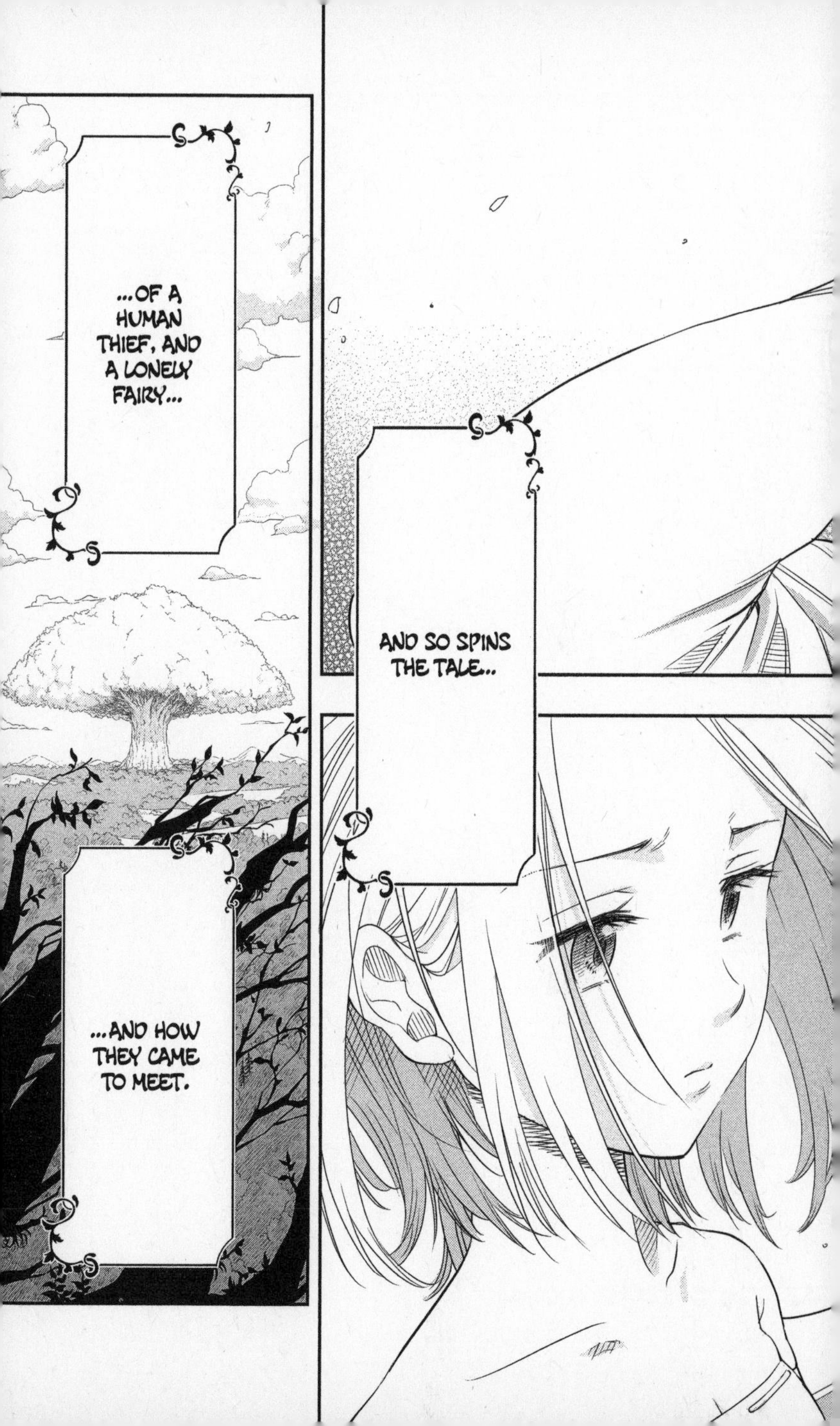
AND SO SPINS THE TALE...
...OF A HUMAN THIEF, AND A LONELY FAIRY...
...AND HOW THEY CAME TO MEET.

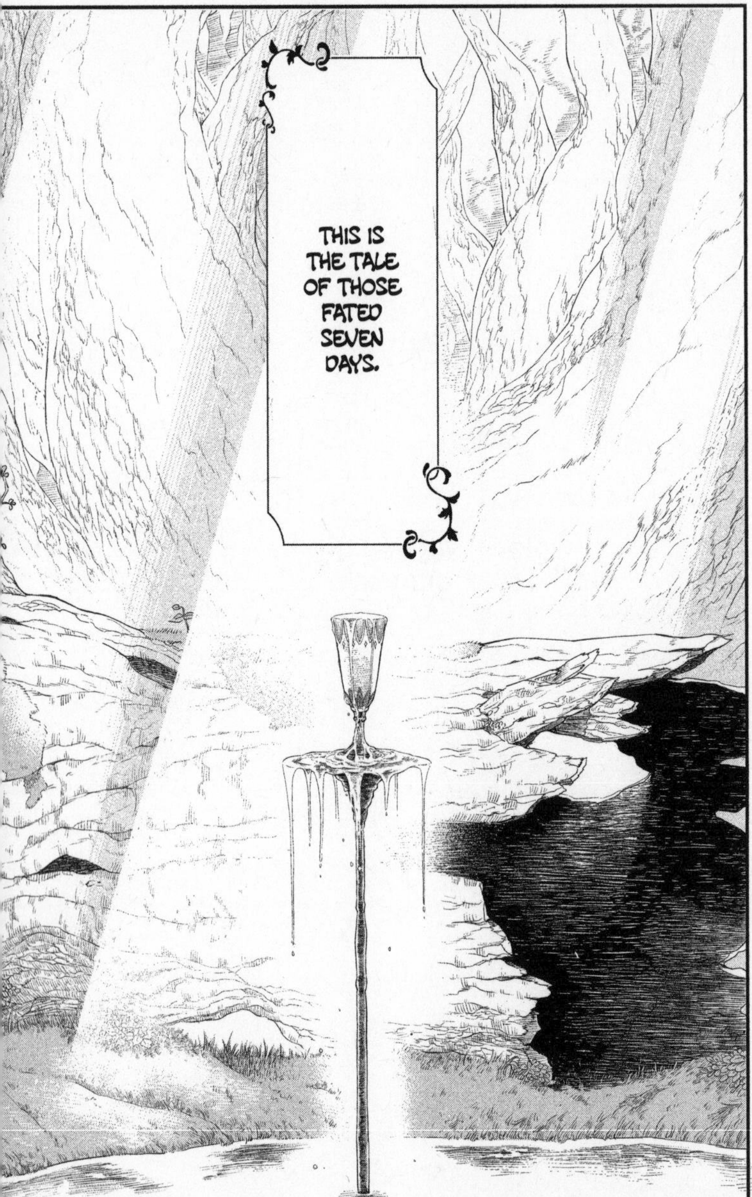
THIS IS THE TALE OF THOSE FATED SEVEN DAYS.

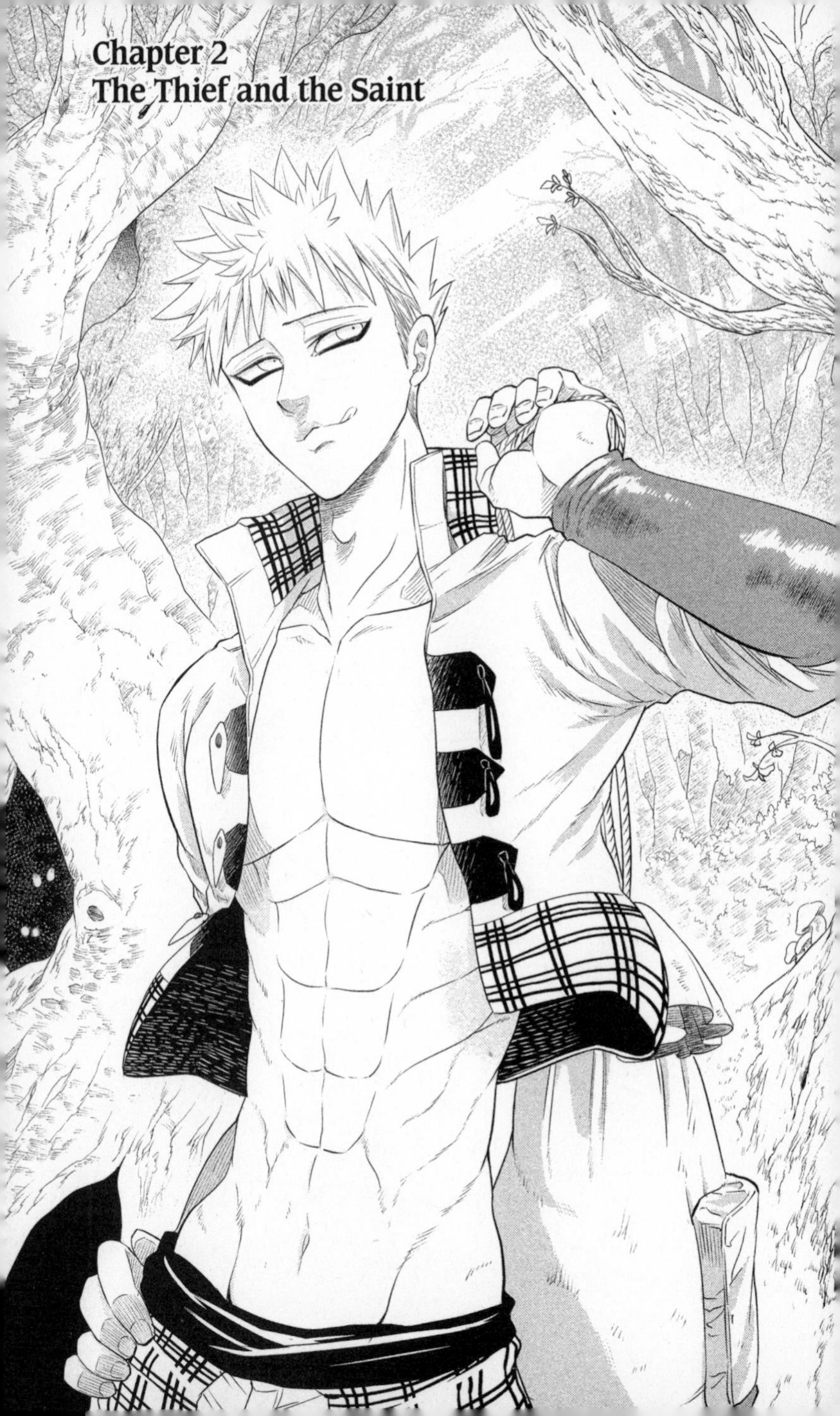
Chapter 2
The Thief and the Saint

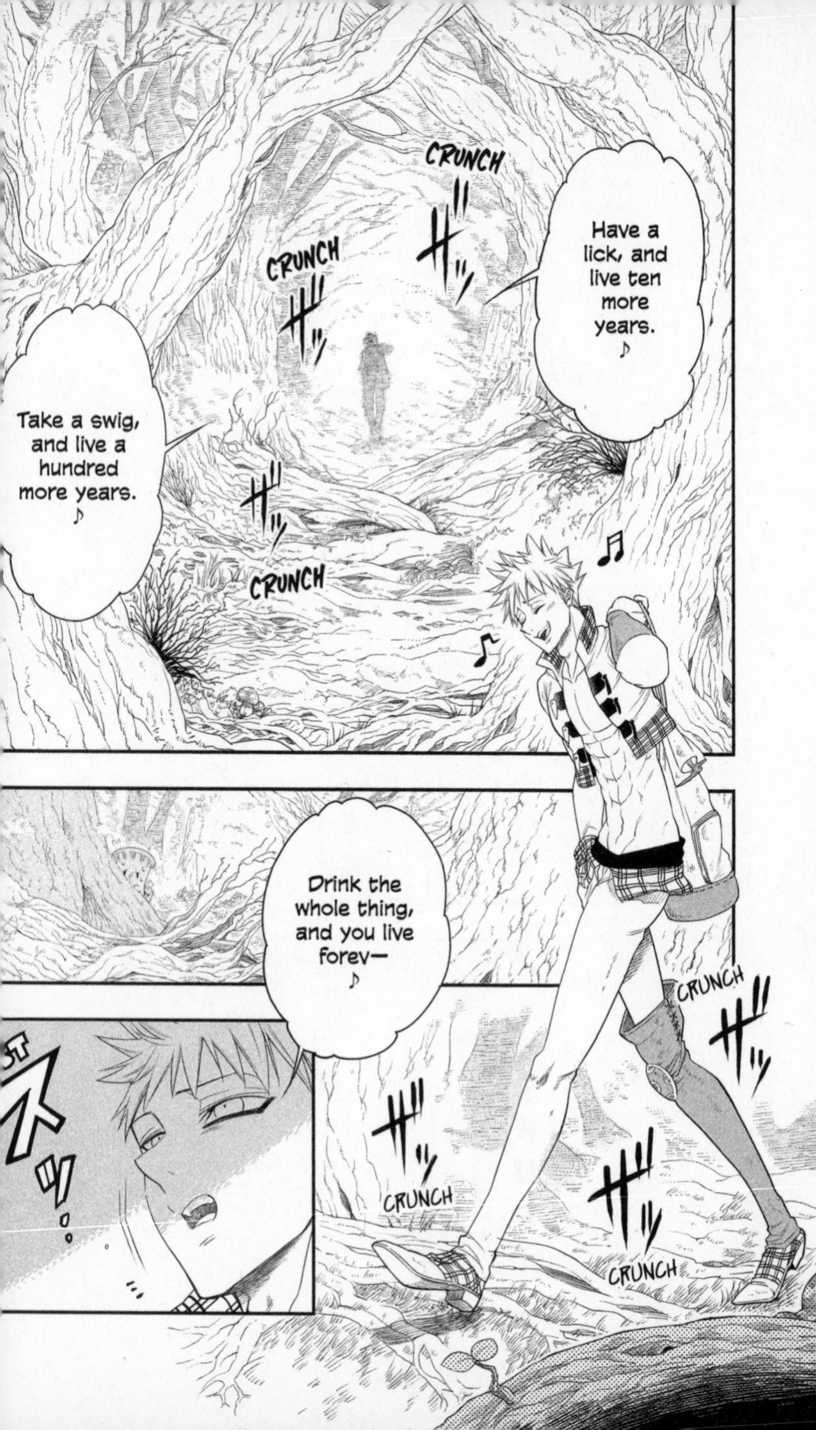
Have a lick, and live ten more years. ♪
CRUNCH
CRUNCH
Take a swig, and live a hundred more years. ♪
CRUNCH
CRUNCH
CRUNCH
Drink the whole thing, and you live forev— ♪
CRUNCH

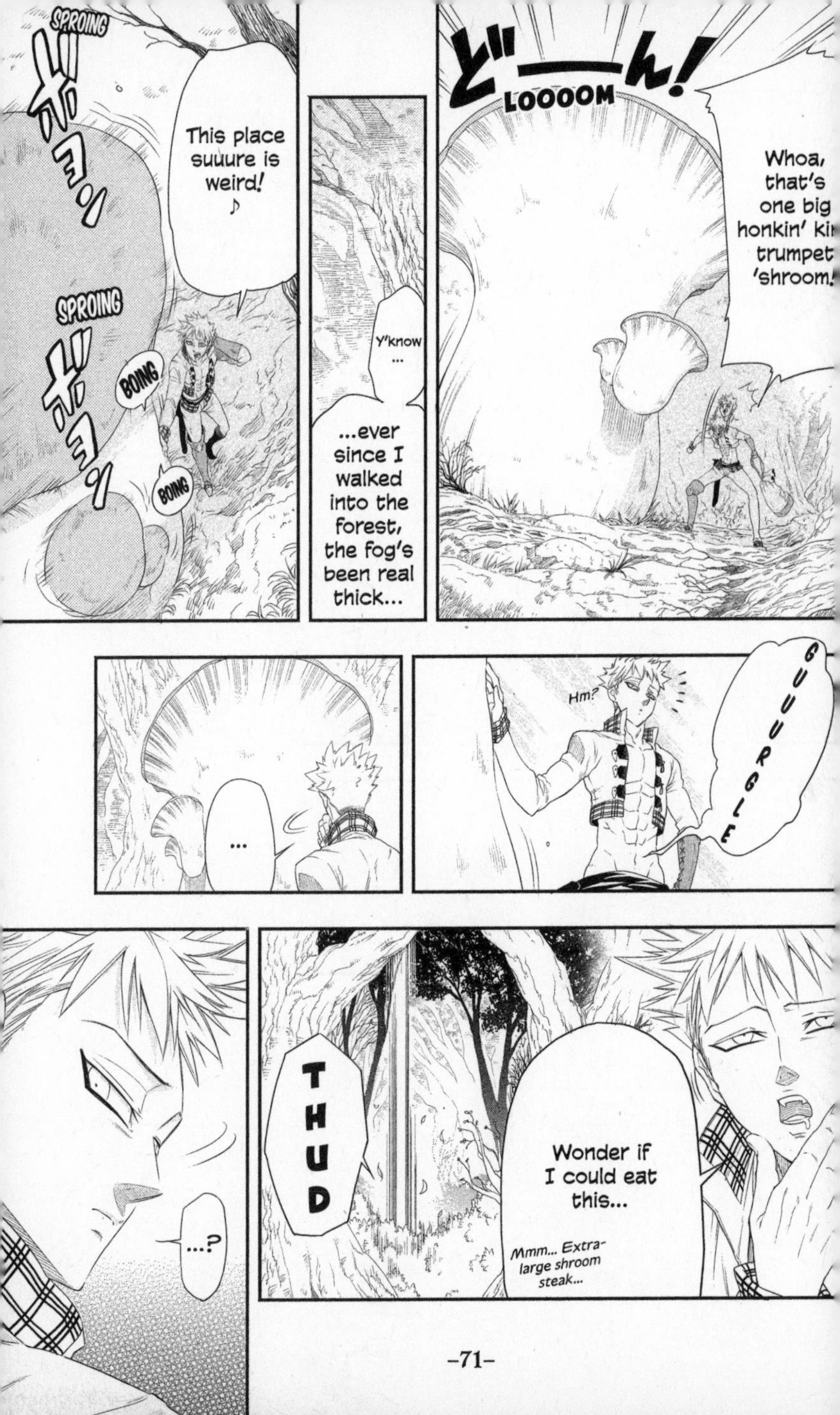
どーーん!
LOOOOM
Whoa, that's one big honkin' ki trumpet 'shroom!
Y'know ...
...ever since I walked into the forest, the fog's been real thick...
SPROING
This place suuure is weird! ♪
SPROING
BOING
BOING
Hm?
GUUURGLE
...
Wonder if I could eat this...
Mmm... Extra-large shroom steak...
THUD
...?

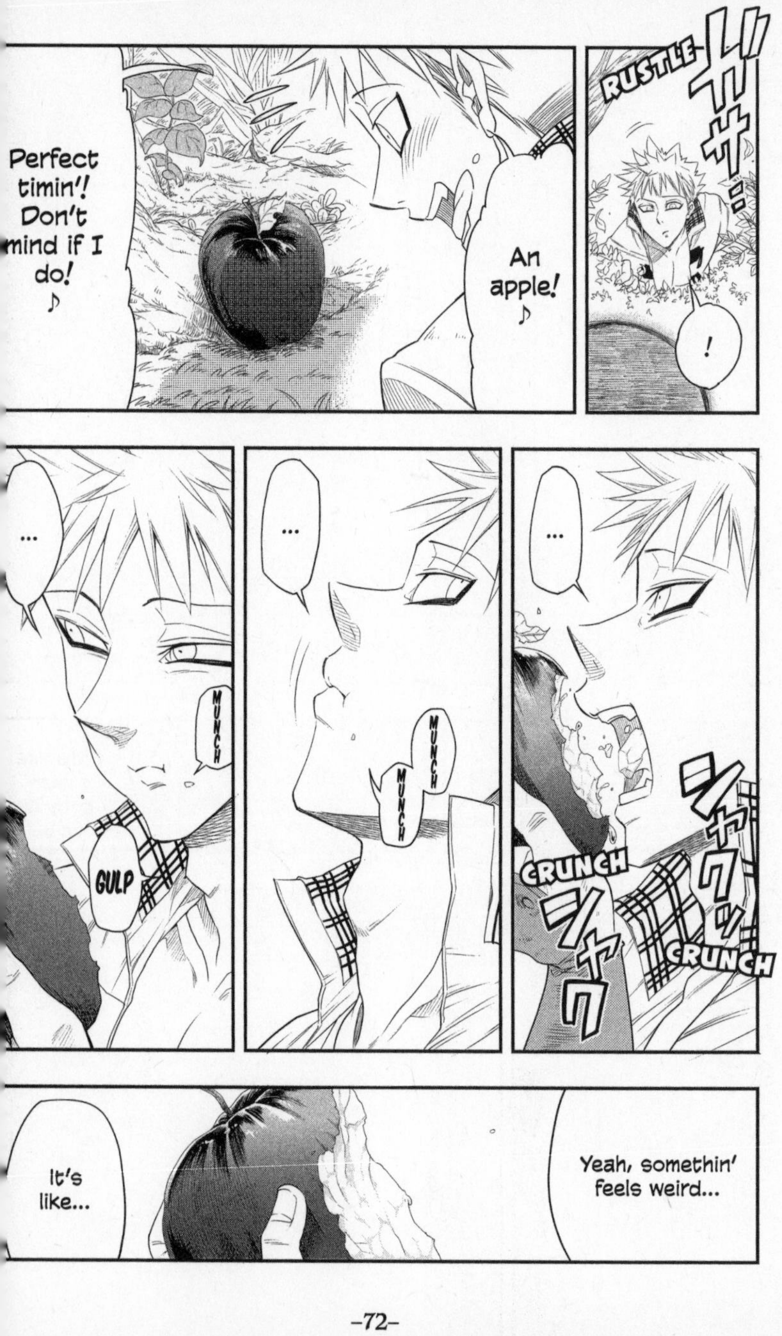
RUSTLE
ガサ
!
An apple! ♪
Perfect timin'! Don't mind if I do! ♪
...
CRUNCH
シャクッ
CRUNCH
シャク
...
MUNCH
MUNCH
...
MUNCH
GULP
Yeah, somethin' feels weird...
It's like...

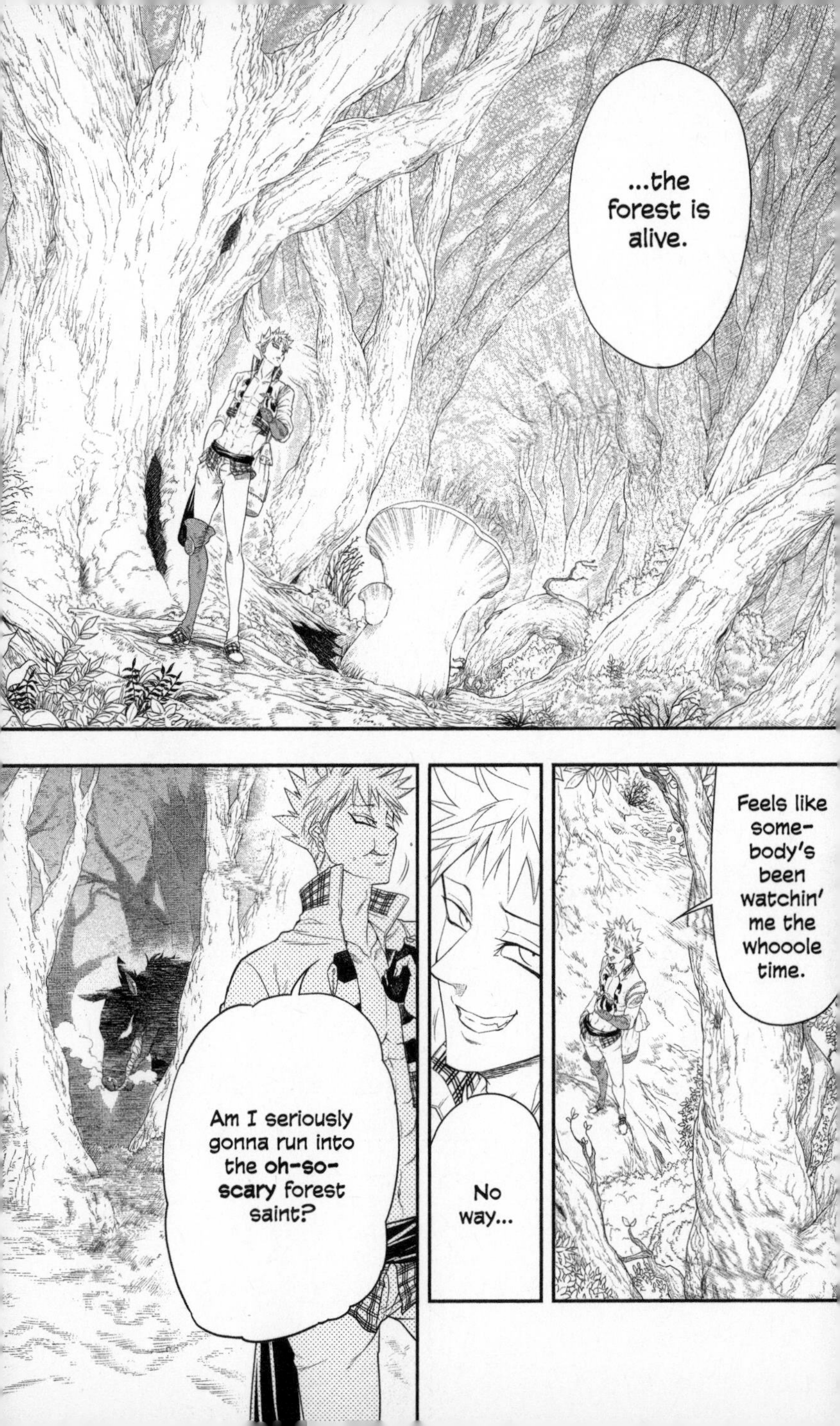
...the forest is alive.
Feels like some-body's been watchin' me the whooole time.
No way...
Am I seriously gonna run into the oh-so-scary forest saint?

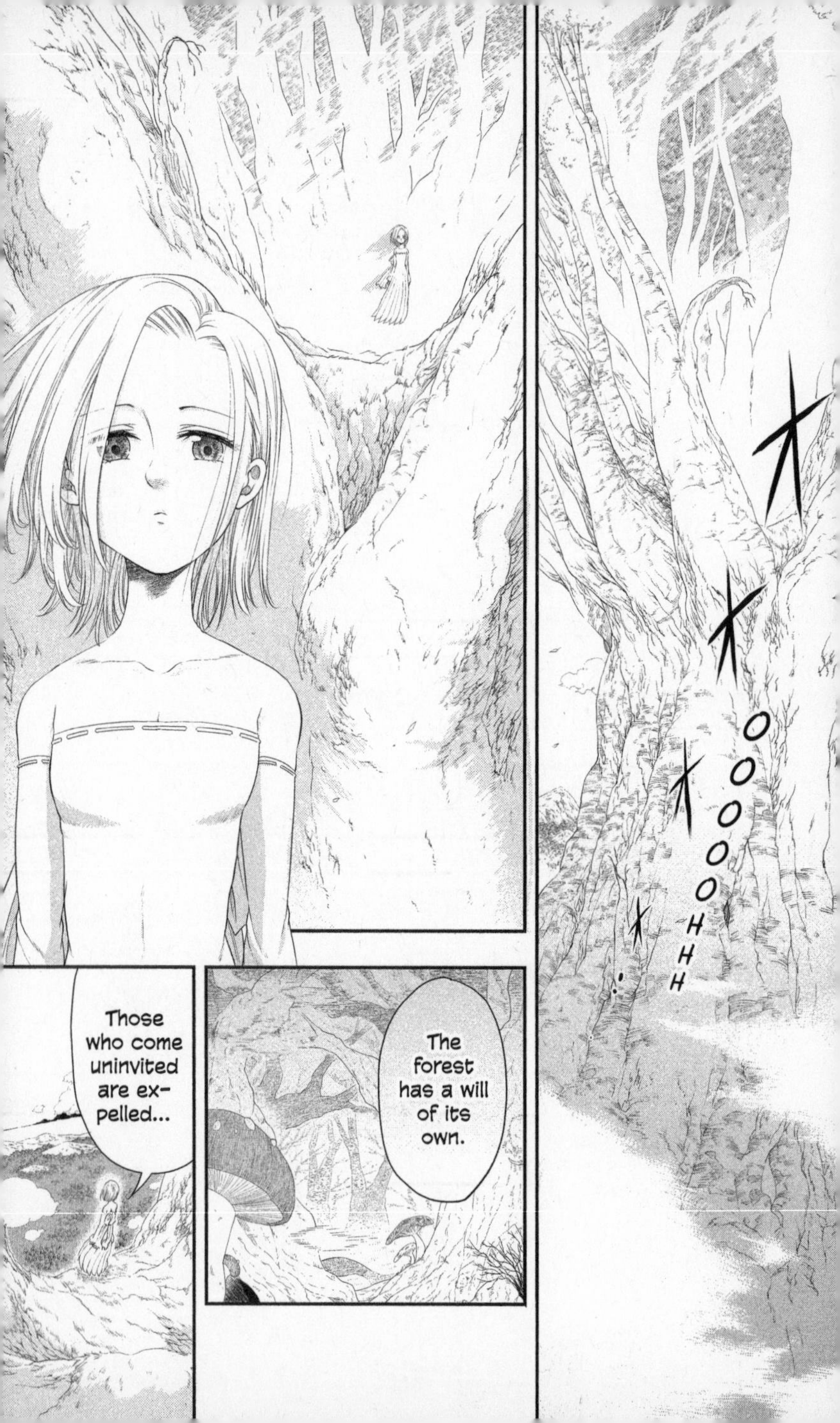
OOOOOOHHH
The forest has a will of its own.
Those who come uninvited are ex-pelled...

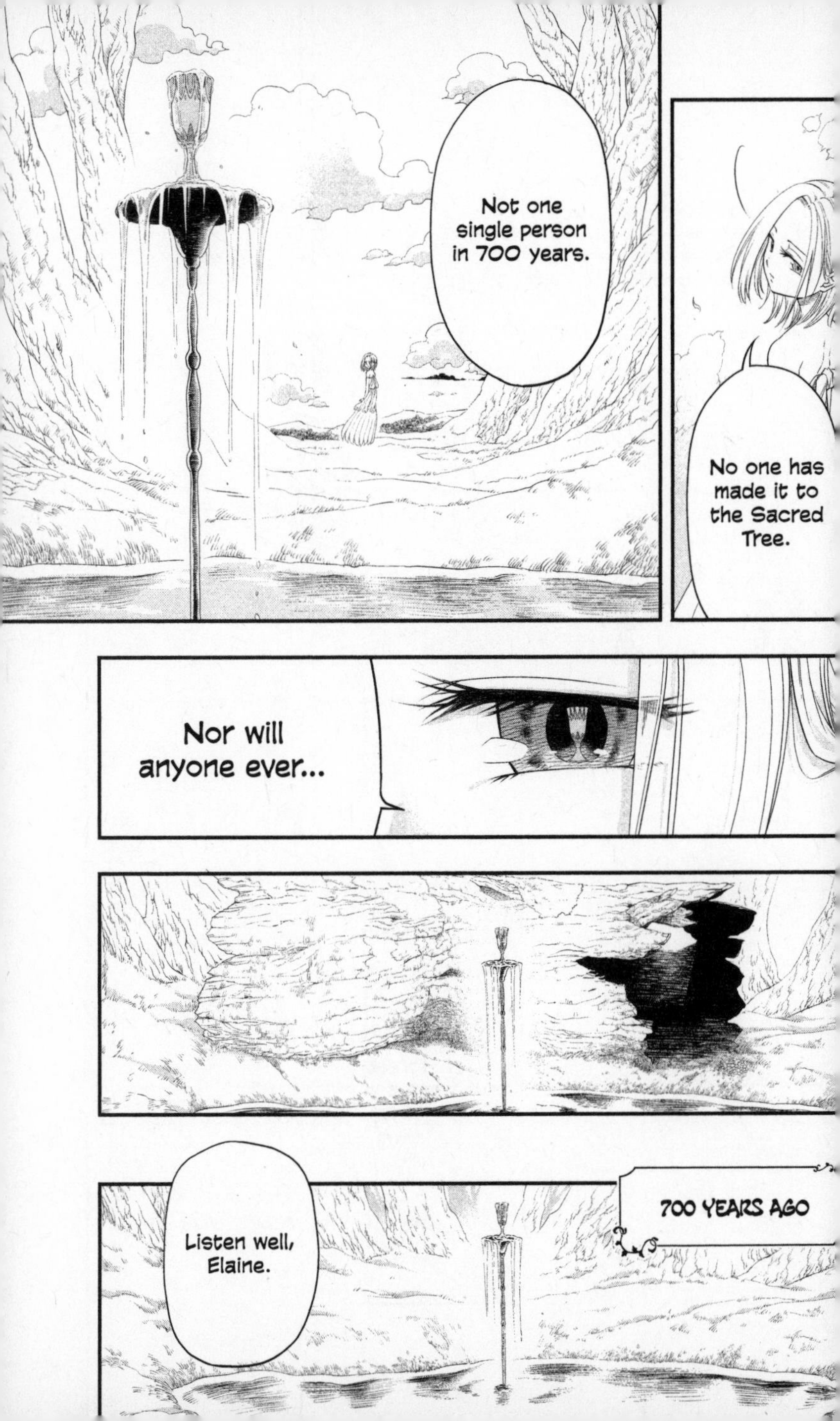
No one has made it to the Sacred Tree.
Not one single person in 700 years.
Nor will anyone ever...
700 YEARS AGO
Listen well, Elaine.

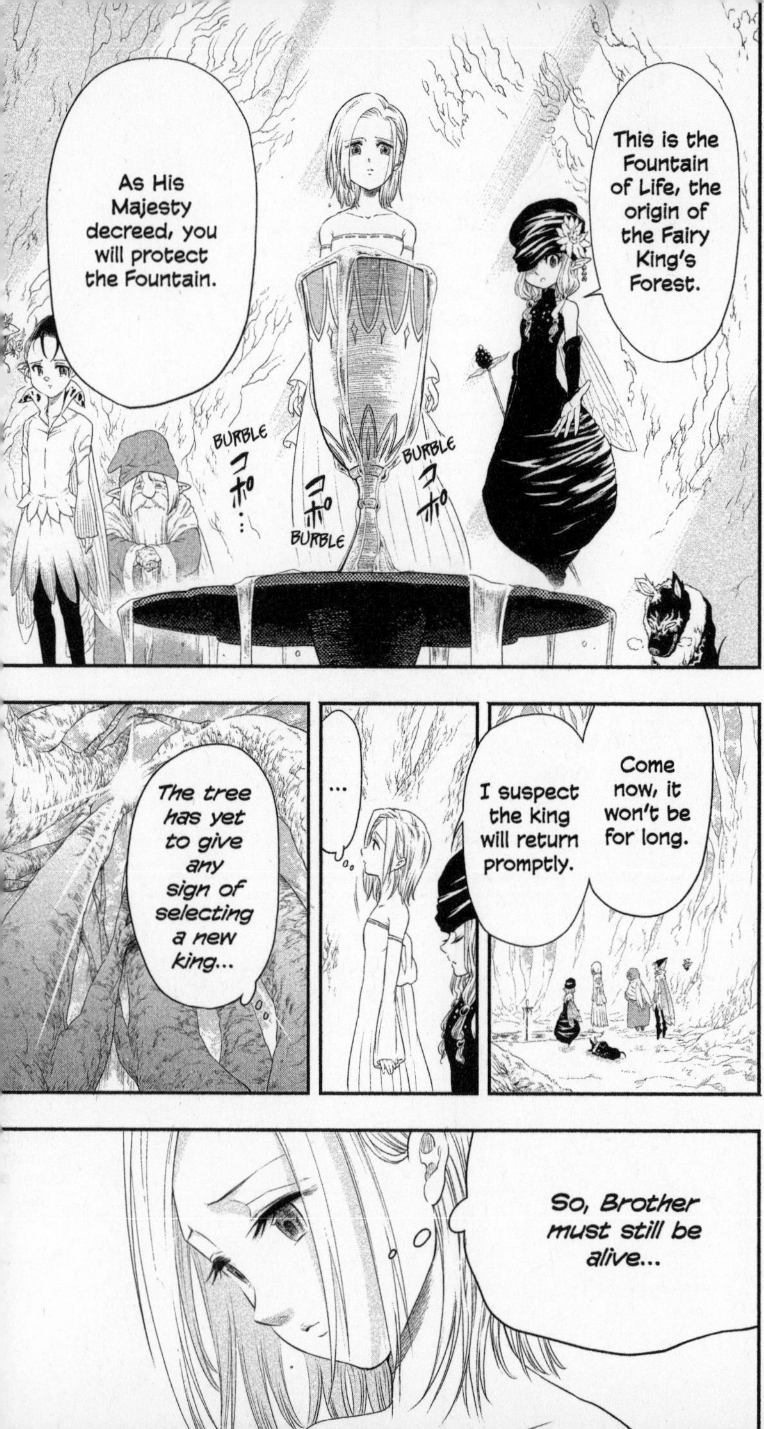
This is the Fountain of Life, the origin of the Fairy King's Forest.
As His Majesty decreed, you will protect the Fountain.
BURBLE
コポ
コポ
BURBLE
BURBLE
コポ…
Come now, it won't be for long.
I suspect the king will return promptly.
…
The tree has yet to give any sign of selecting a new king…
So, Brother must still be alive…

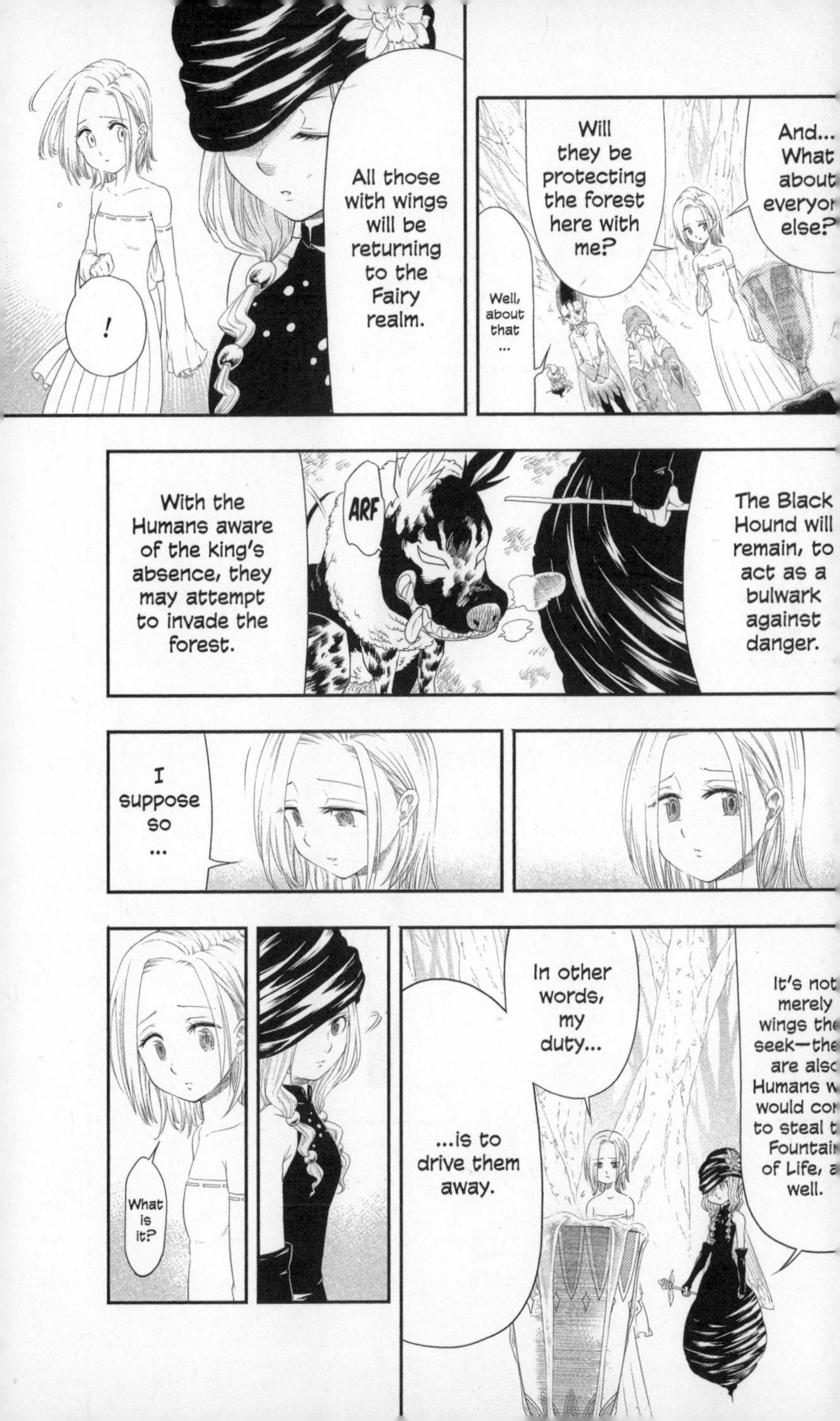
And... What about everyor else?
Will they be protecting the forest here with me?
Well, about that ...
All those with wings will be returning to the Fairy realm.
!
The Black Hound will remain, to act as a bulwark against danger.
ARF
With the Humans aware of the king's absence, they may attempt to invade the forest.
I suppose so ...
It's not merely wings the seek—the are also Humans w would cor to steal t Fountai of Life, a well.
In other words, my duty...
...is to drive them away.
What is it?

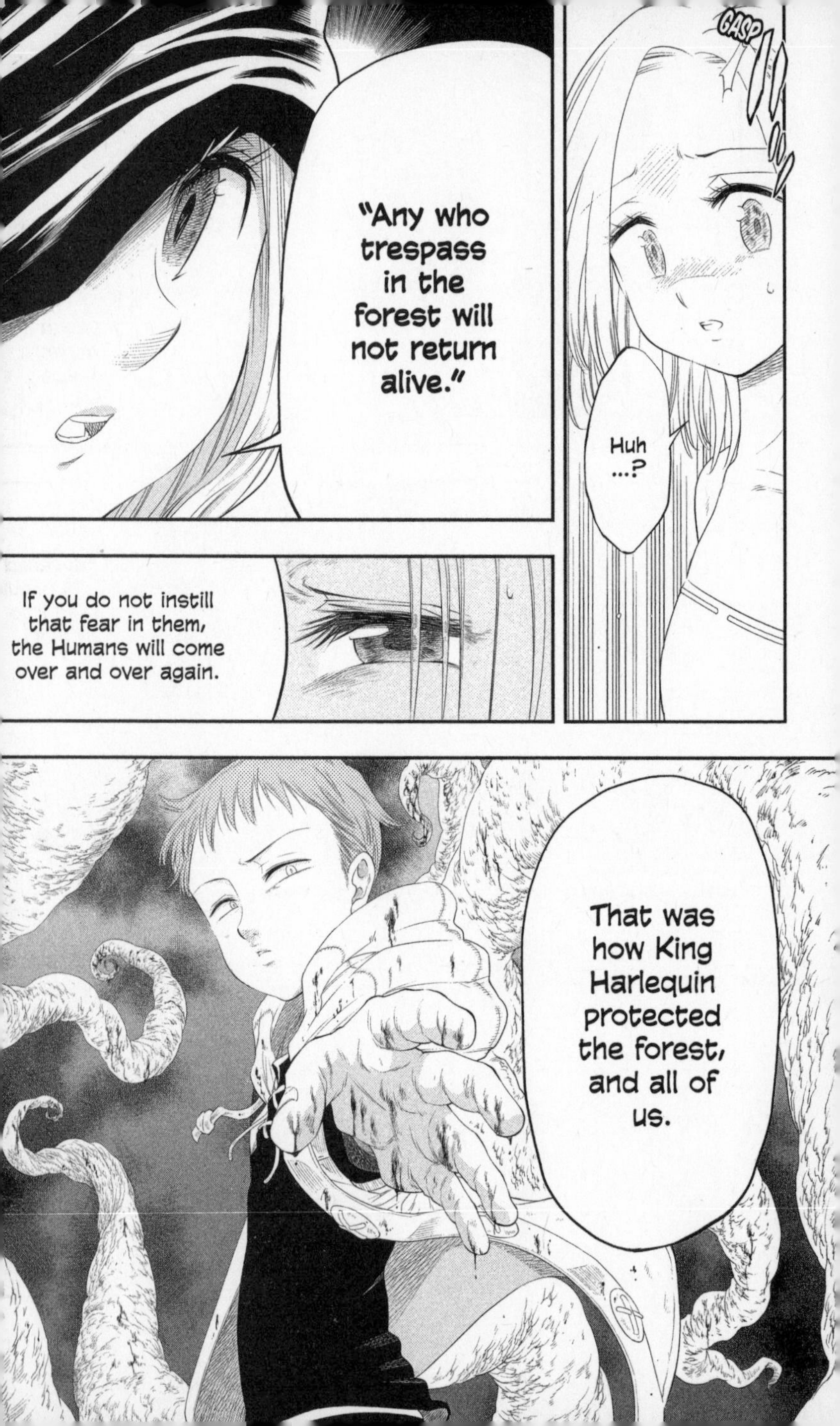
GASP
Huh ...?
"Any who trespass in the forest will not return alive."
If you do not instill that fear in them, the Humans will come over and over again.
That was how King Harlequin protected the forest, and all of us.

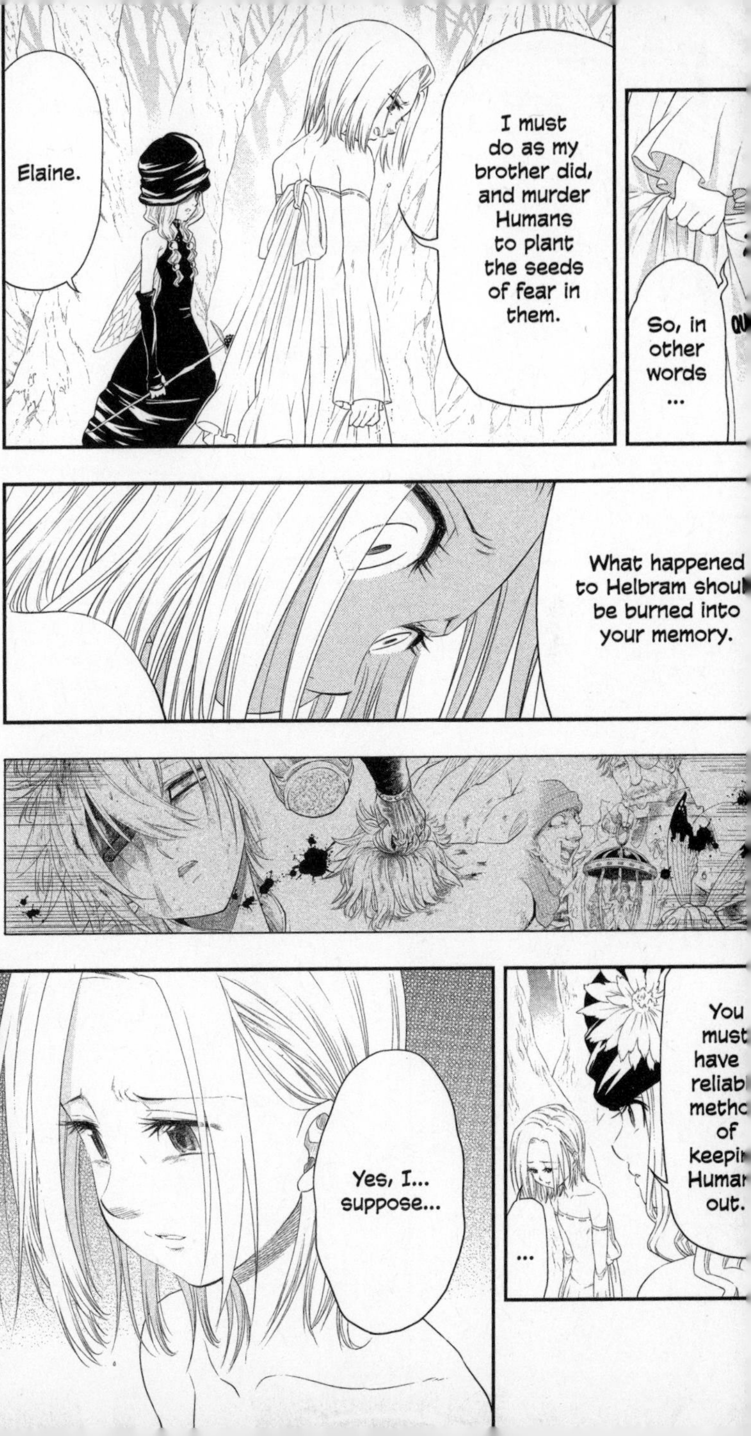
So, in other words ...
I must do as my brother did, and murder Humans to plant the seeds of fear in them.
Elaine.
What happened to Helbram shoul be burned into your memory.
You must have reliab metho of keepi Huma out.
...
Yes, I... suppose...

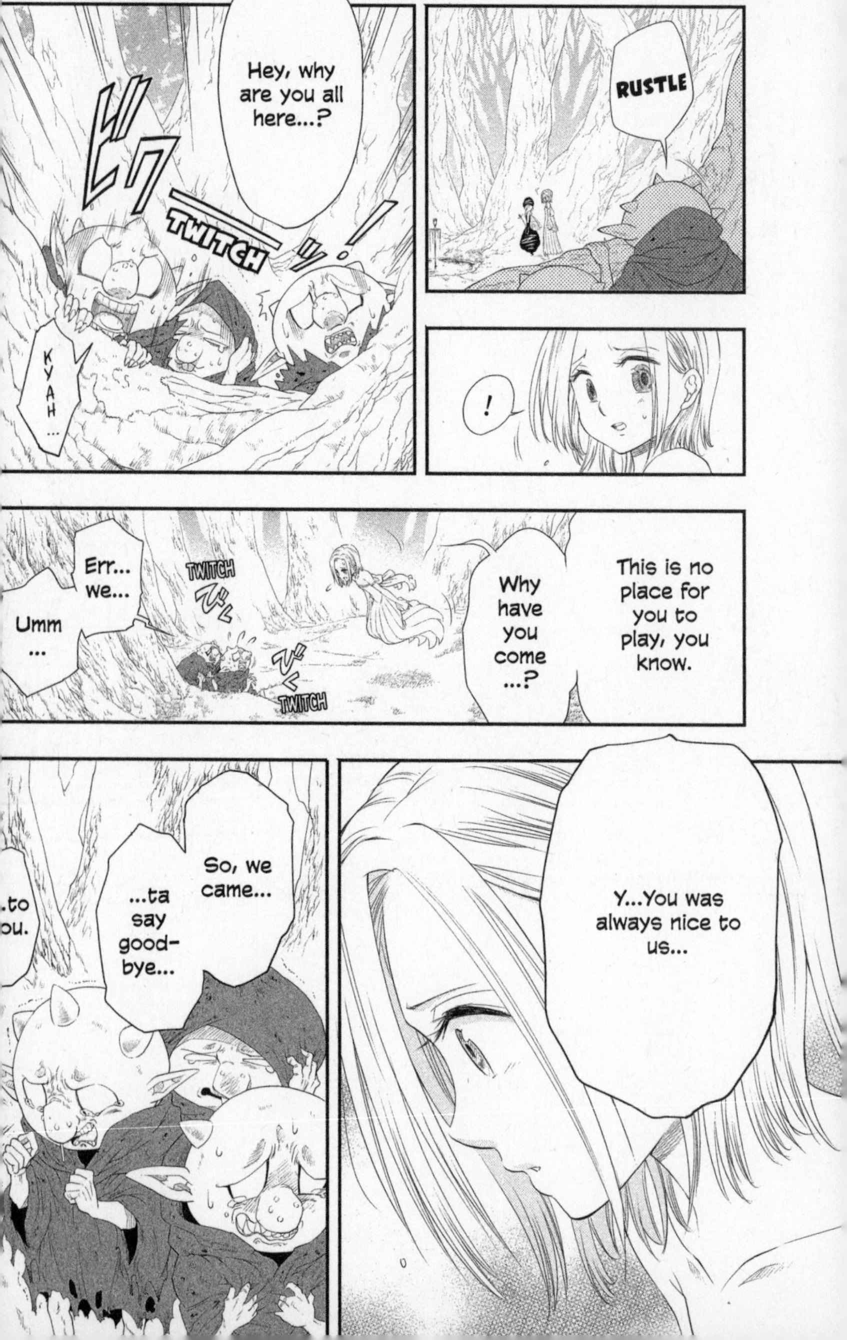
RUSTLE
!
Hey, why are you all here...?
TWITCH
KYAH...
This is no place for you to play, you know.
Why have you come ...?
TWITCH
TWITCH
Err... we...
Umm ...
Y...You was always nice to us...
So, we came...
...ta say good-bye...
.to ou.

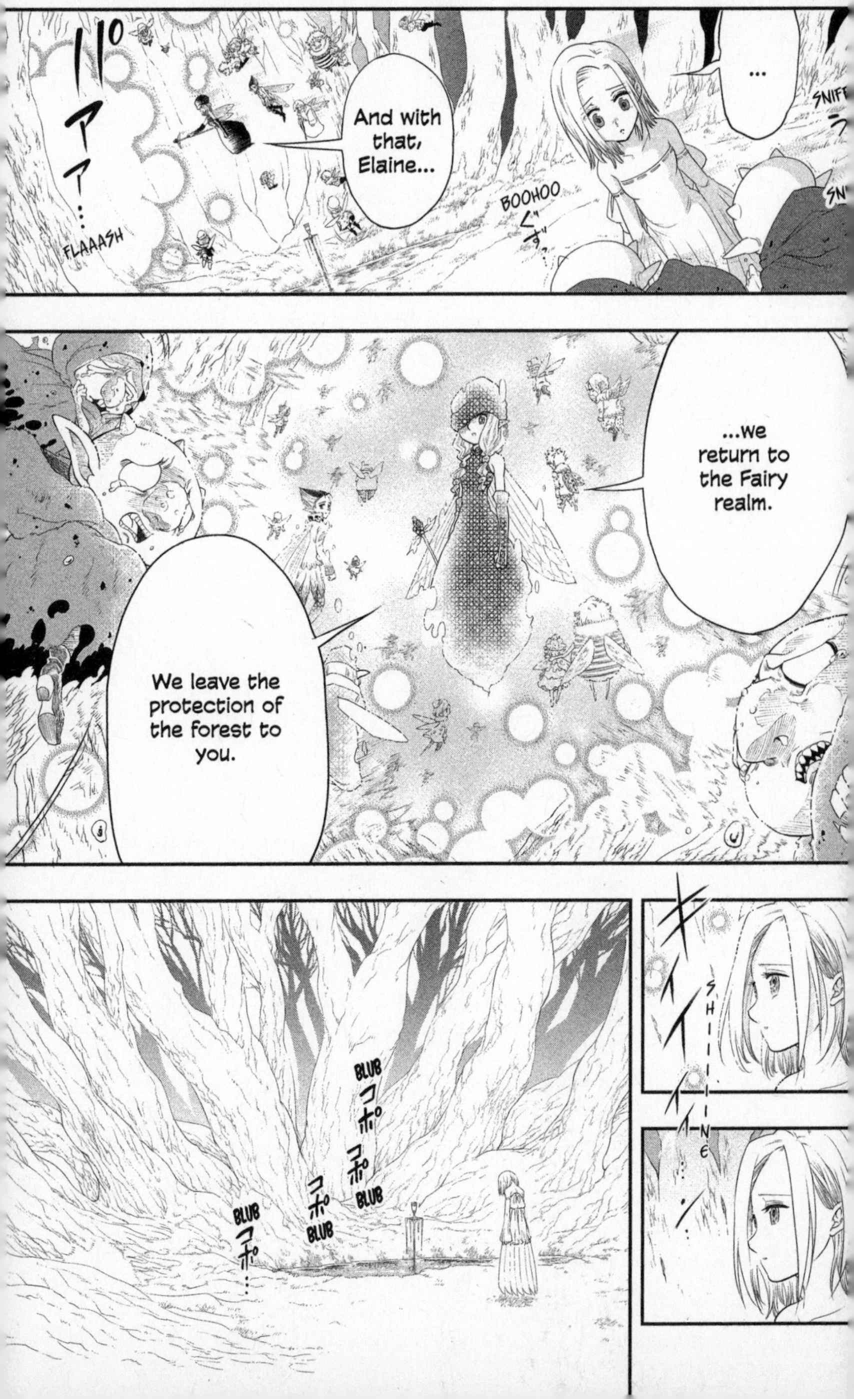
...
SNIFF
BOOHOO
ぐずっ…
And with that, Elaine...
パアア…
FLAAASH
...we return to the Fairy realm.
We leave the protection of the forest to you.
キイイイ…
SHI-I-I-I-NE
BLUB
コポ
コポ
BLUB
コポ
BLUB
BLUB
コポ…

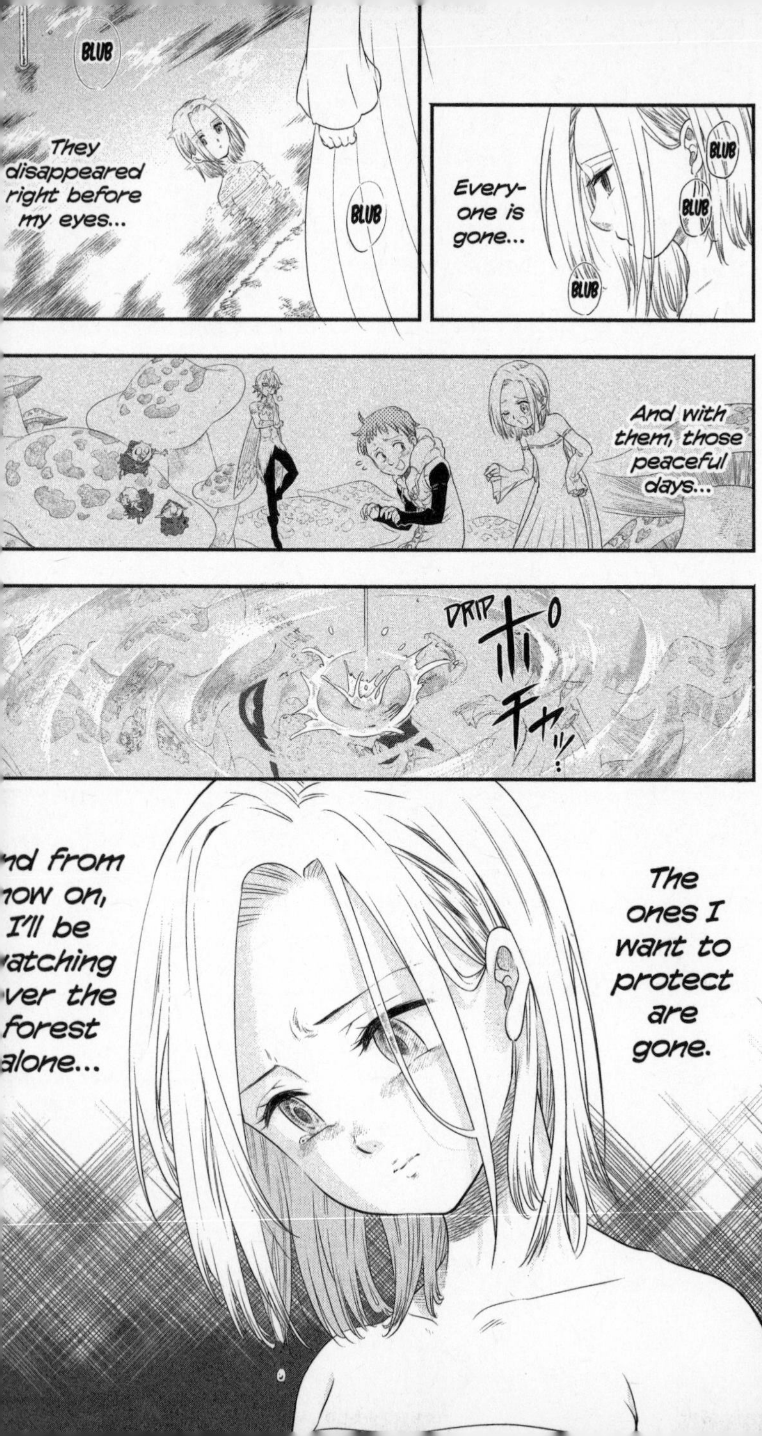
BLUB
BLUB
Every-one is gone...
BLUB
BLUB
BLUB
They disappeared right before my eyes...
And with them, those peaceful days...
DRIP
ポチャッ
The ones I want to protect are gone.
nd from now on, I'll be atching ver the forest alone...

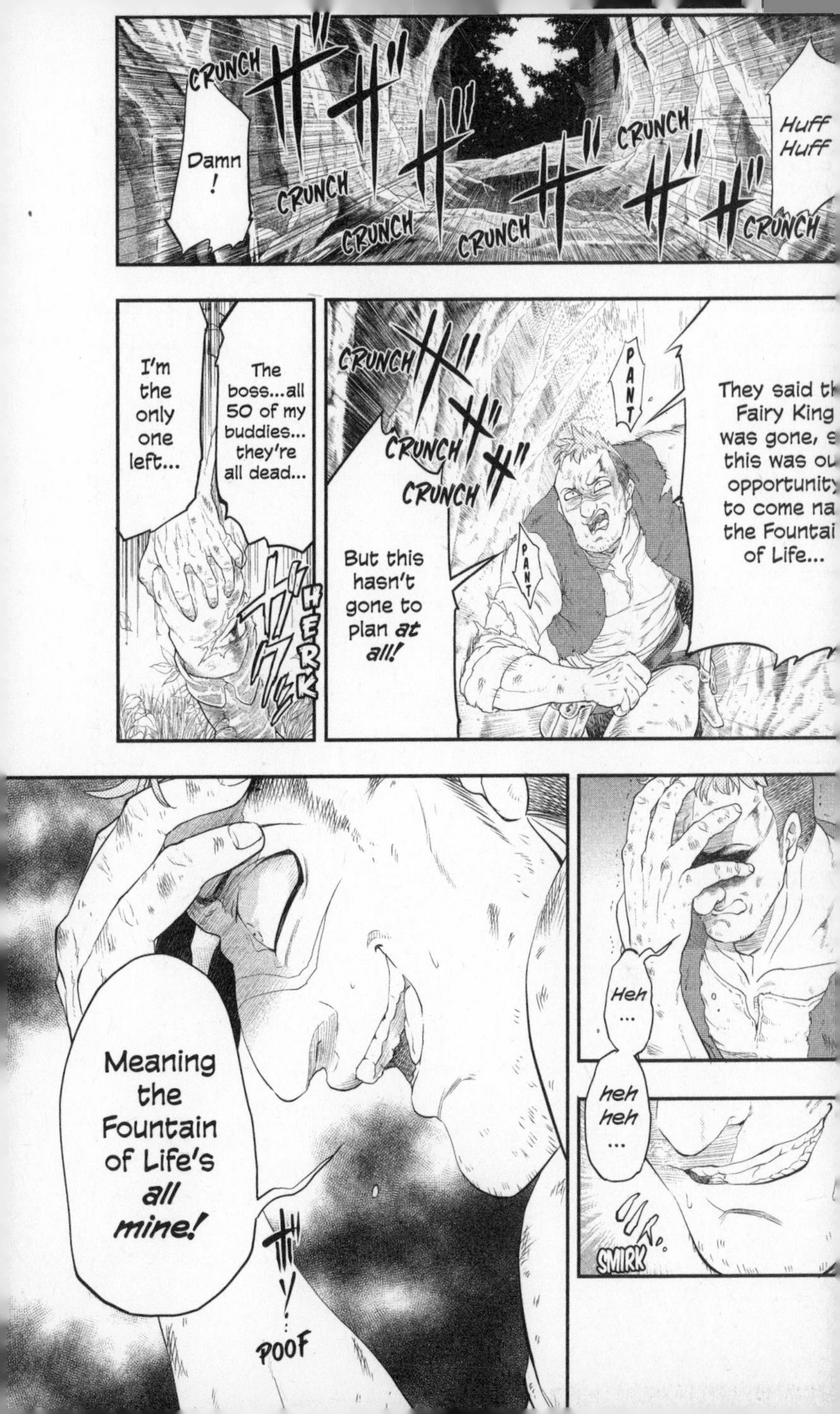
Huff
Huff
CRUNCH
CRUNCH
CRUNCH
CRUNCH
CRUNCH
CRUNCH
Damn!
They said th
Fairy King
was gone, s
this was ou
opportunity
to come na
the Fountai
of Life...
PANT
CRUNCH
CRUNCH
CRUNCH
PANT
But this hasn't gone to plan *at all!*
The boss...all 50 of my buddies... they're all dead...
I'm the only one left...
HERK
Heh...
heh heh...
SMIRK
Meaning the Fountain of Life's *all mine!*
POOF

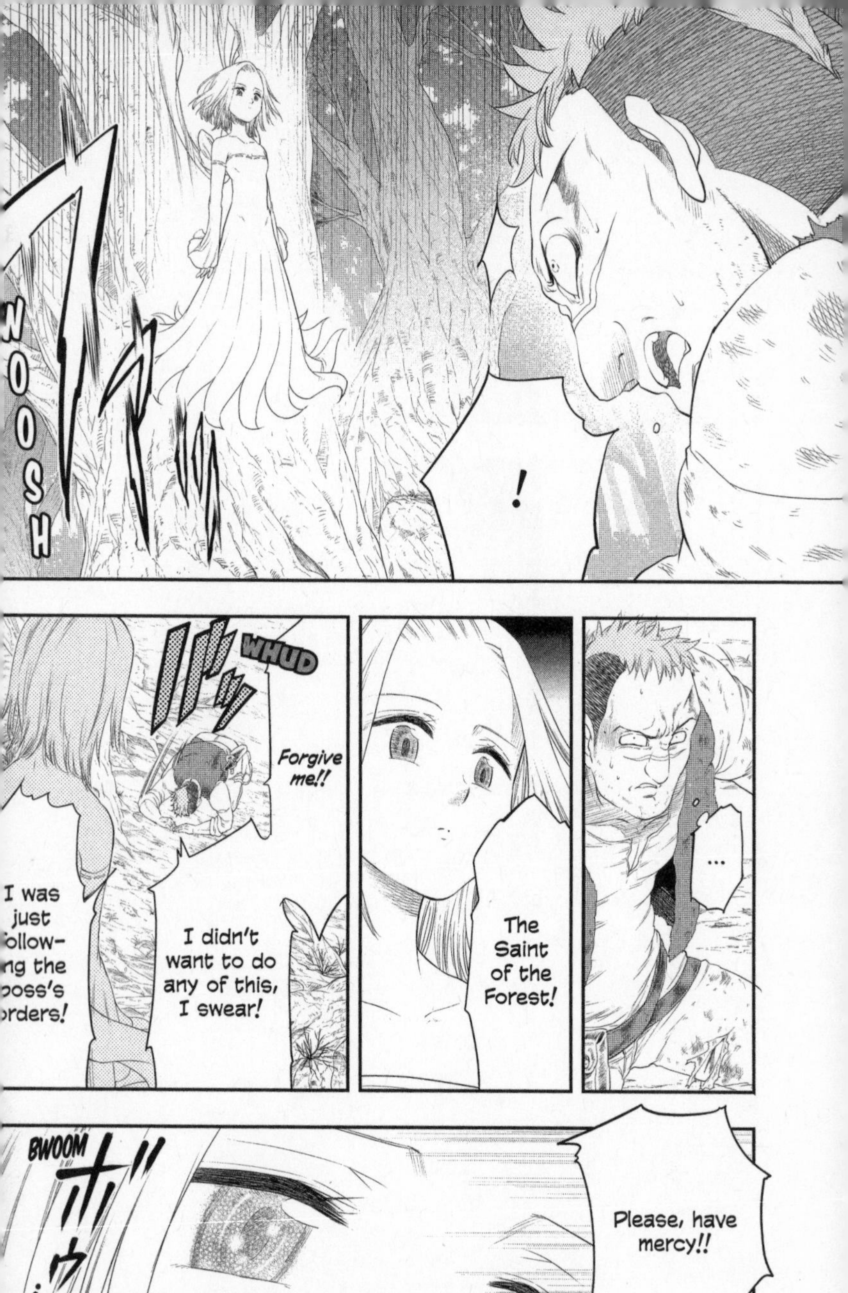
!
WOOSH
...
The Saint of the Forest!
WHUD
Forgive me!!
I didn't want to do any of this, I swear!
I was just ollow- ng the oss's rders!
Please, have mercy!!
BWOOM
...

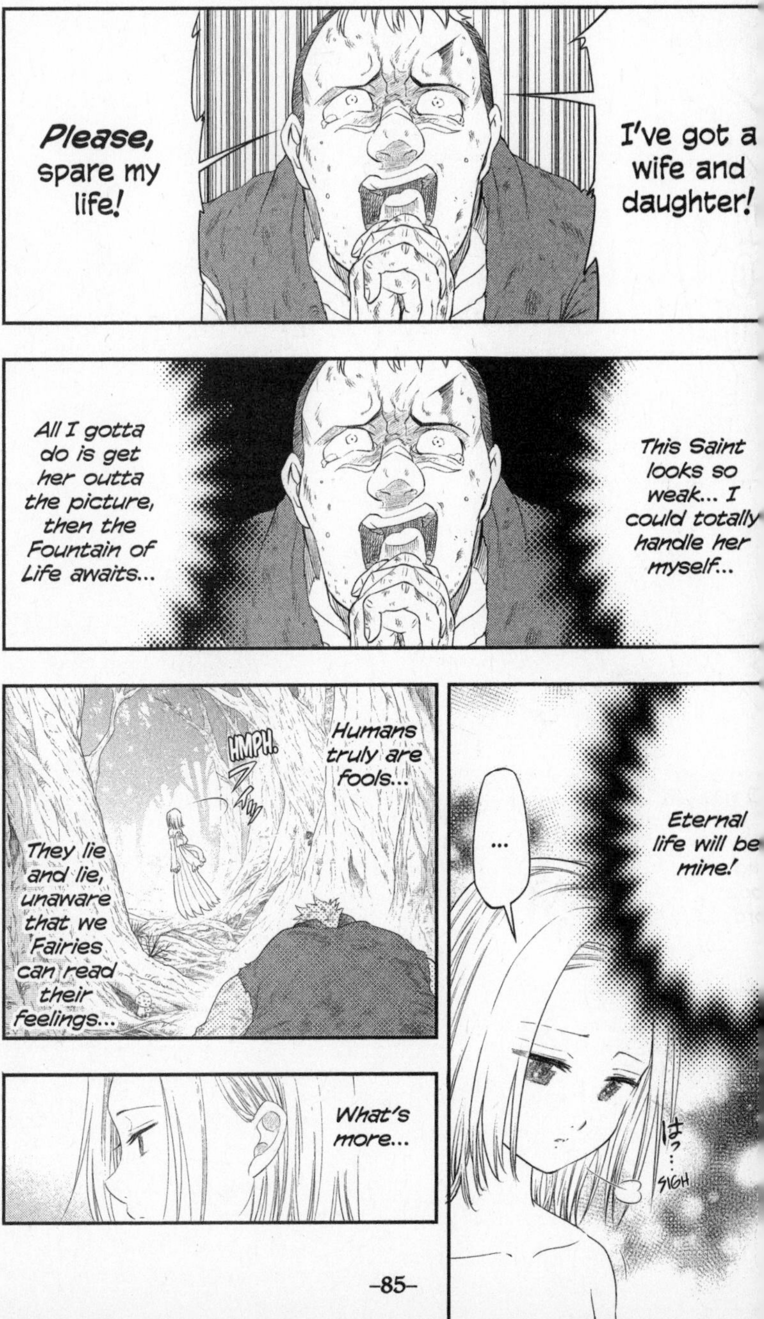
I've got a wife and daughter!
Please, spare my life!
This Saint looks so weak... I could totally handle her myself...
All I gotta do is get her outta the picture, then the Fountain of Life awaits...
Eternal life will be mine!
...
はっ... SIGH
Humans truly are fools...
HMPH.
They lie and lie, unaware that we Fairies can read their feelings...
What's more...

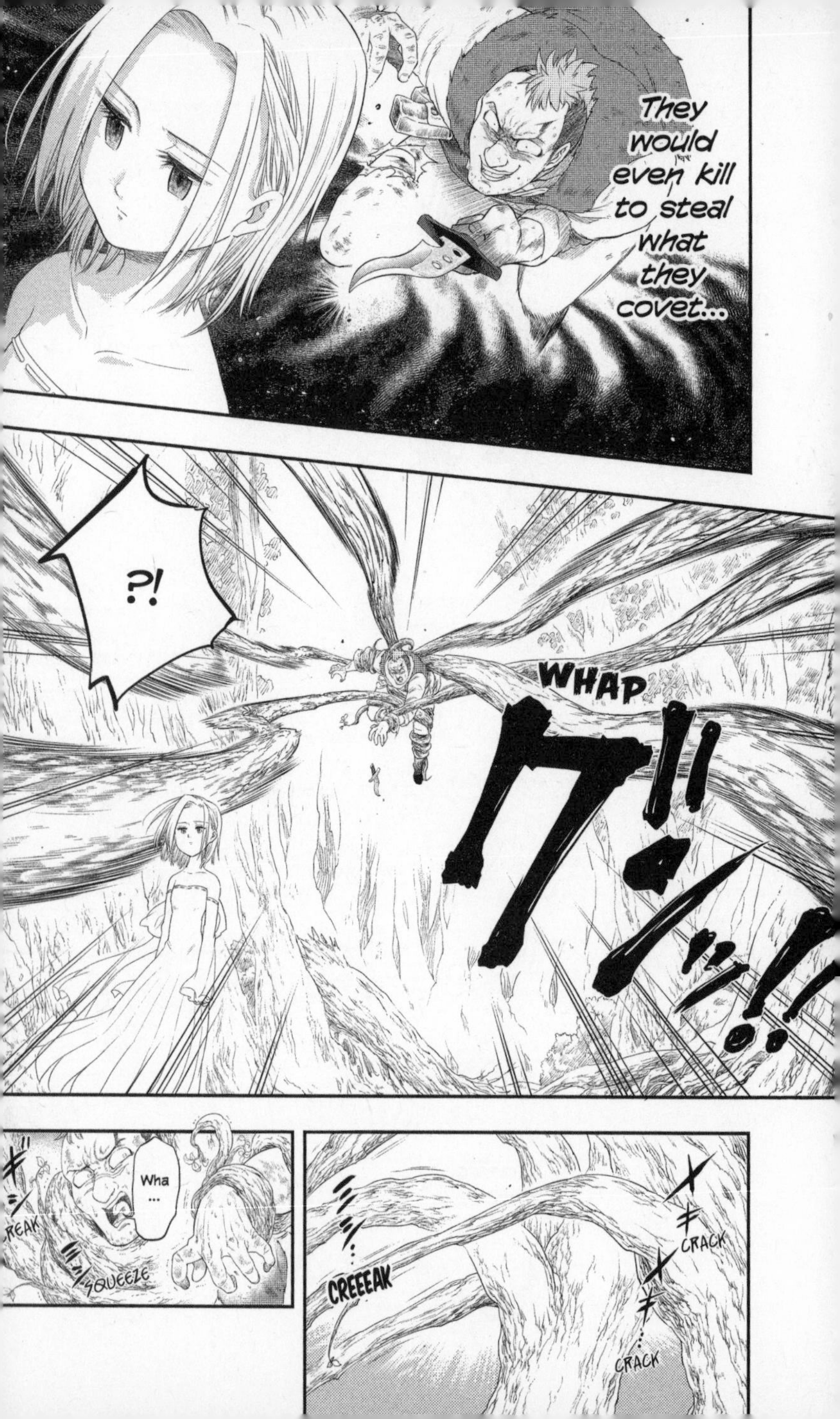
They would even kill to steal what they covet...
?!
WHAP
CRACK
CRACK
CREEEAK
Wha ...
REAK
SQUEEZE

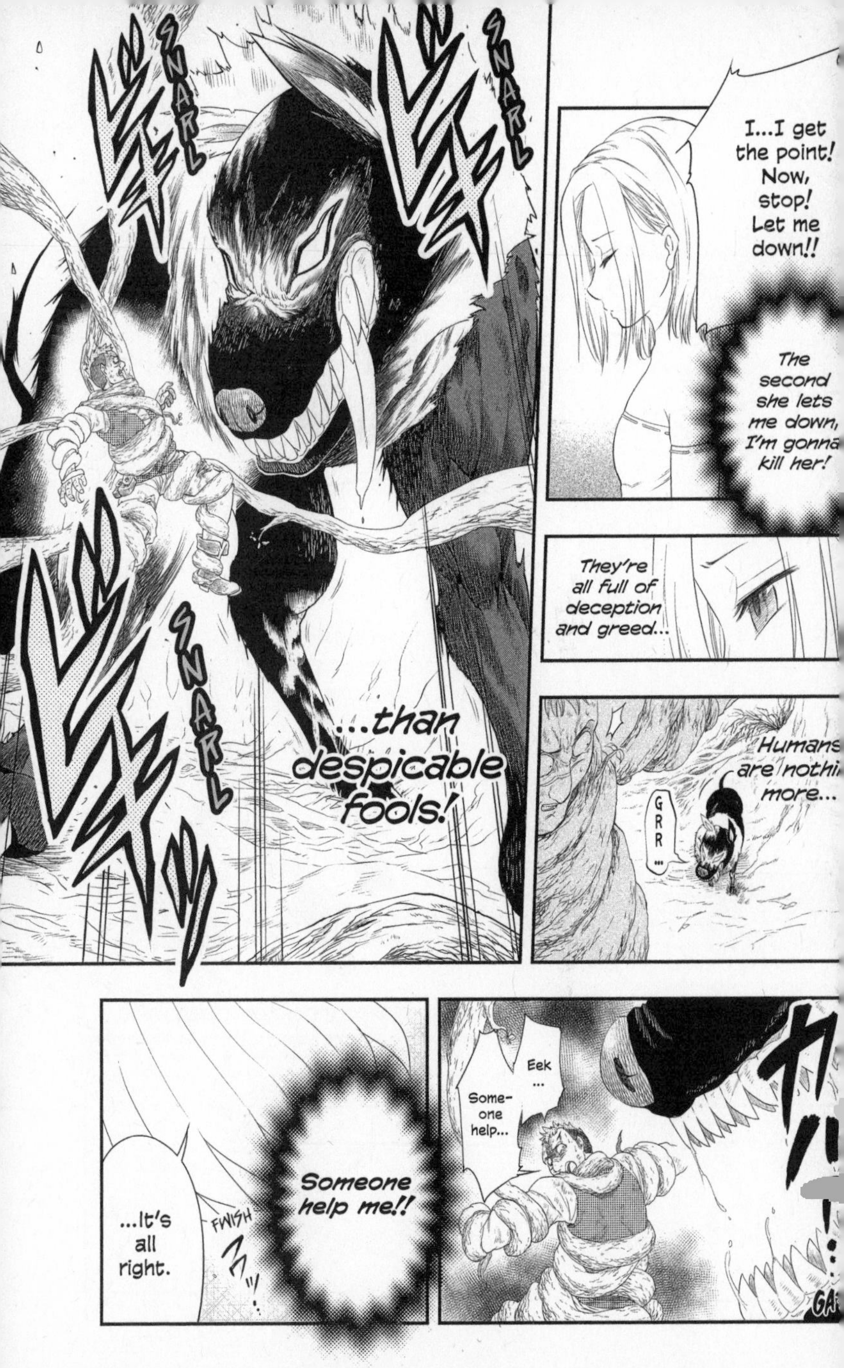
I...I get the point! Now, stop! Let me down!!
The second she lets me down, I'm gonna kill her!
They're all full of deception and greed...
Humans are nothi more...
GRR...
SNARL
SNARL
SNARL
...than despicable fools!
Eek...
Some-one help...
GA
Someone help me!!
FWISH
...It's all right.

AAAAAAAAGGGGGGGHHHHH!!

You may die, but the forest you'll become part of will live forever.

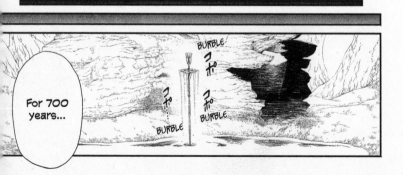

For 700 years...

BURBLE

BURBLE

BURBLE

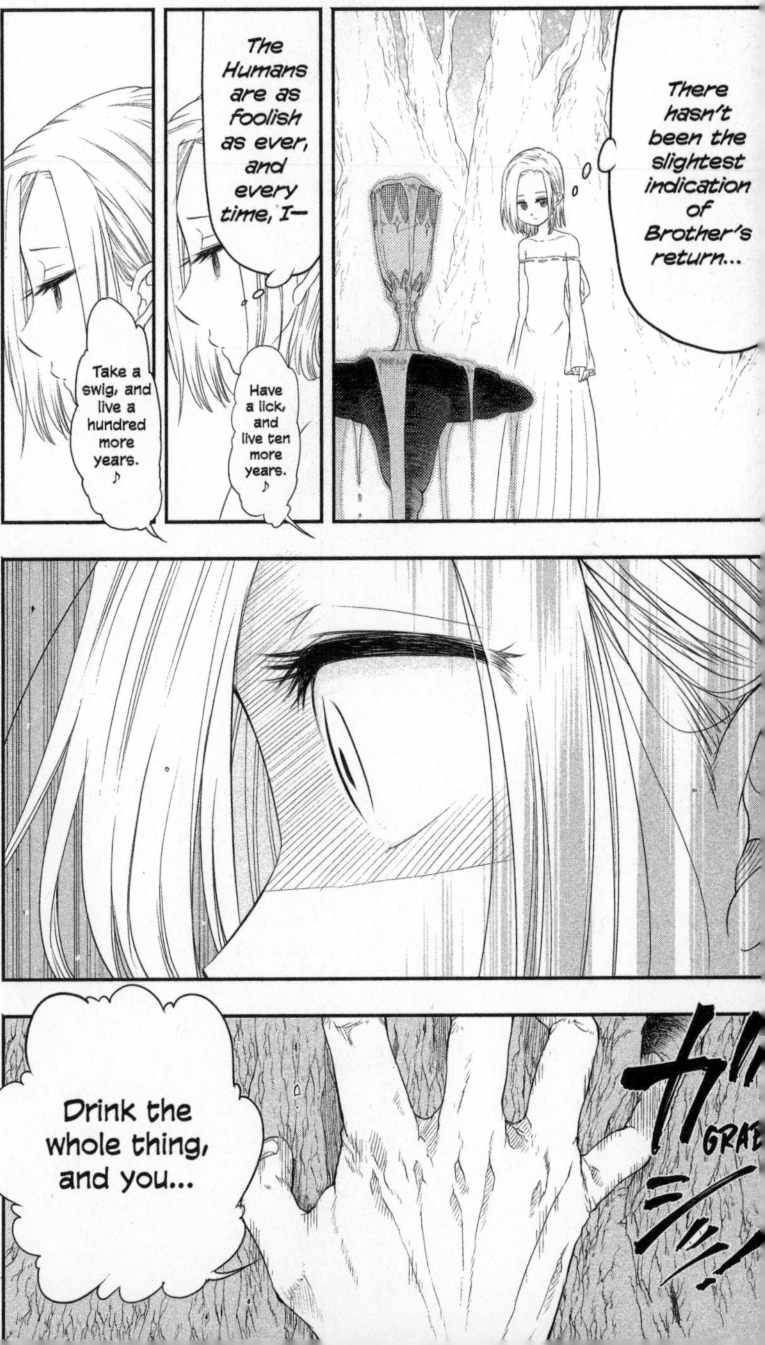
There hasn't been the slightest indication of Brother's return...
The Humans are as foolish as ever, and every time, I—
Have a lick, and live ten more years. ♪
Take a swig, and live a hundred more years. ♪
Drink the whole thing, and you...

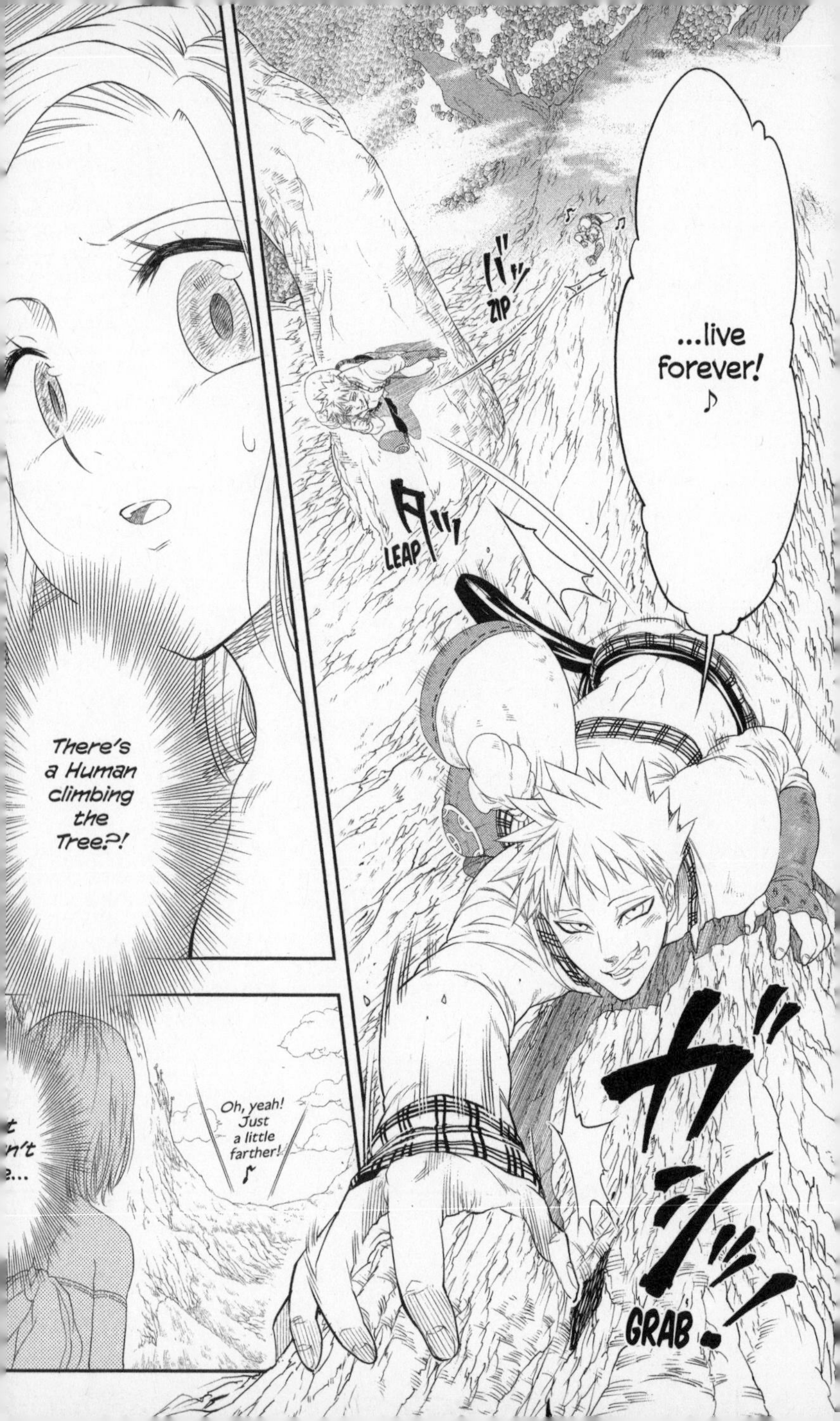
...live forever! ♪
ZIP
LEAP
GRAB
There's a Human climbing the Tree?!
Oh, yeah! Just a little farther! ♪

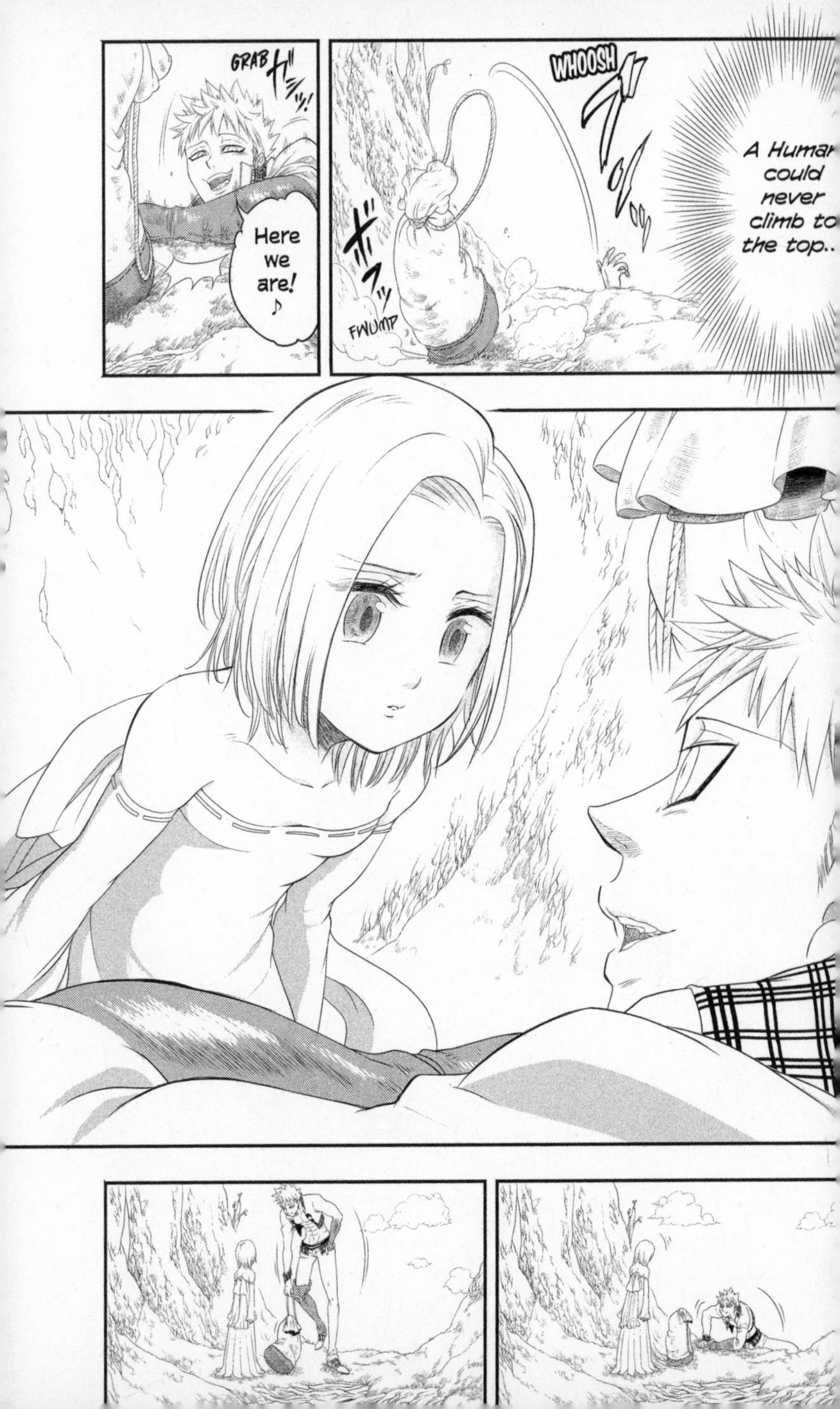
A Human could never climb to the top..
WHOOSH
FWUMP
GRAB
Here we are! ♪

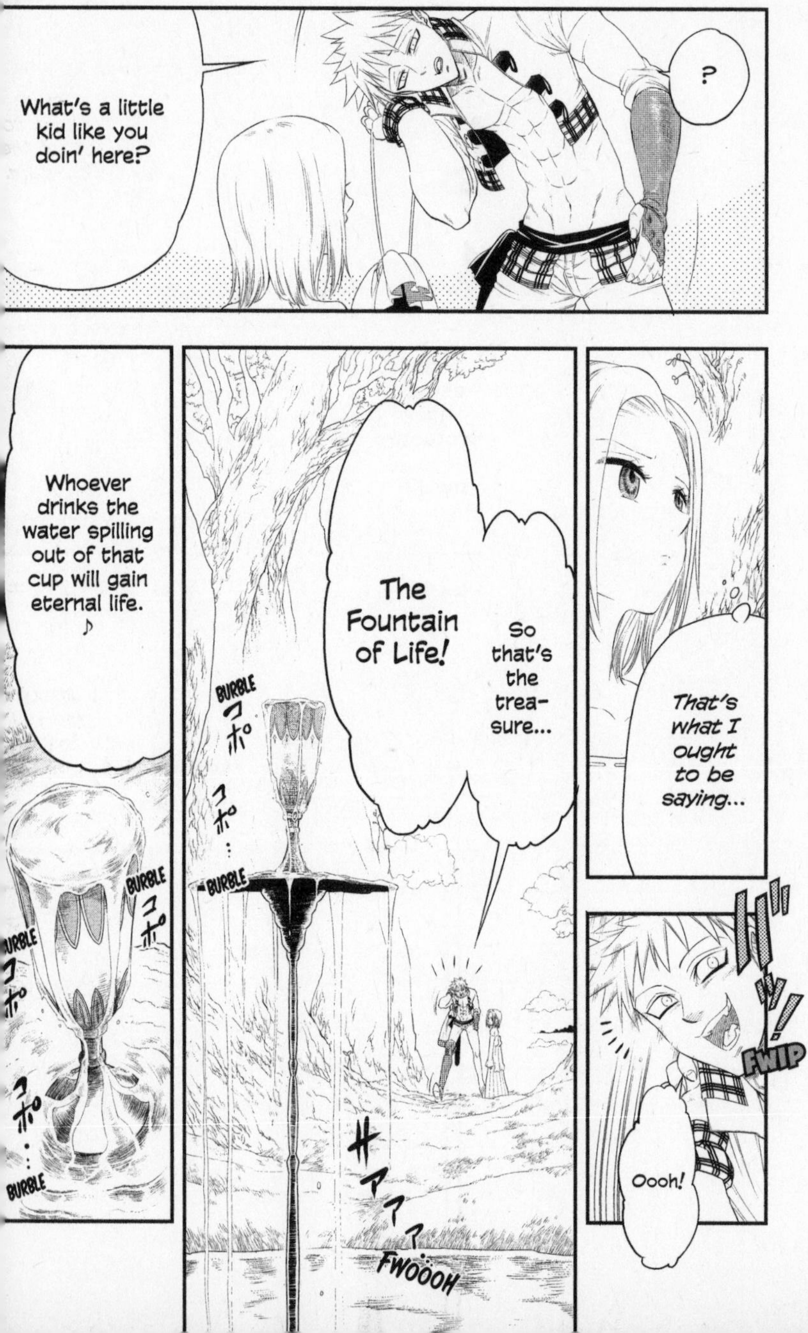
?
What's a little kid like you doin' here?
That's what I ought to be saying...
FWIP
Oooh!
So that's the treasure...
The Fountain of Life!
BURBLE
BURBLE
FWOOOH
Whoever drinks the water spilling out of that cup will gain eternal life. ♪
BURBLE
BURBLE
BURBLE

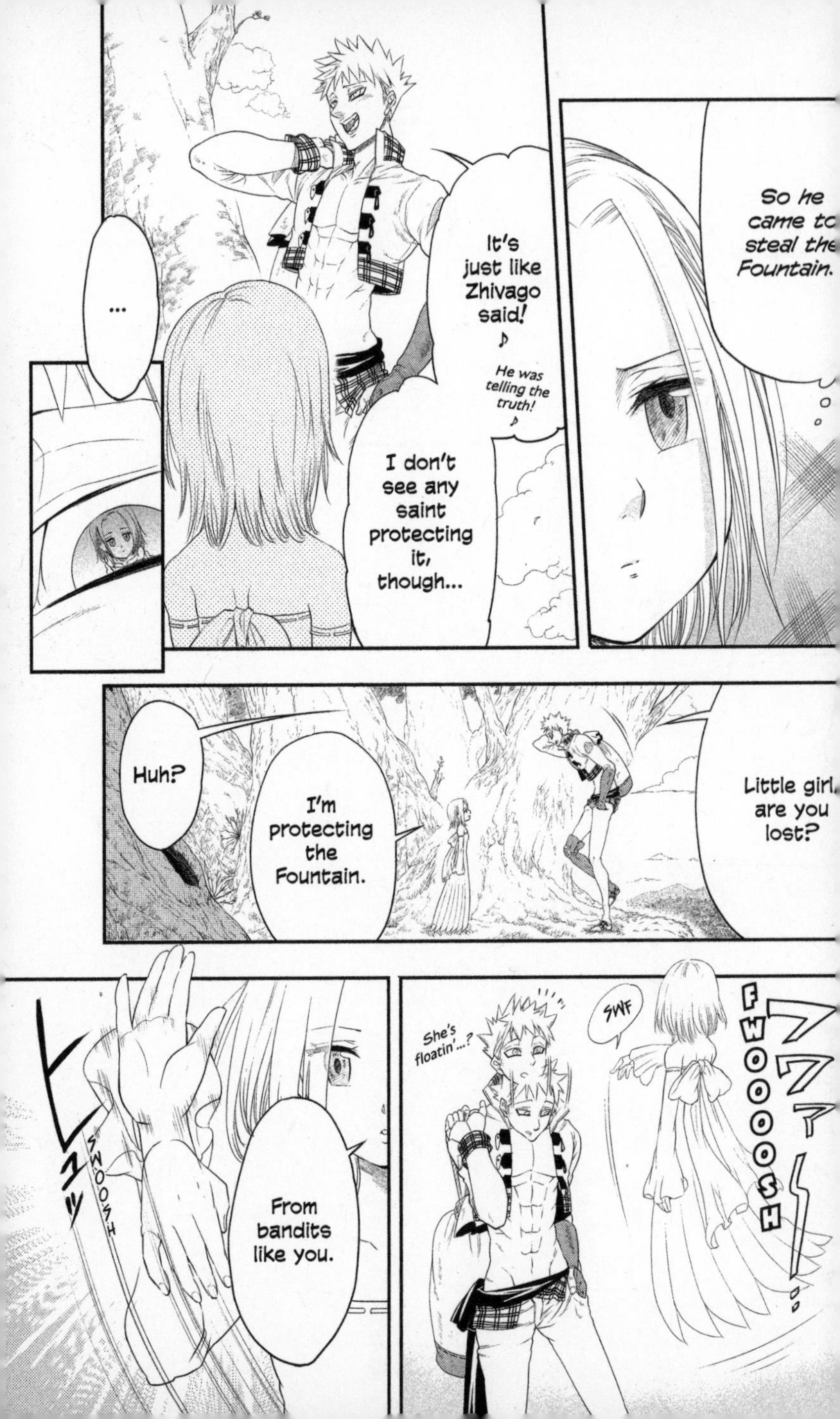
So he came to steal the Fountain.
It's just like Zhivago said! ♪
He was telling the truth! ♪
I don't see any saint protecting it, though...
...
Little girl, are you lost?
I'm protecting the Fountain.
Huh?
FWOOOOOSH
SWF
She's floatin'...?
SWOOSH
From bandits like you.

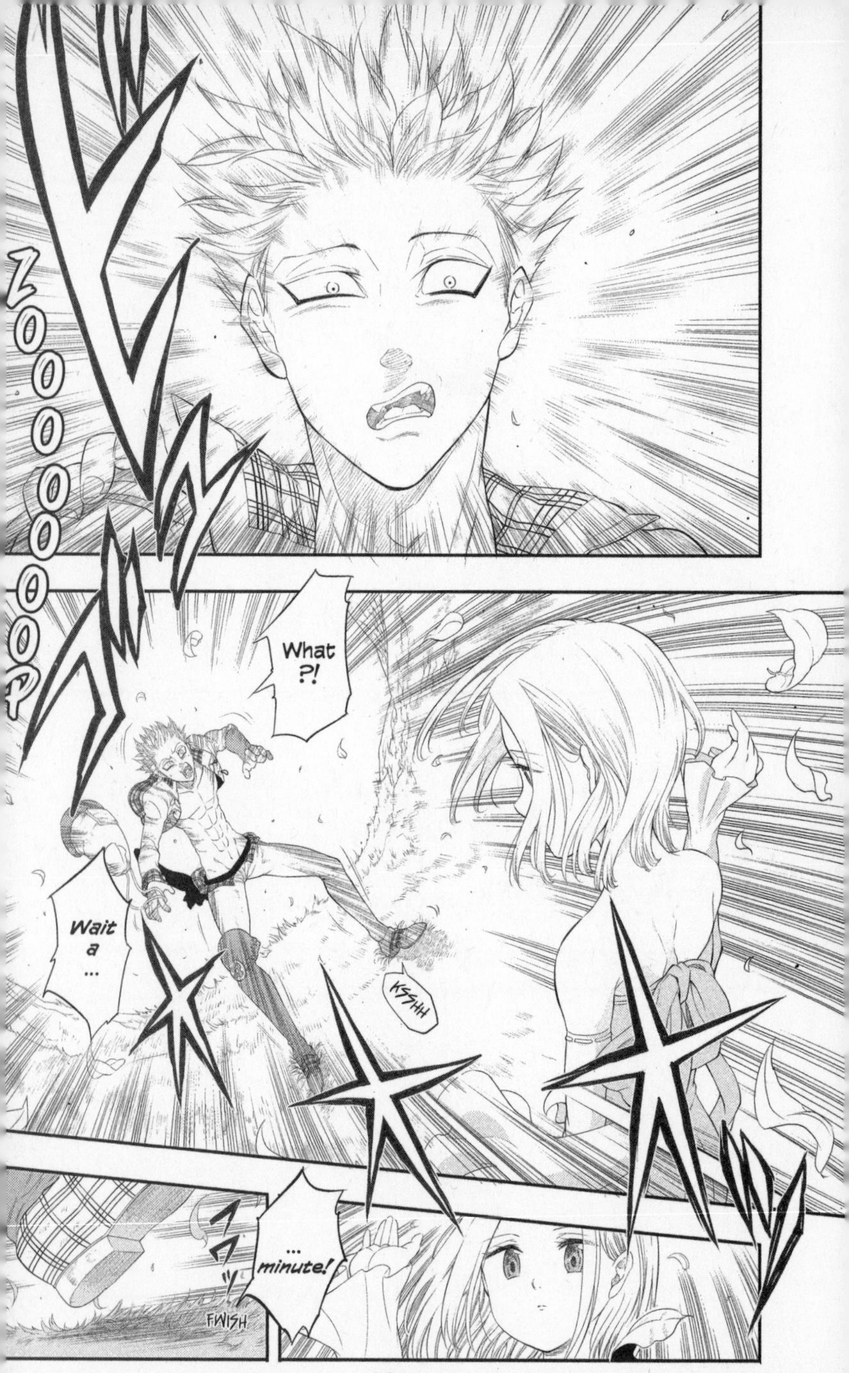
ZOOOOOOOP
What ?!
Wait a ...
KSSHH
... minute!
FWISH

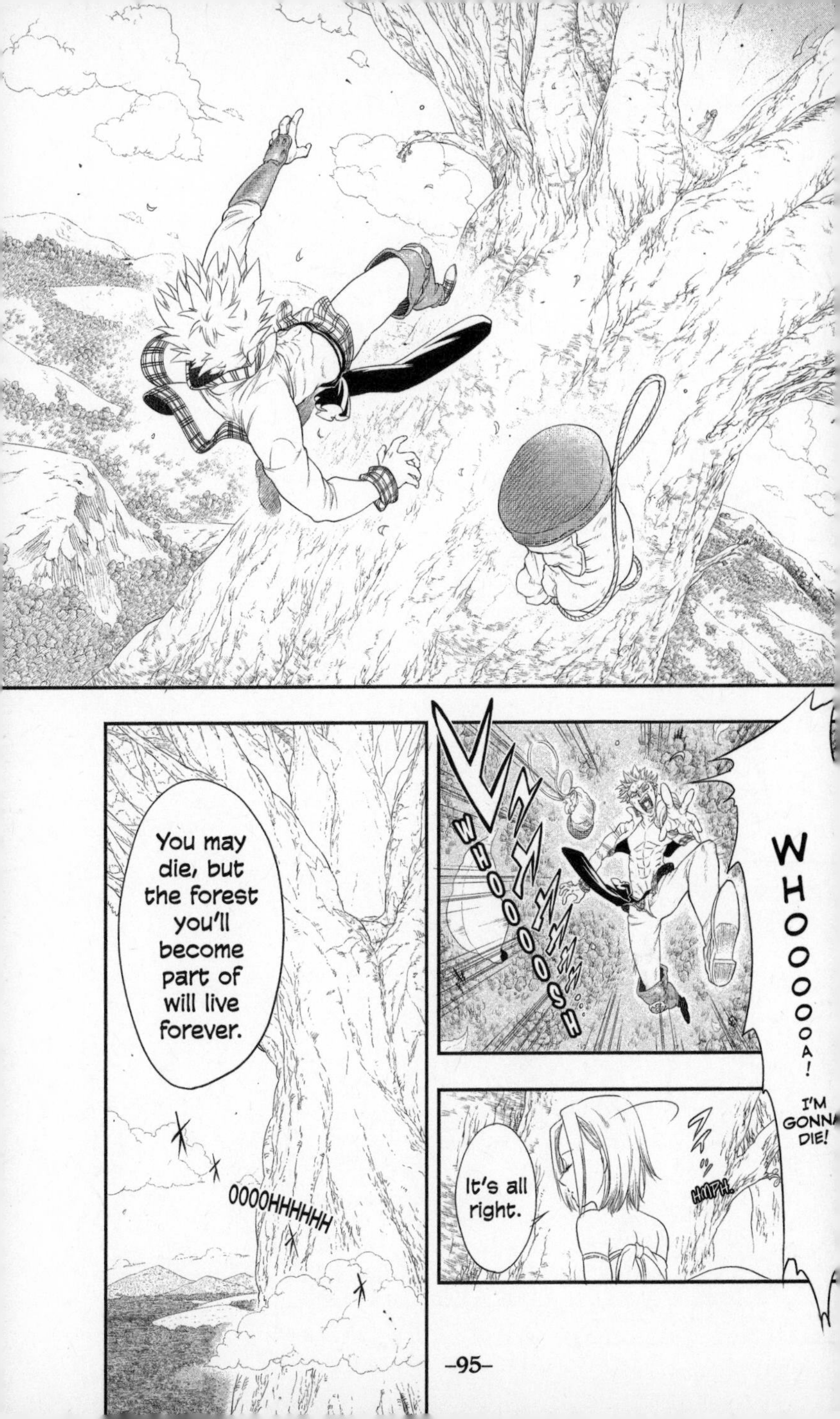
WHOOOOSH
WHOOOOOOA!
I'M GONNA DIE!
HMPH.
It's all right.
You may die, but the forest you'll become part of will live forever.
OOOOHHHHHH

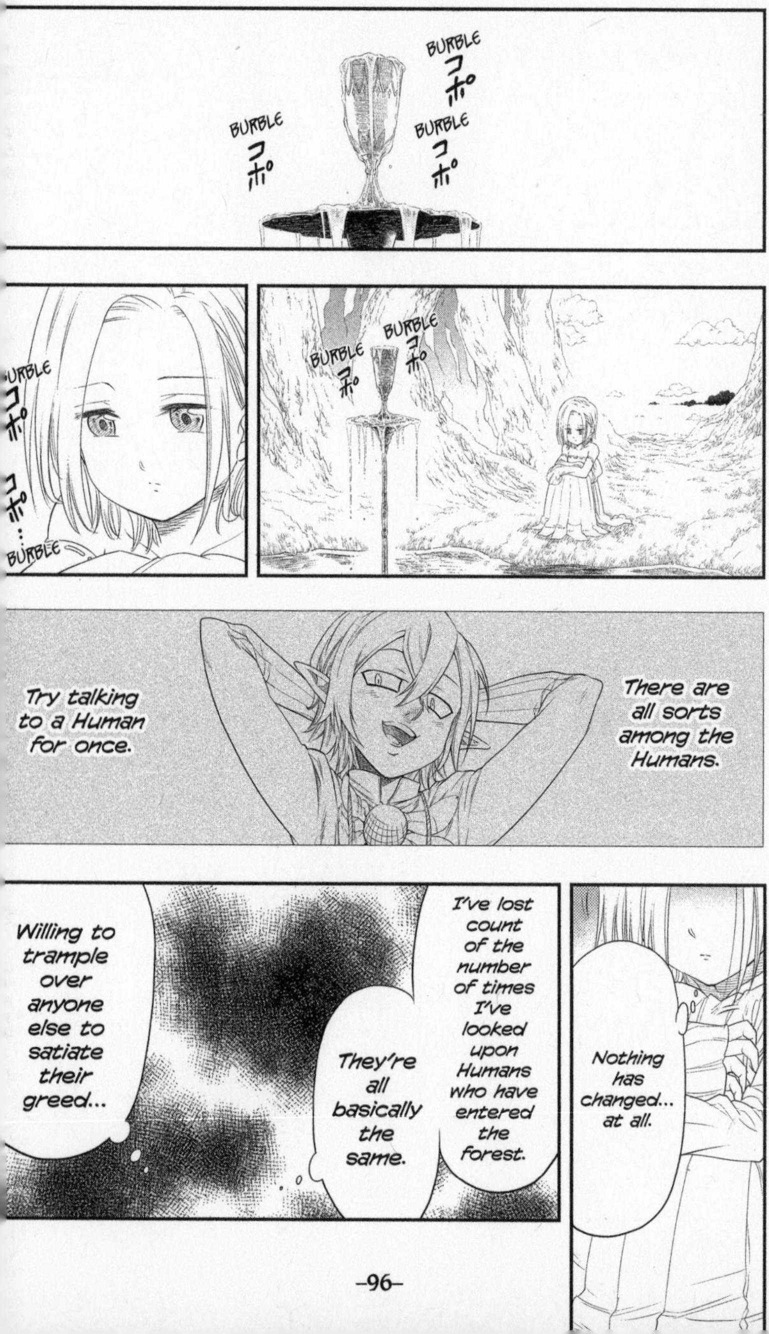
BURBLE
コポ
BURBLE
コポ
BURBLE
コポ
BURBLE
コポ
BURBLE
コポ
BURBLE
コポ
コポ…
BURBLE
There are all sorts among the Humans.
Try talking to a Human for once.
Nothing has changed... at all.
I've lost count of the number of times I've looked upon Humans who have entered the forest.
They're all basically the same.
Willing to trample over anyone else to satiate their greed...

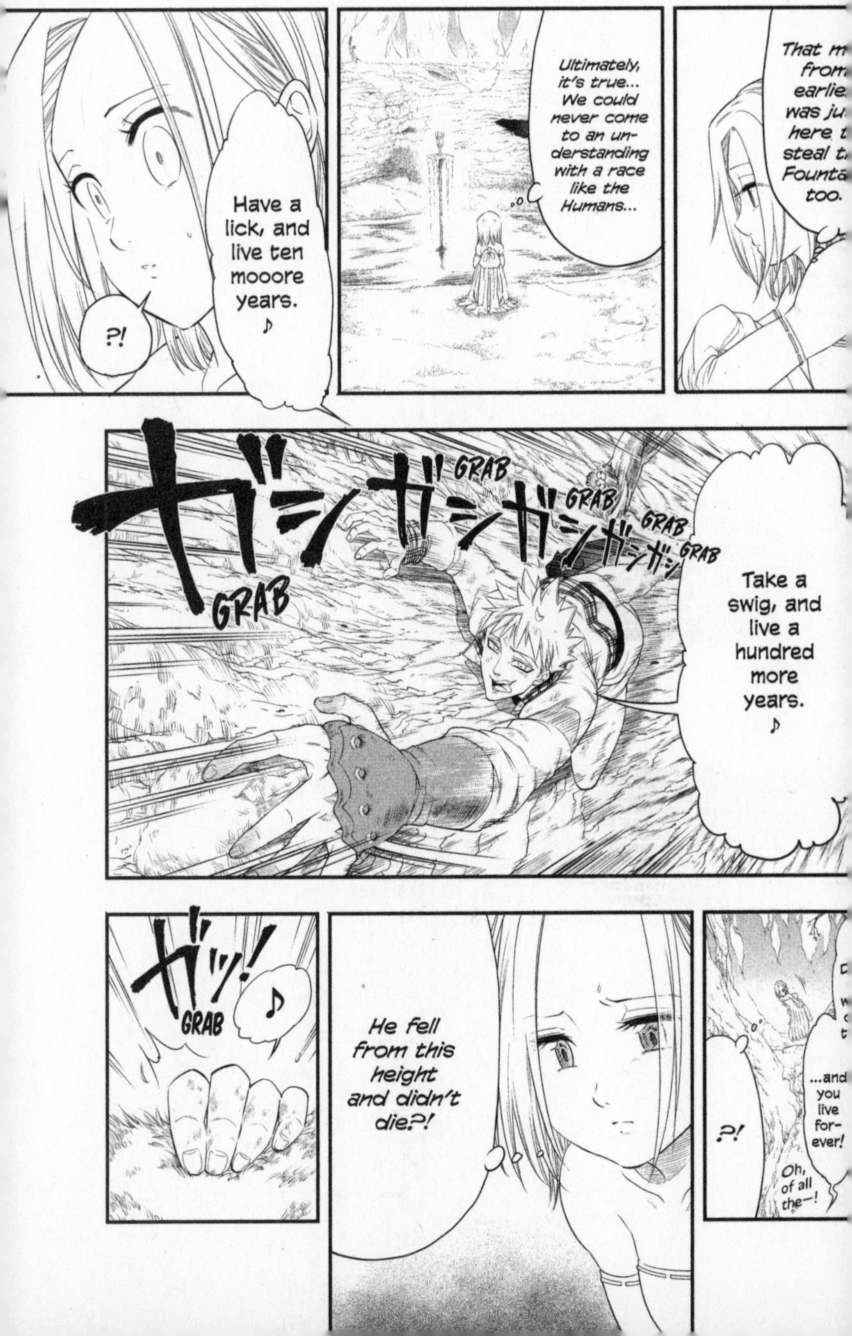
That m
from
earlie
was ju
here t
steal t
Founta
too.
Ultimately, it's true... We could never come to an understanding with a race like the Humans...
Have a lick, and live ten mooore years. ♪
?!
Take a swig, and live a hundred more years. ♪
GRAB
GRAB
GRAB
GRAB
GRAB
...and you live forever!
Oh, of all the—!
?!
He fell from this height and didn't die?!
♪
GRAB

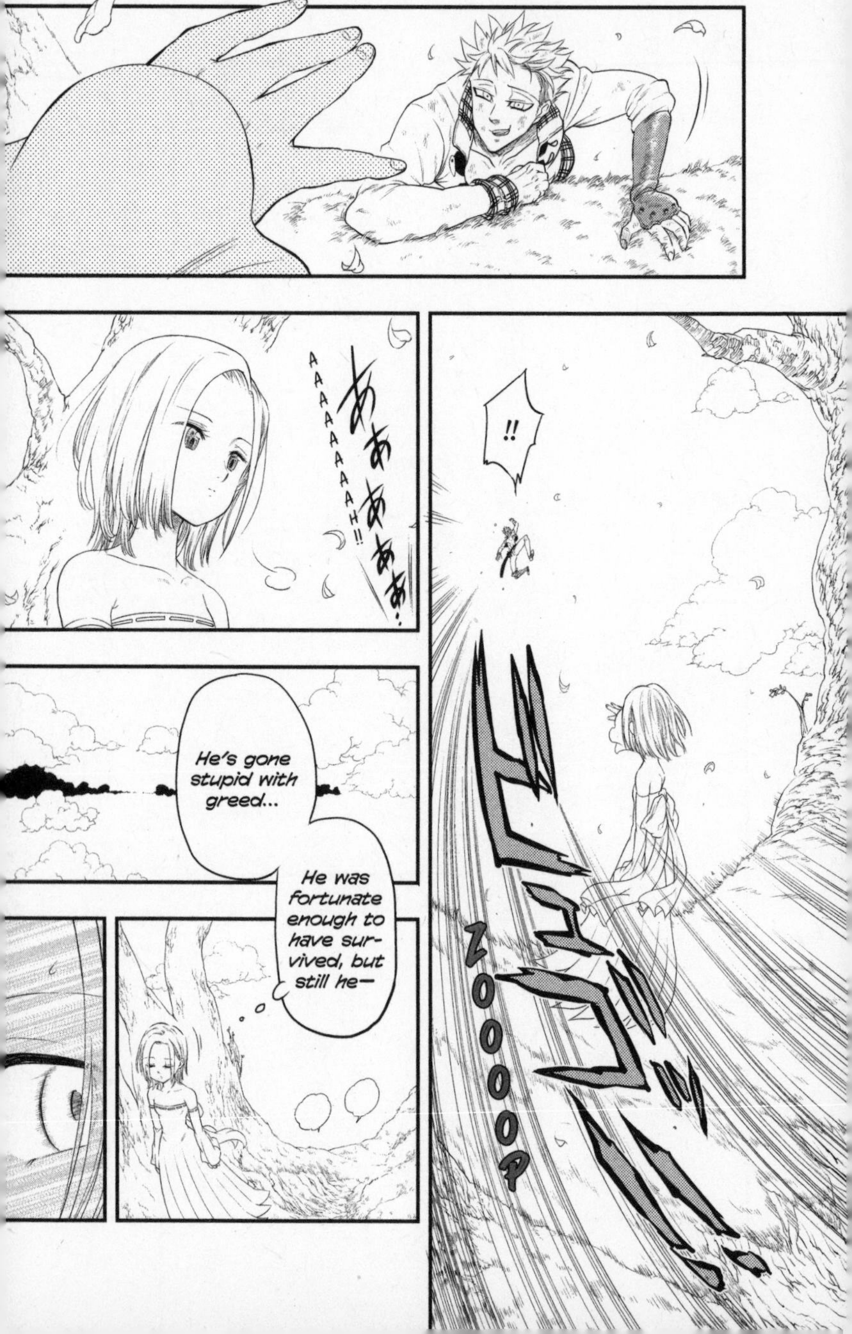

!!
ZOOOOOP
ああああぁ
AAAAAAAAAH!!
He's gone stupid with greed...
He was fortunate enough to have survived, but still he—

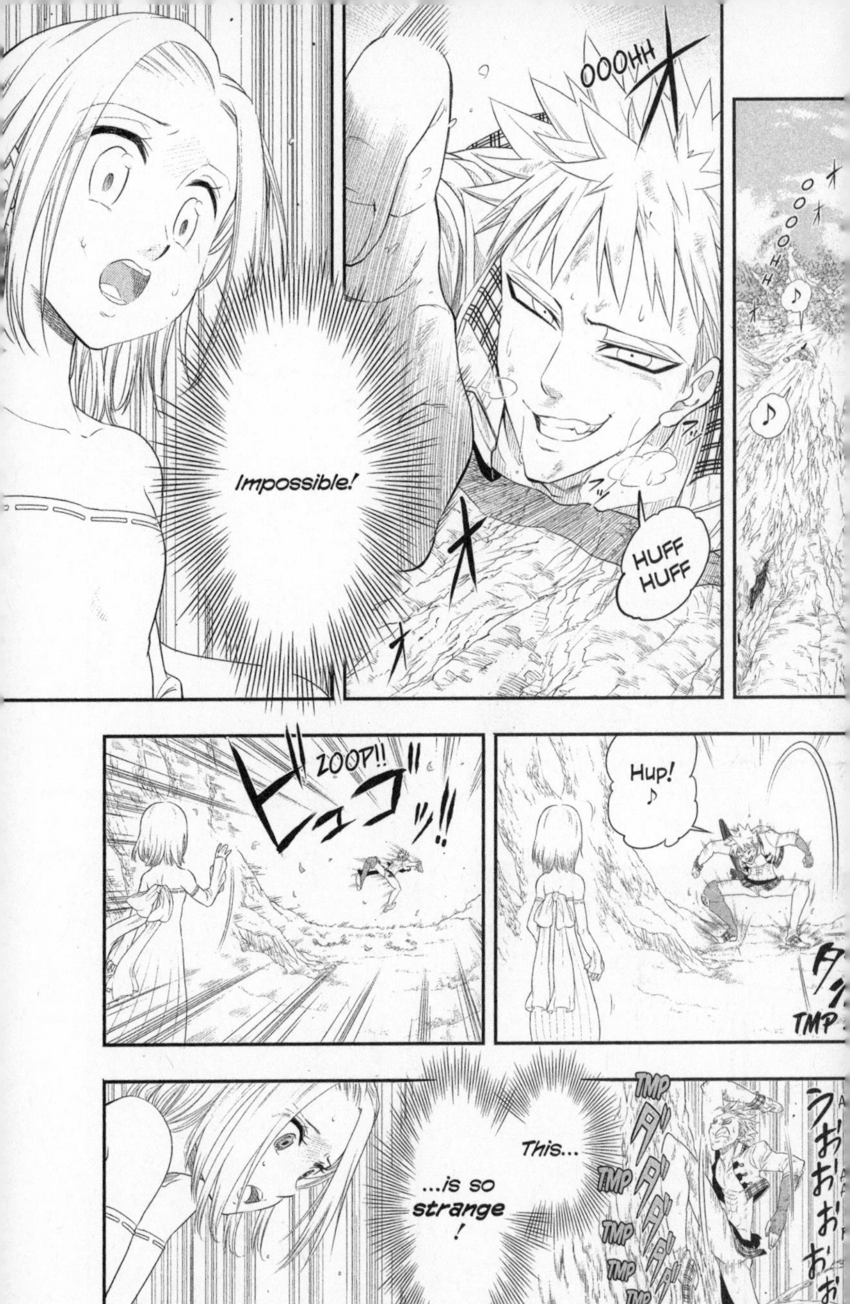

OOOOHH
♪
♪
OOOHH
HUFF HUFF
Impossible!
Hup! ♪
TMP
ZOOP!!
TMP
TMP
TMP
TMP
TMP
This...
...is so strange!

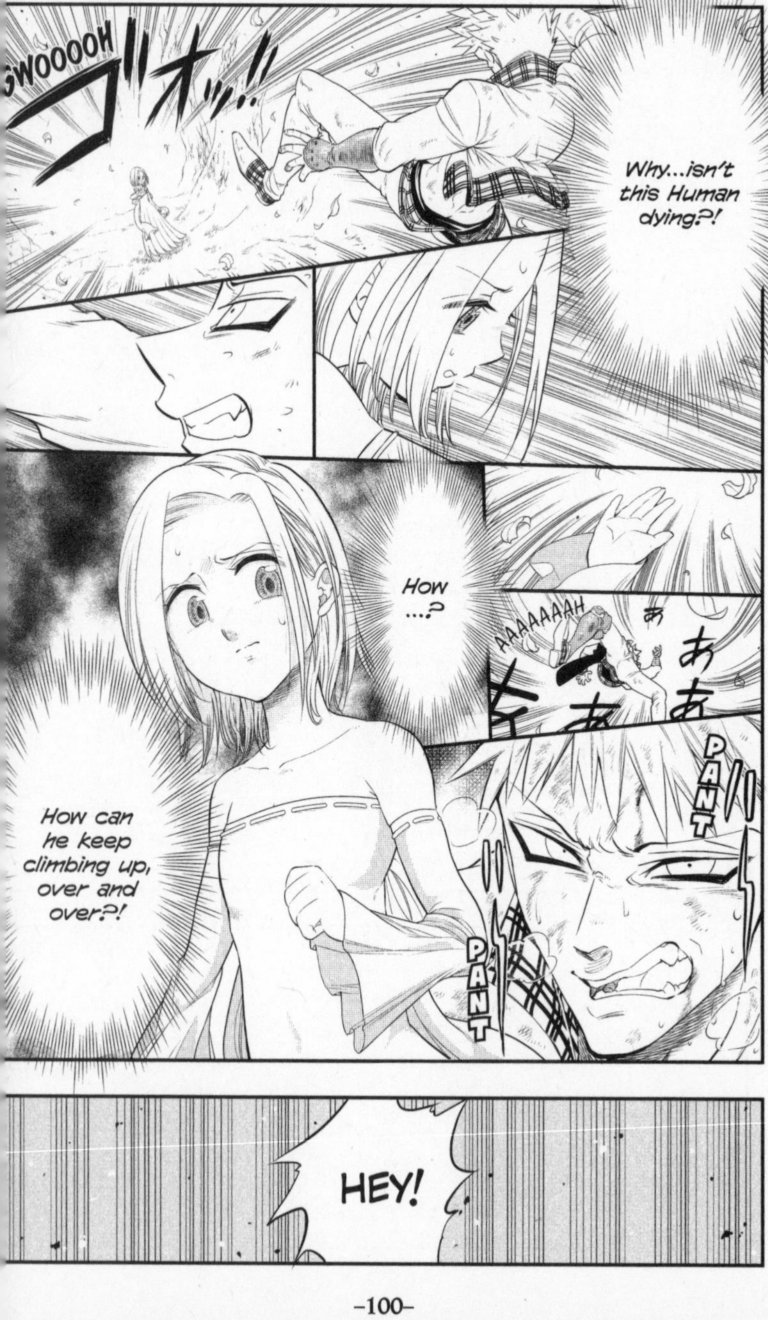
GWOOOOH
ゴオッ!!
Why...isn't this Human dying?!
AAAAAAAH
PANT
PANT
How ...?
How can he keep climbing up, over and over?!
HEY!

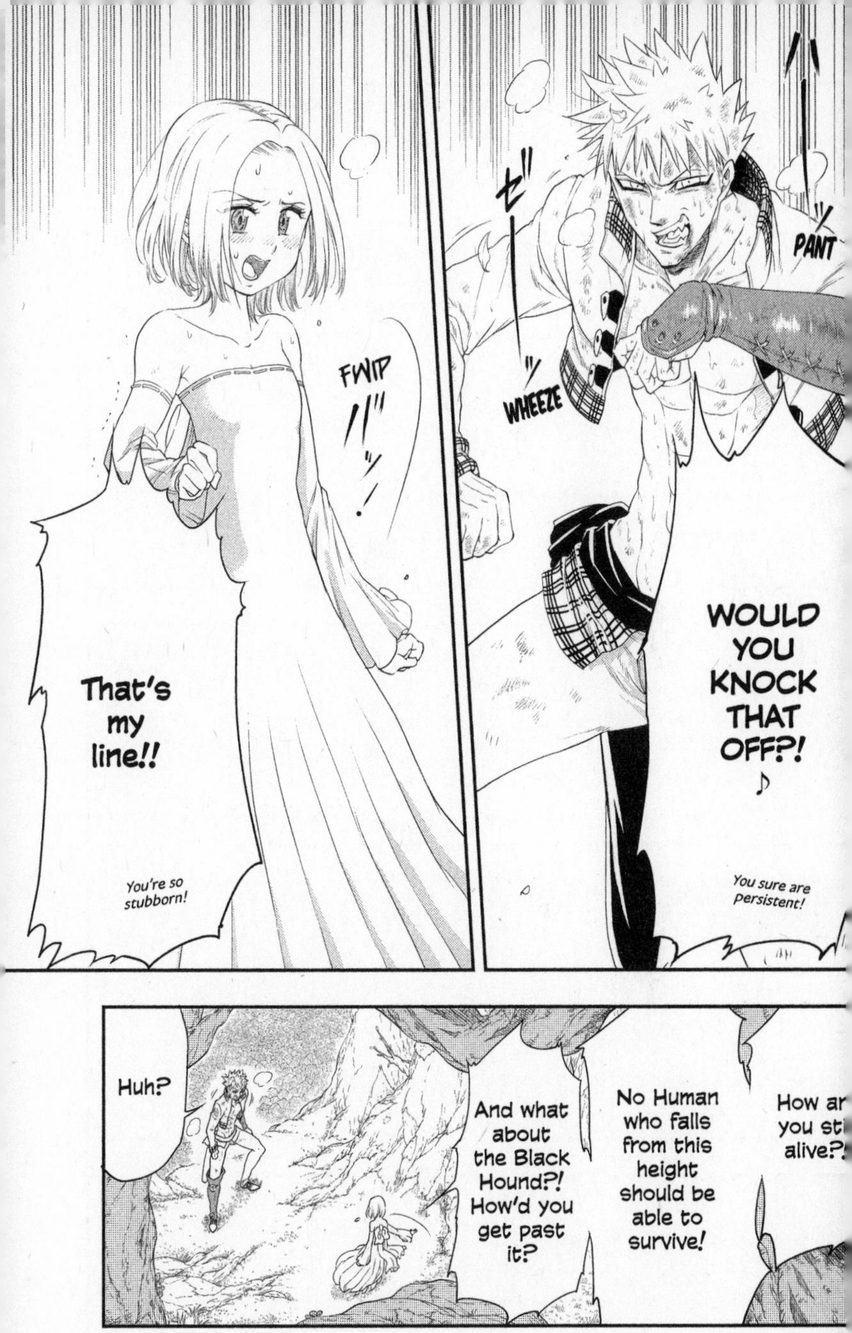
PANT
WHEEZE
WOULD YOU KNOCK THAT OFF?! ♪
You sure are persistent!
FWIP
That's my line!!
You're so stubborn!
How ar you st alive?!
No Human who falls from this height should be able to survive!
And what about the Black Hound?! How'd you get past it?
Huh?

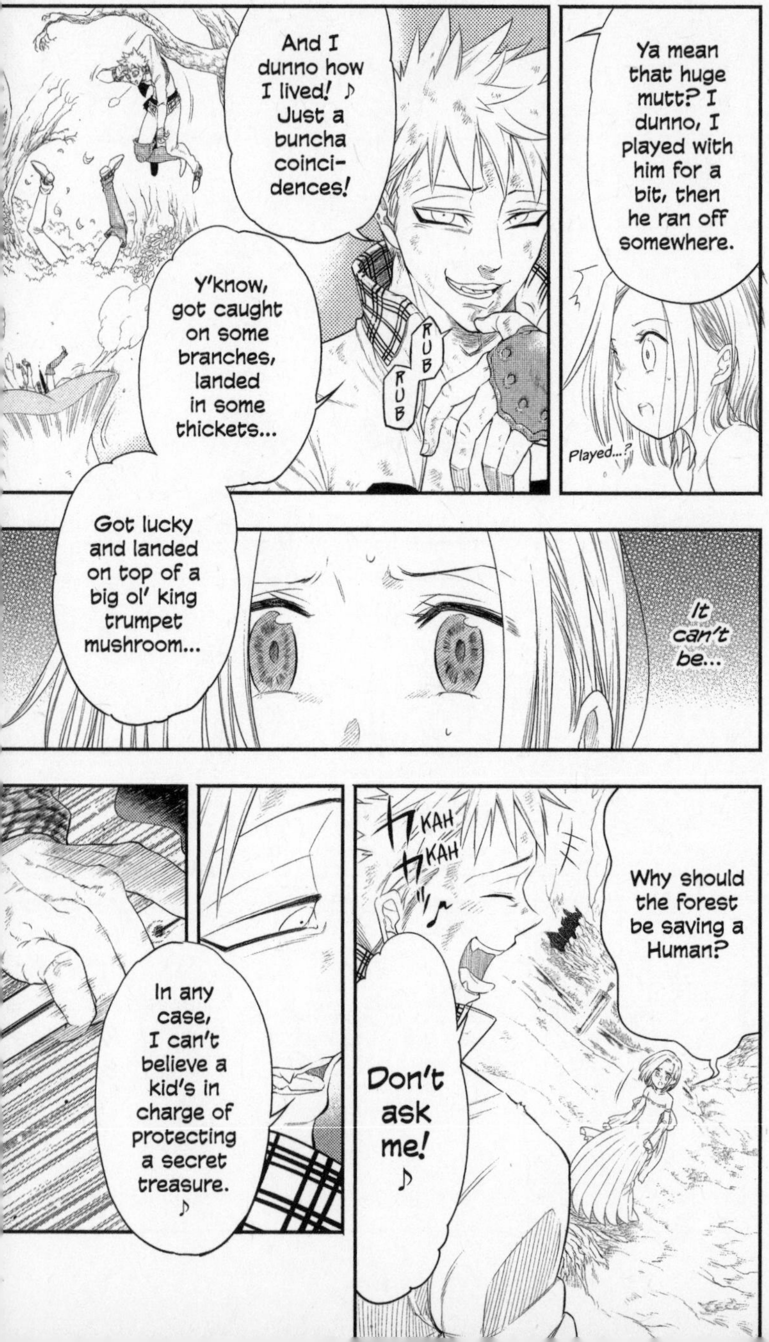
Ya mean that huge mutt? I dunno, I played with him for a bit, then he ran off somewhere.
Played...?
And I dunno how I lived! ♪ Just a buncha coinci-dences!
RUB RUB
Y'know, got caught on some branches, landed in some thickets...
Got lucky and landed on top of a big ol' king trumpet mushroom...
It can't be...
Why should the forest be saving a Human?
KAH KAH
Don't ask me! ♪
In any case, I can't believe a kid's in charge of protecting a secret treasure. ♪

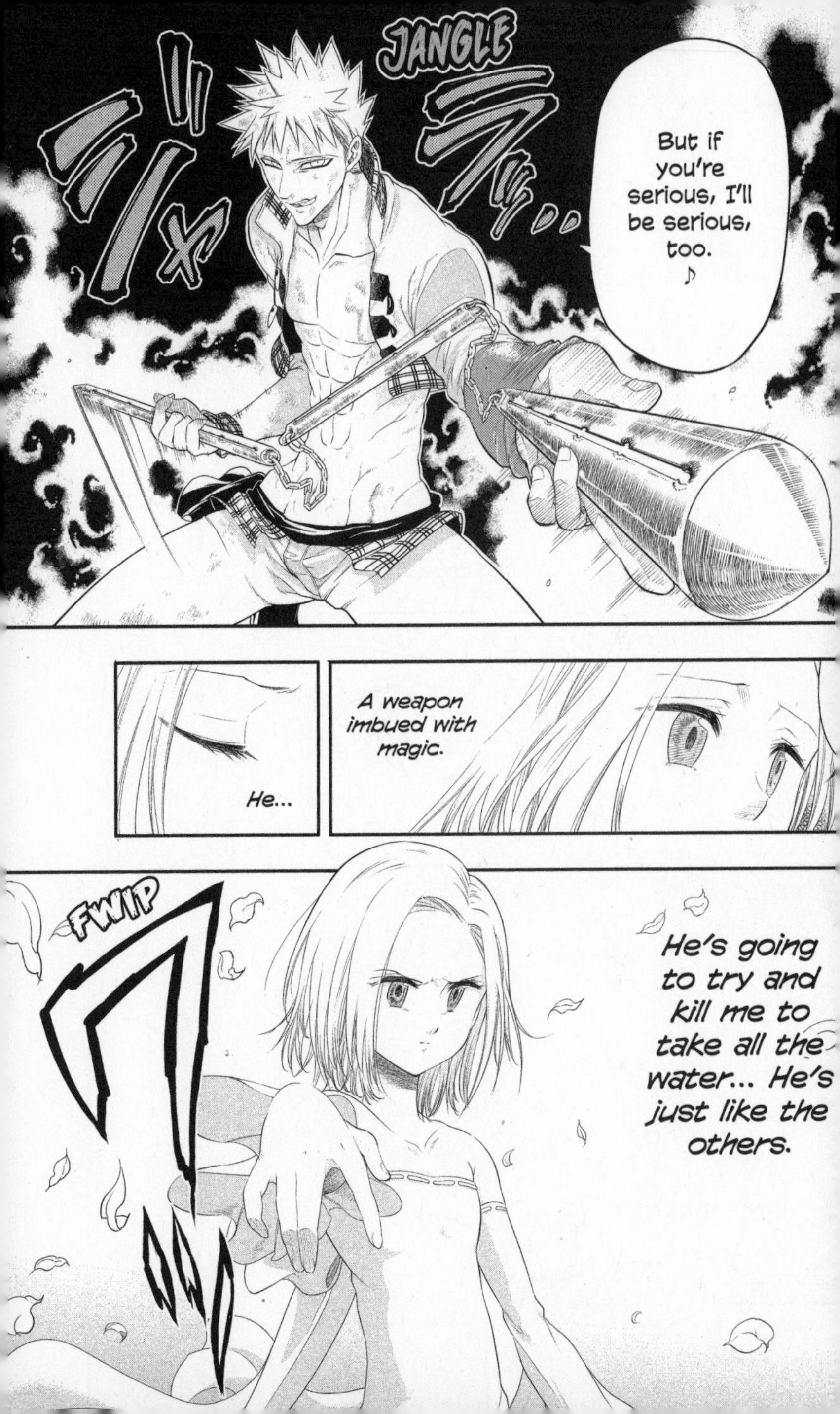
JANGLE
But if you're serious, I'll be serious, too. ♪
A weapon imbued with magic.
He...
He's going to try and kill me to take all the water... He's just like the others.
FWIP

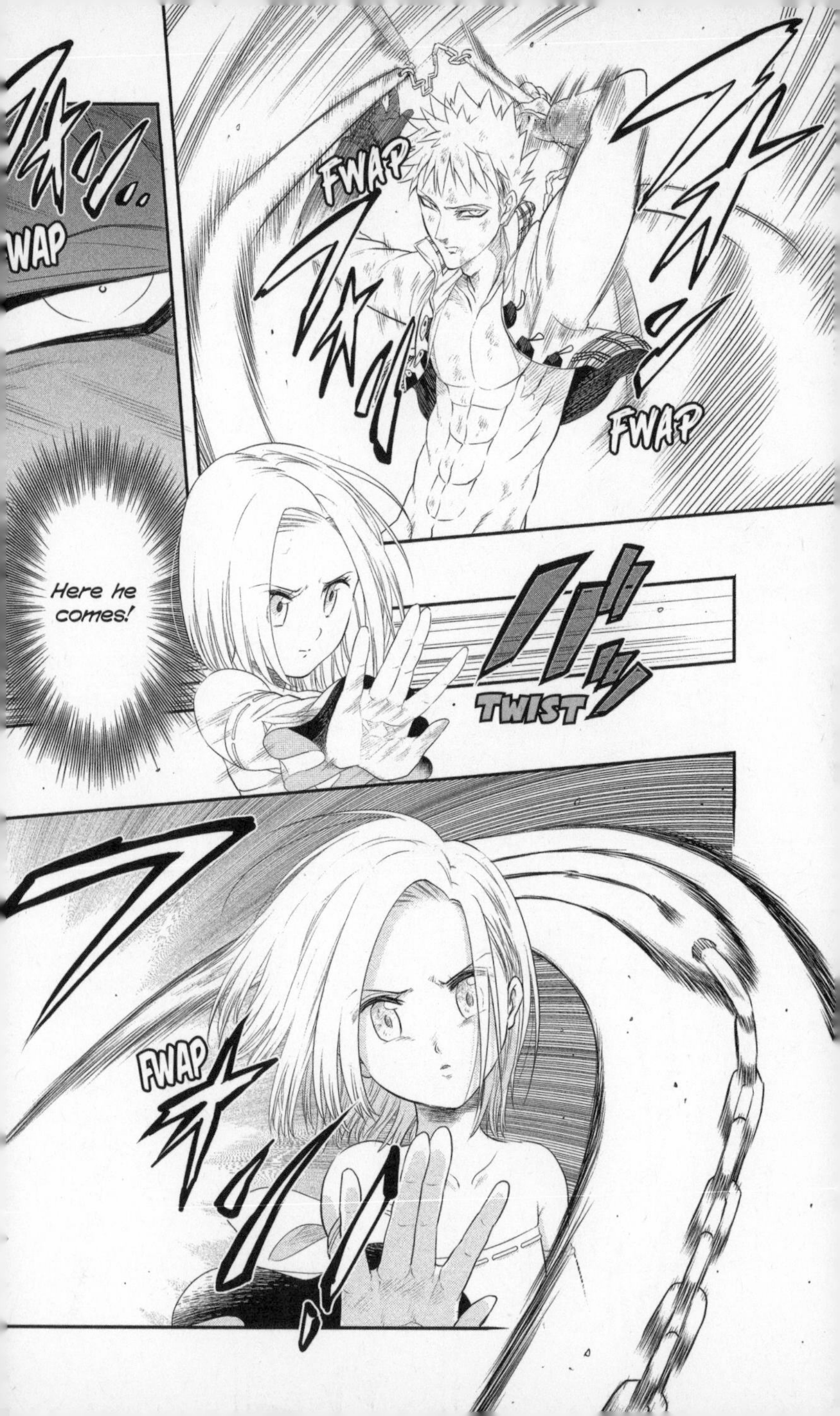
FWAP
FWAP
WAP
TWIST
Here he comes!
FWAP

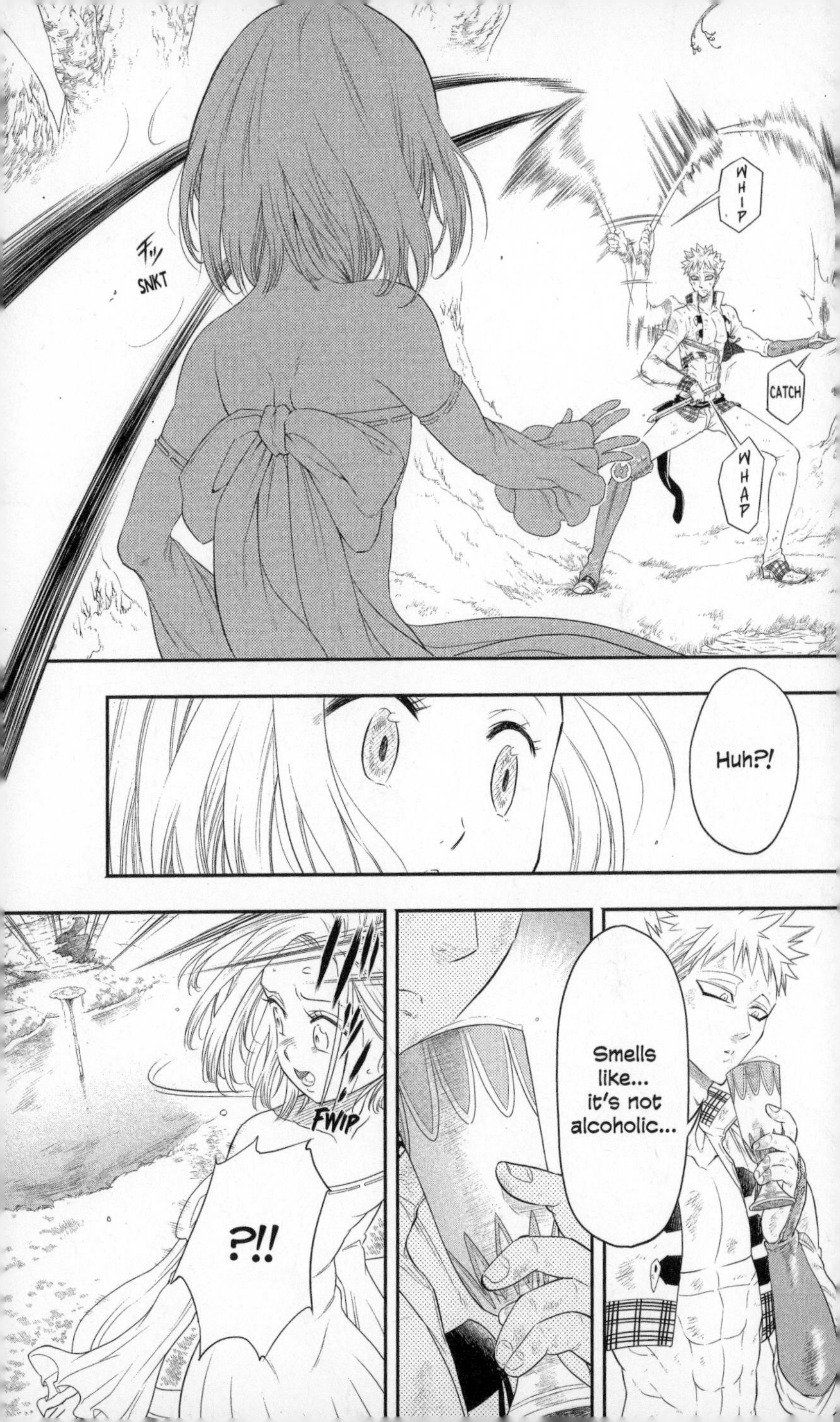
WHIP
CATCH
WHAP
チッ
SNKT
Huh?!
Smells like... it's not alcoholic...
FWIP
?!!

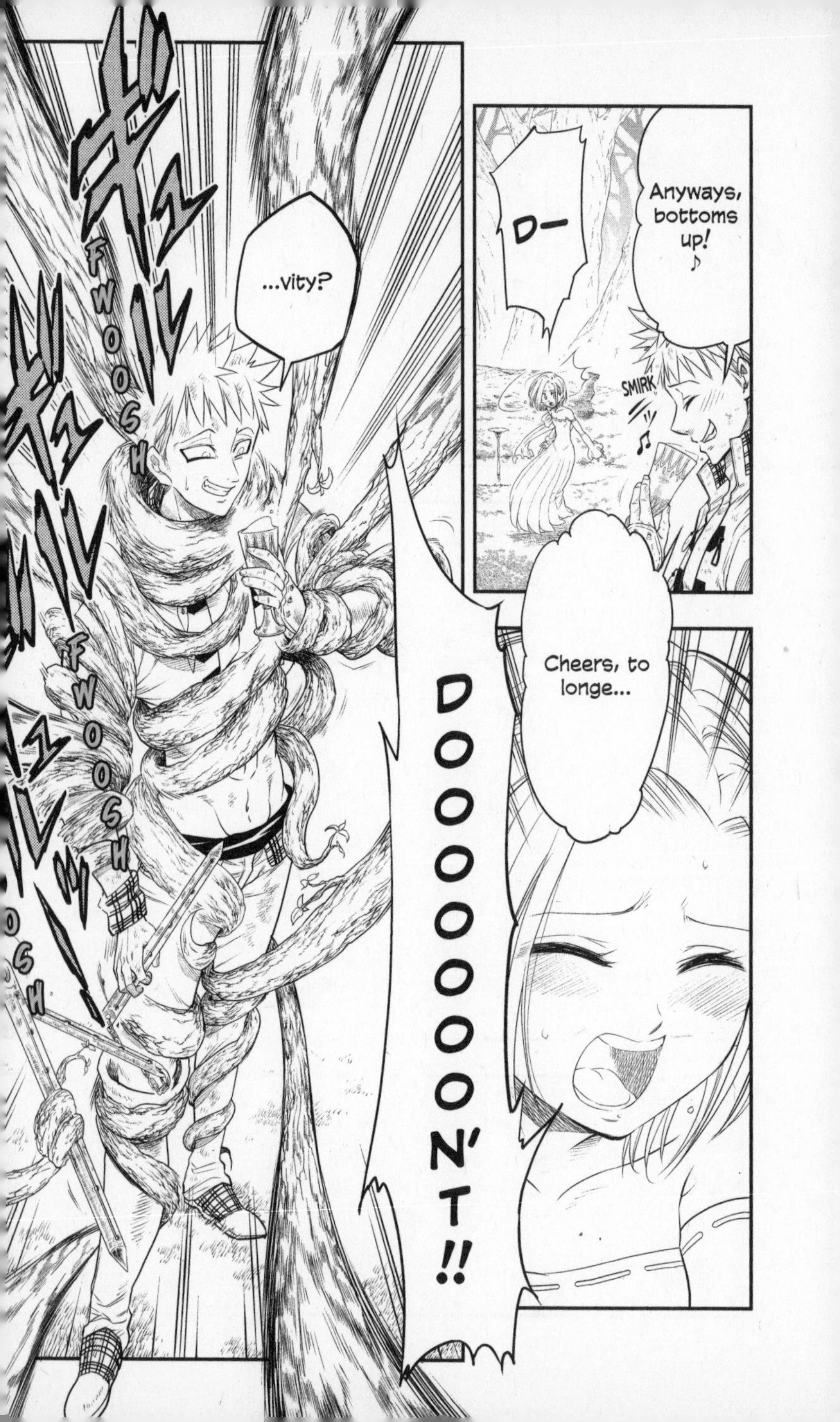
Anyways, bottoms up! ♪
D—
SMIRK
Cheers, to longe...
DOOOOOOON'T!!
...vity?
FWOOSH
FWOOSH
OSH

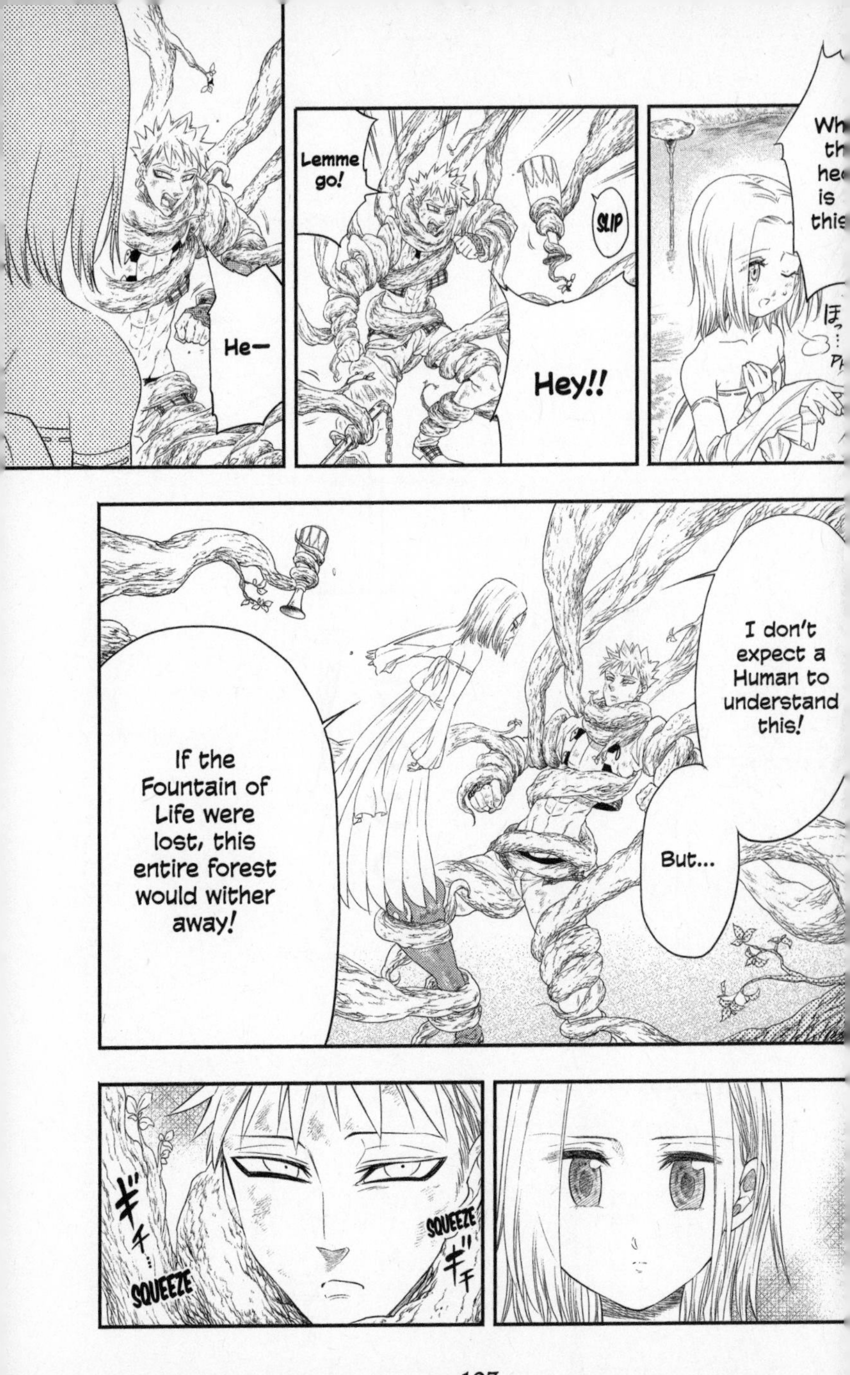
ほっ…
Lemme go!
SLIP
Hey!!
He—
I don't expect a Human to understand this!
But...
If the Fountain of Life were lost, this entire forest would wither away!
SQUEEZE
ギチ
ギチ…
SQUEEZE

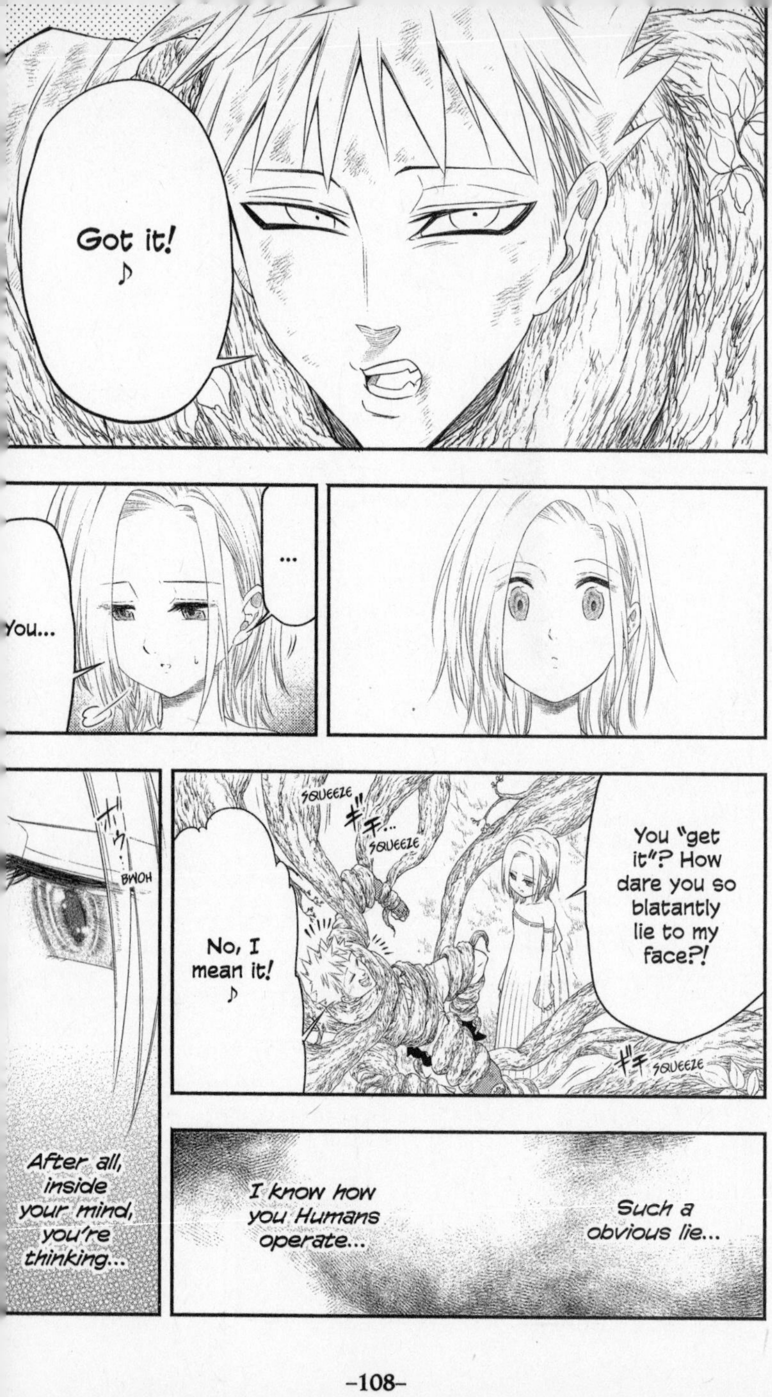

Got it! ♪
...
You...
You "get it"? How dare you so blatantly lie to my face?!
SQUEEZE
SQUEEZE
No, I mean it! ♪
SQUEEZE
Such a obvious lie...
I know how you Humans operate...
BWOH
After all, inside your mind, you're thinking...

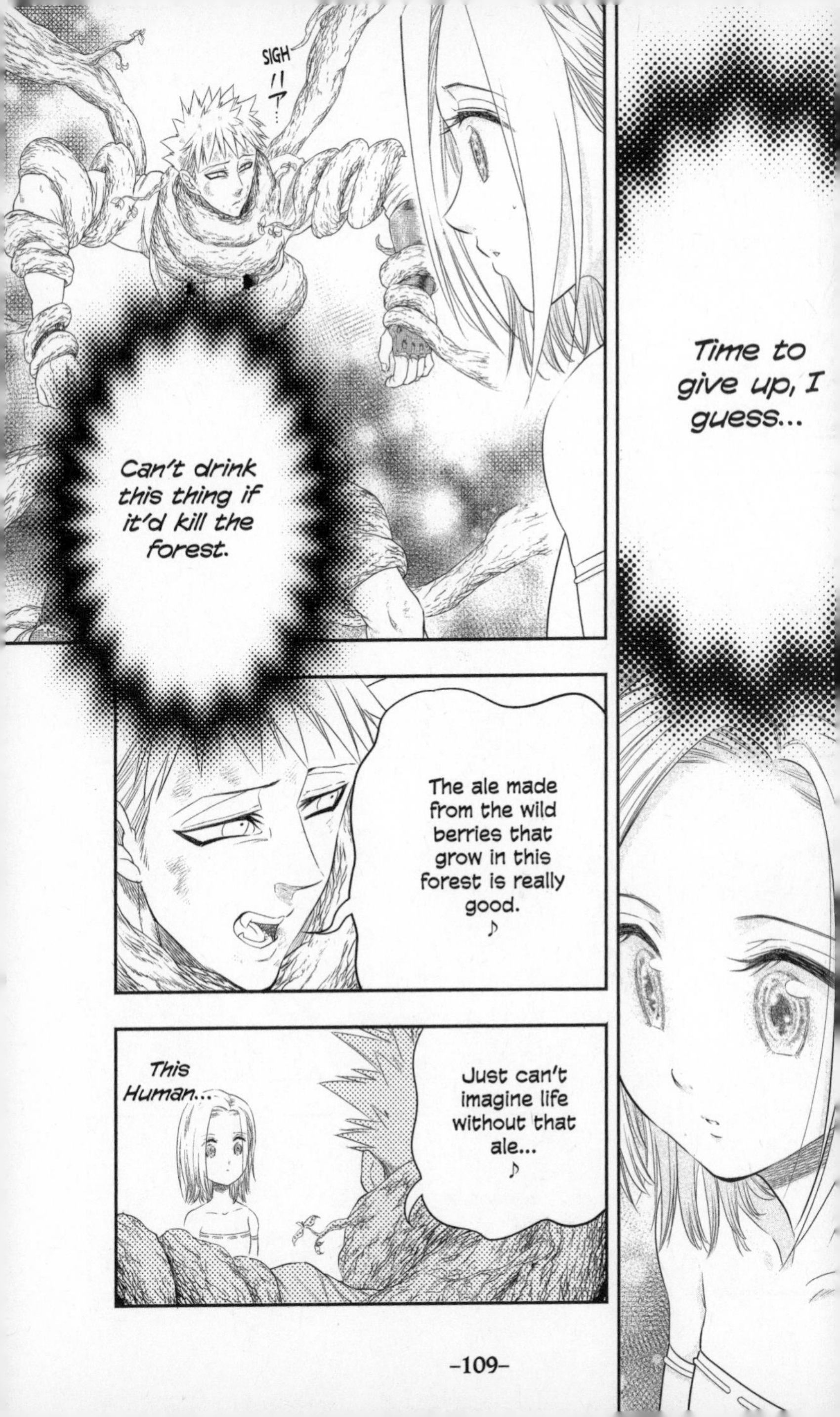
Time to give up, I guess...
SIGH
Can't drink this thing if it'd kill the forest.
The ale made from the wild berries that grow in this forest is really good. ♪
Just can't imagine life without that ale... ♪
This Human...

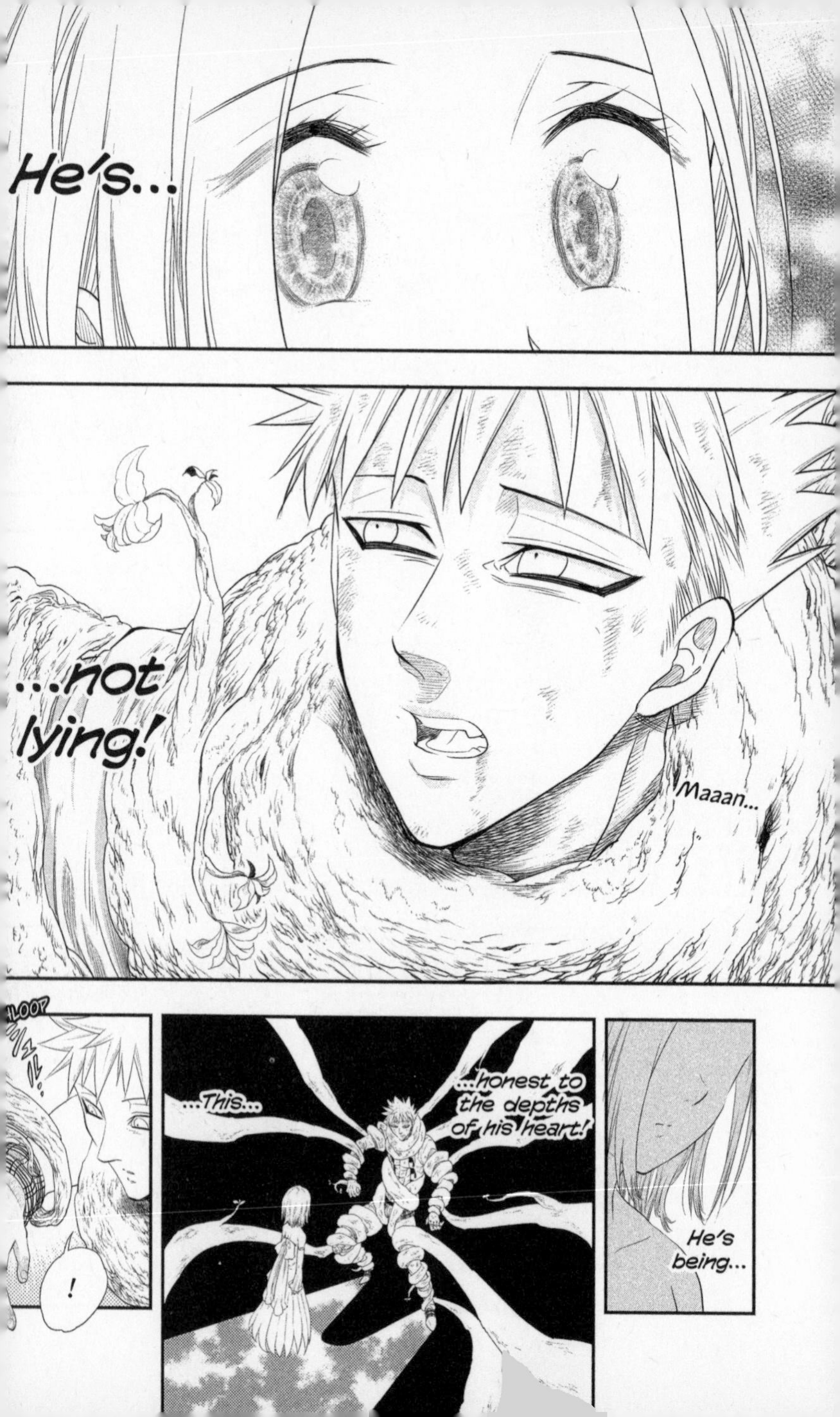
He's...
...not lying!
Maaan...
He's being...
...honest to the depths of his heart!
...This...
HLOOP
!

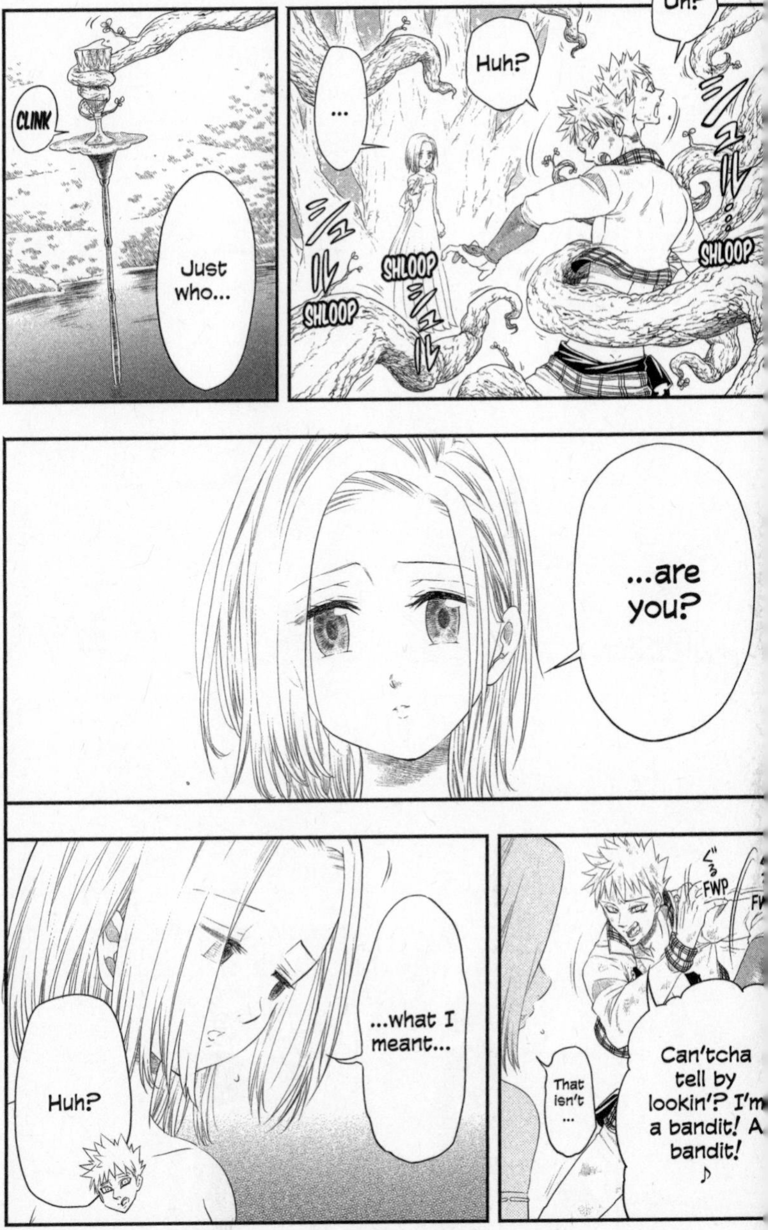
Uh?
SHLOOP
Huh?
...
SHLOOP
SHLOOP
CLINK
Just who...
...are you?
FWP
Can'tcha tell by lookin'? I'm a bandit! A bandit! ♪
That isn't ...
...what I meant...
Huh?

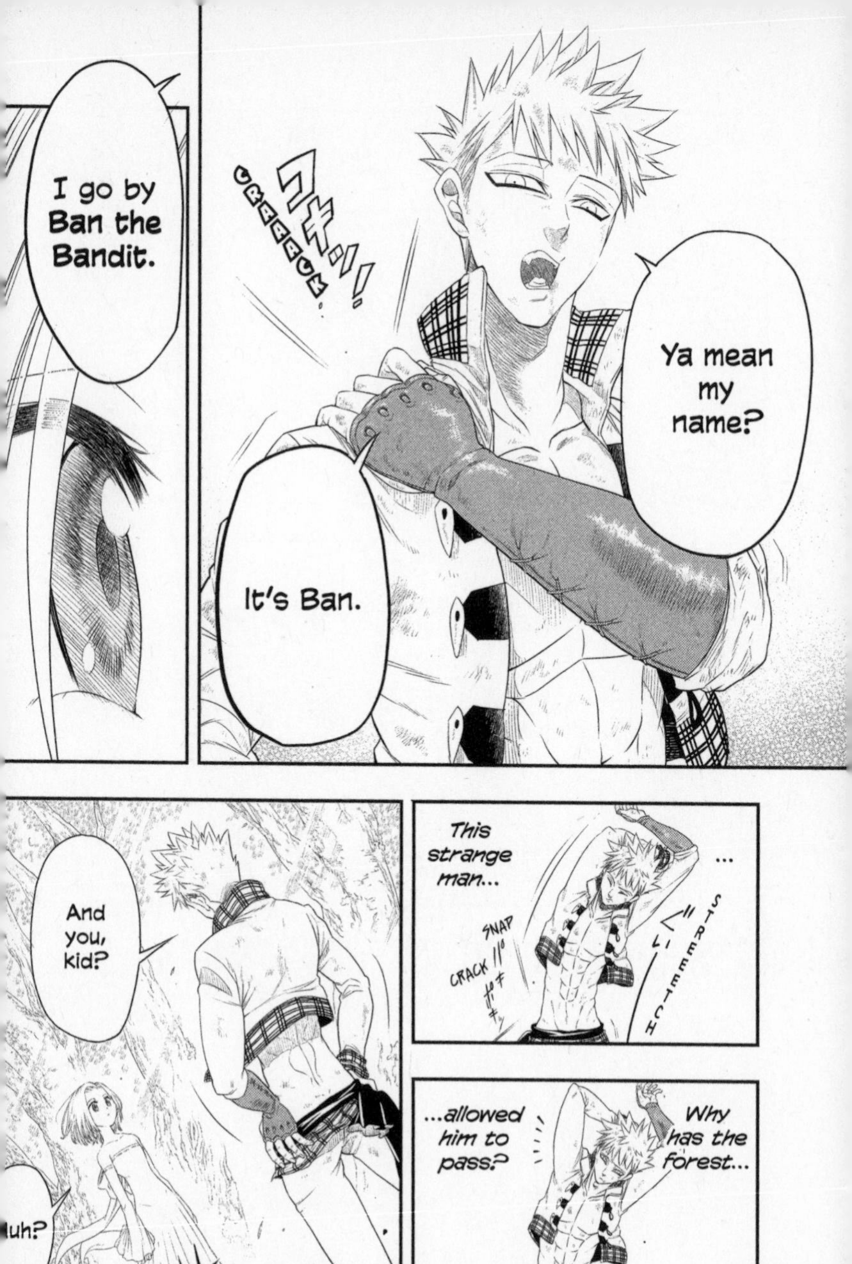
Ya mean my name?
GRAAAACK
It's Ban.
I go by Ban the Bandit.
...
STREEEETCH
SNAP
CRACK
This strange man...
Why has the forest...
...allowed him to pass?
And you, kid?
uh?
FWOOOH

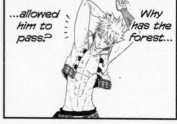

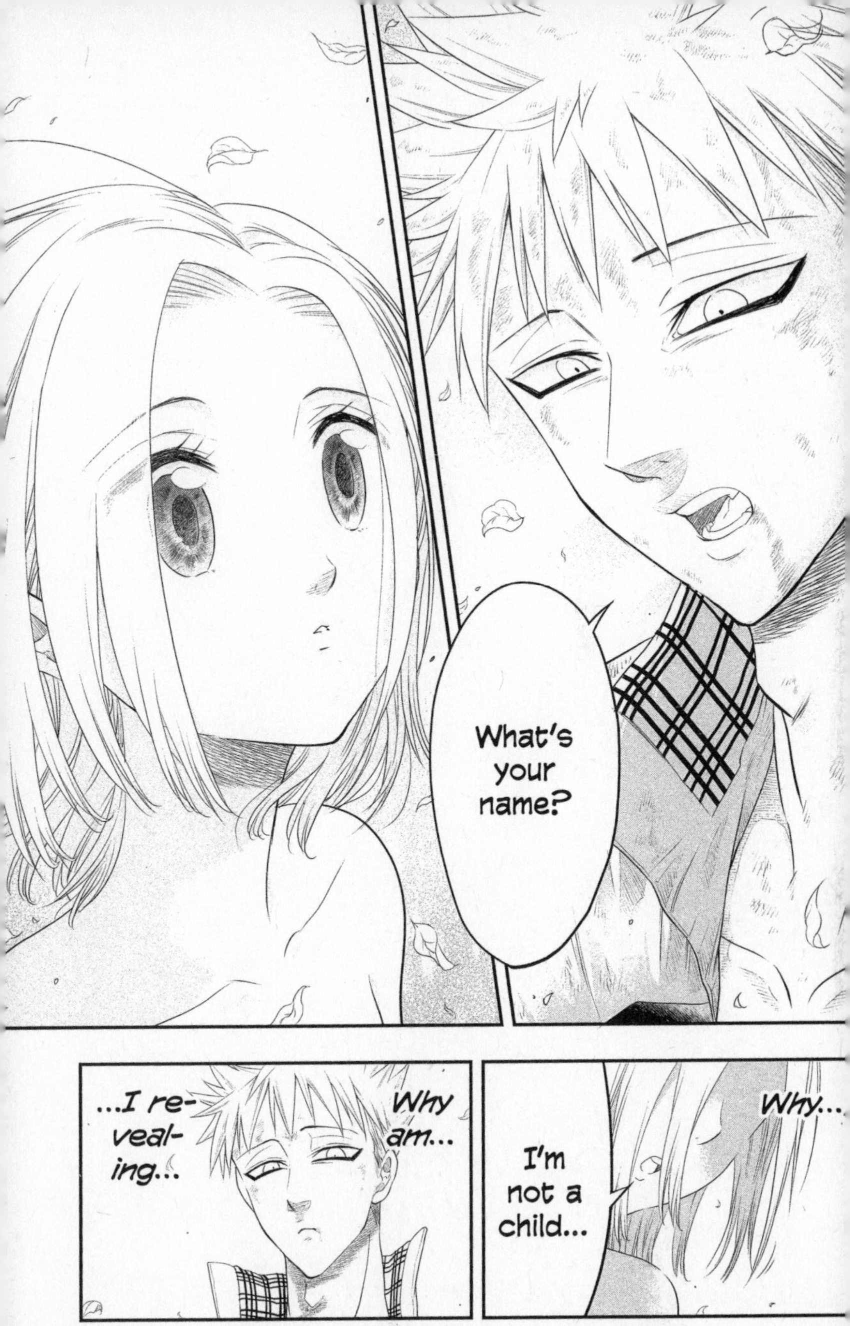
What's your name?
Why...
I'm not a child...
Why am...
...I re-vealing...

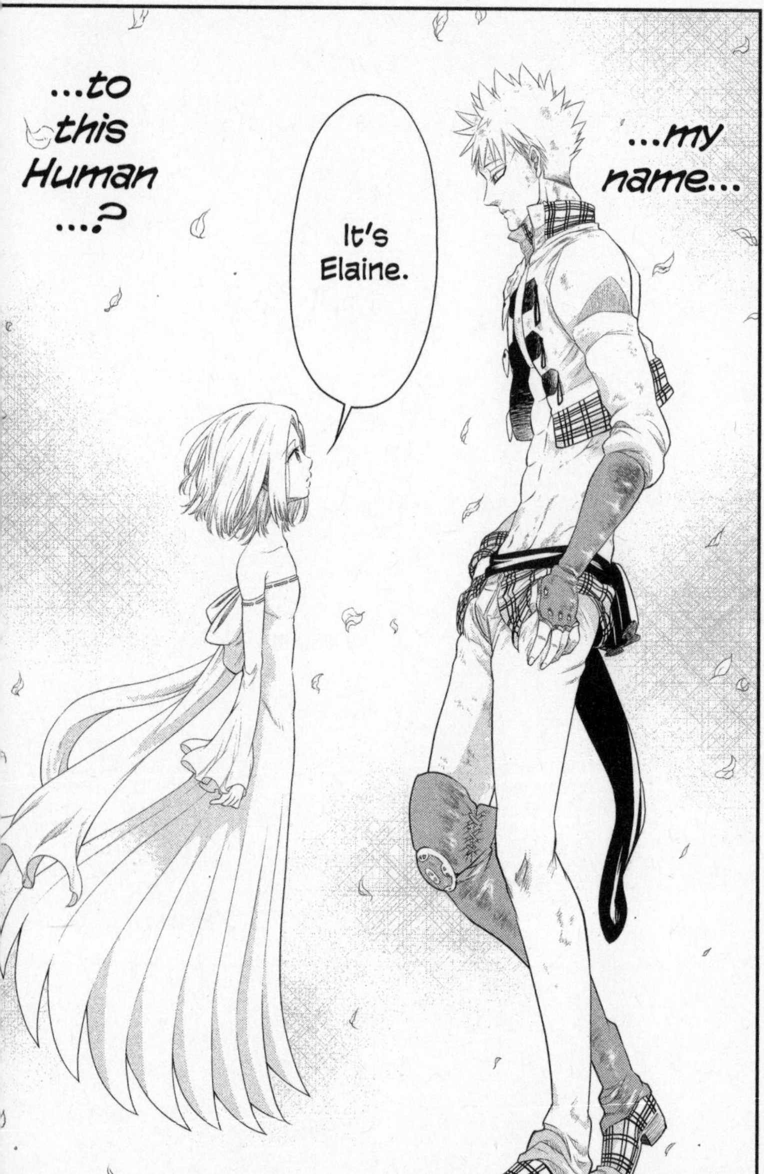
...my name...
It's Elaine.
...to this Human ...?

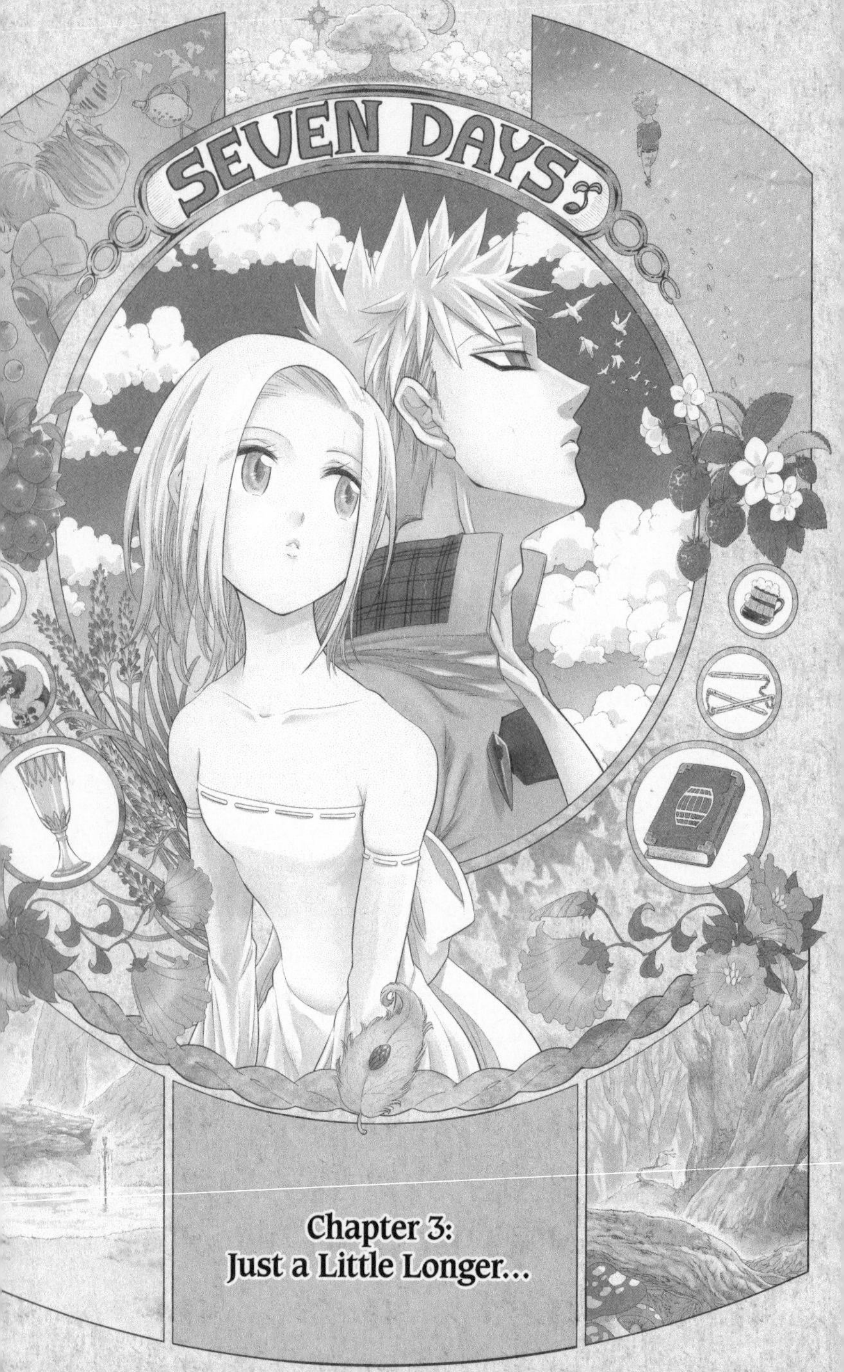
SEVEN DAYS
Chapter 3:
Just a Little Longer...

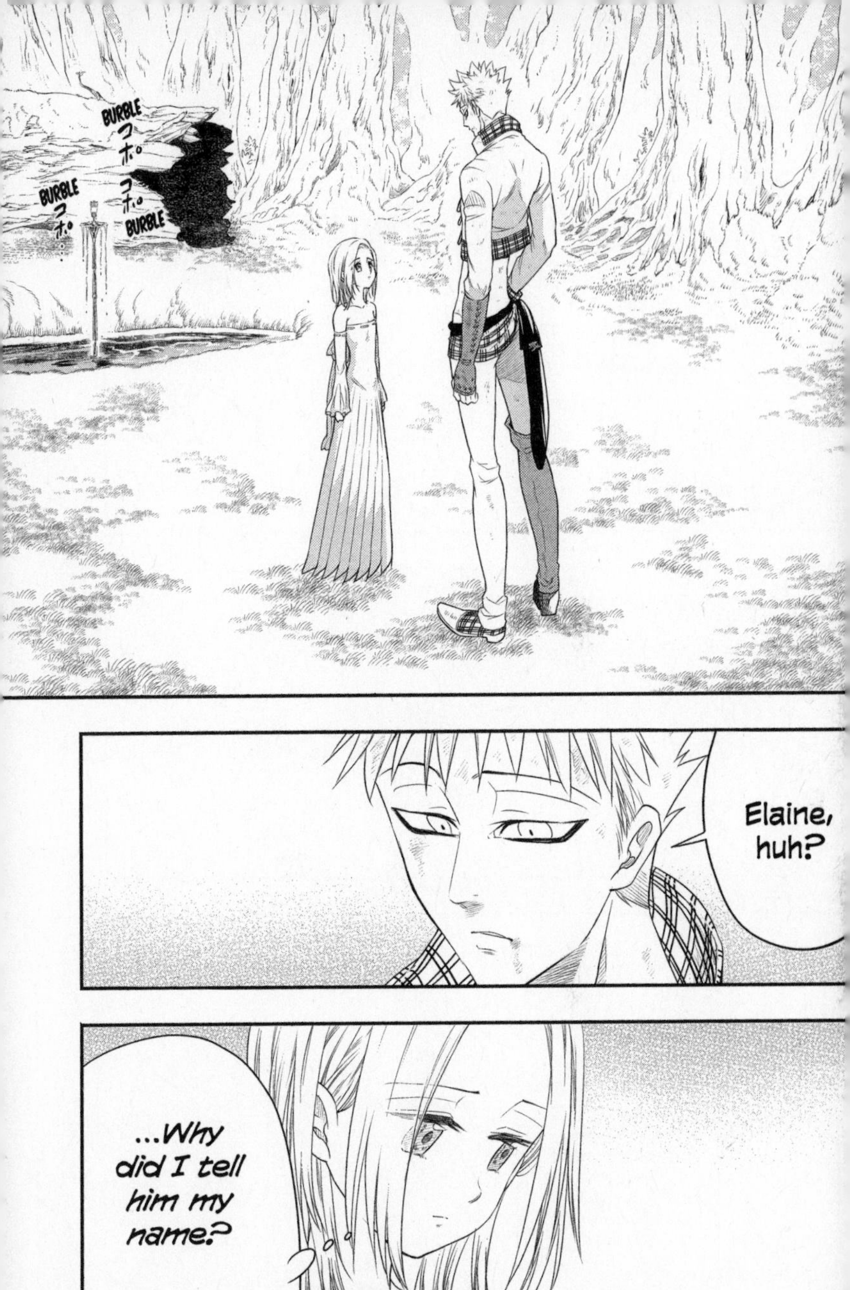
BURBLE コポ
コポ BURBLE
BURBLE コポ…
Elaine, huh?
...Why did I tell him my name?

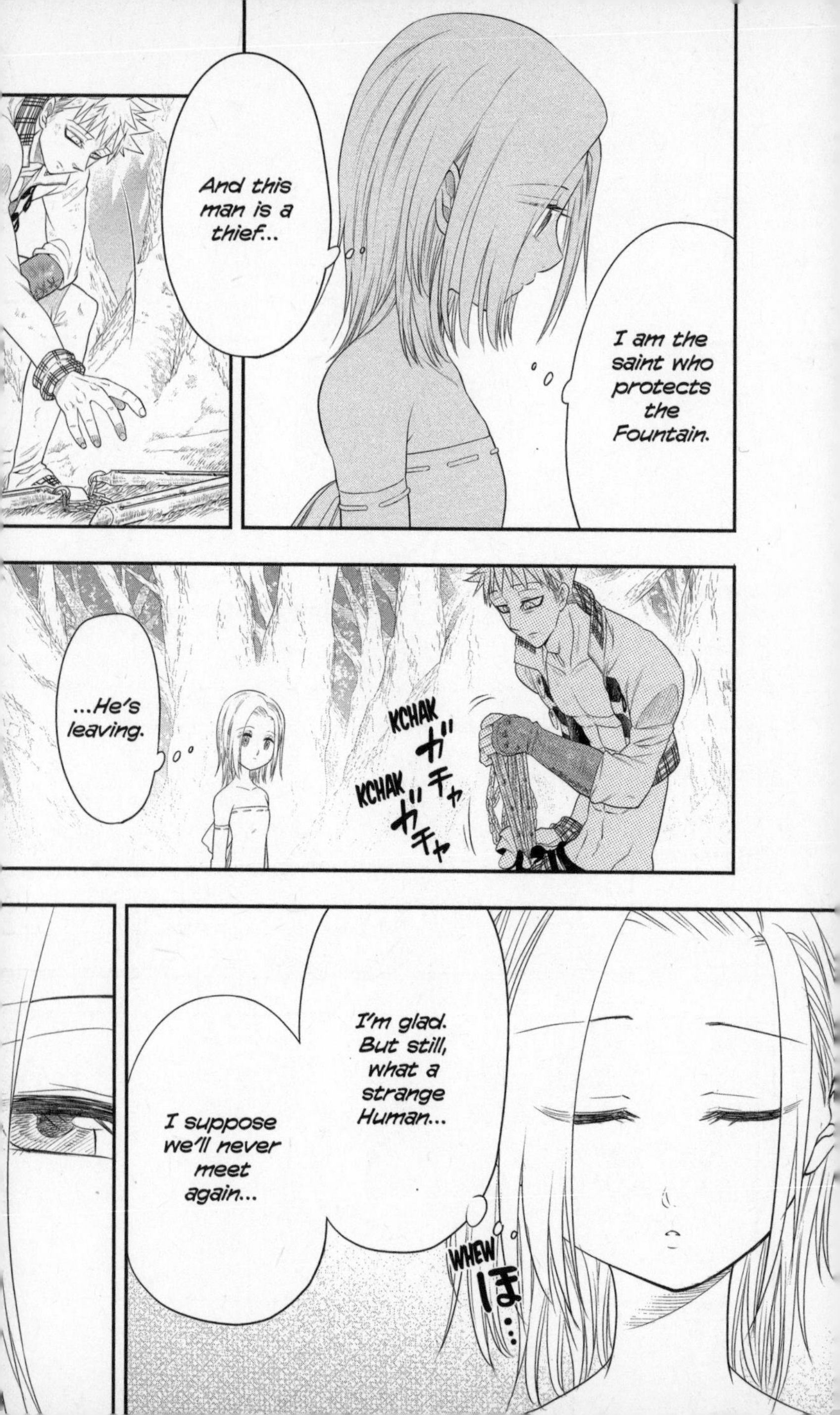

I am the saint who protects the Fountain.
And this man is a thief...
KCHAK
ガチャ
KCHAK
ガチャ
...He's leaving.
I'm glad. But still, what a strange Human...
I suppose we'll never meet again...
WHEW
ほ...

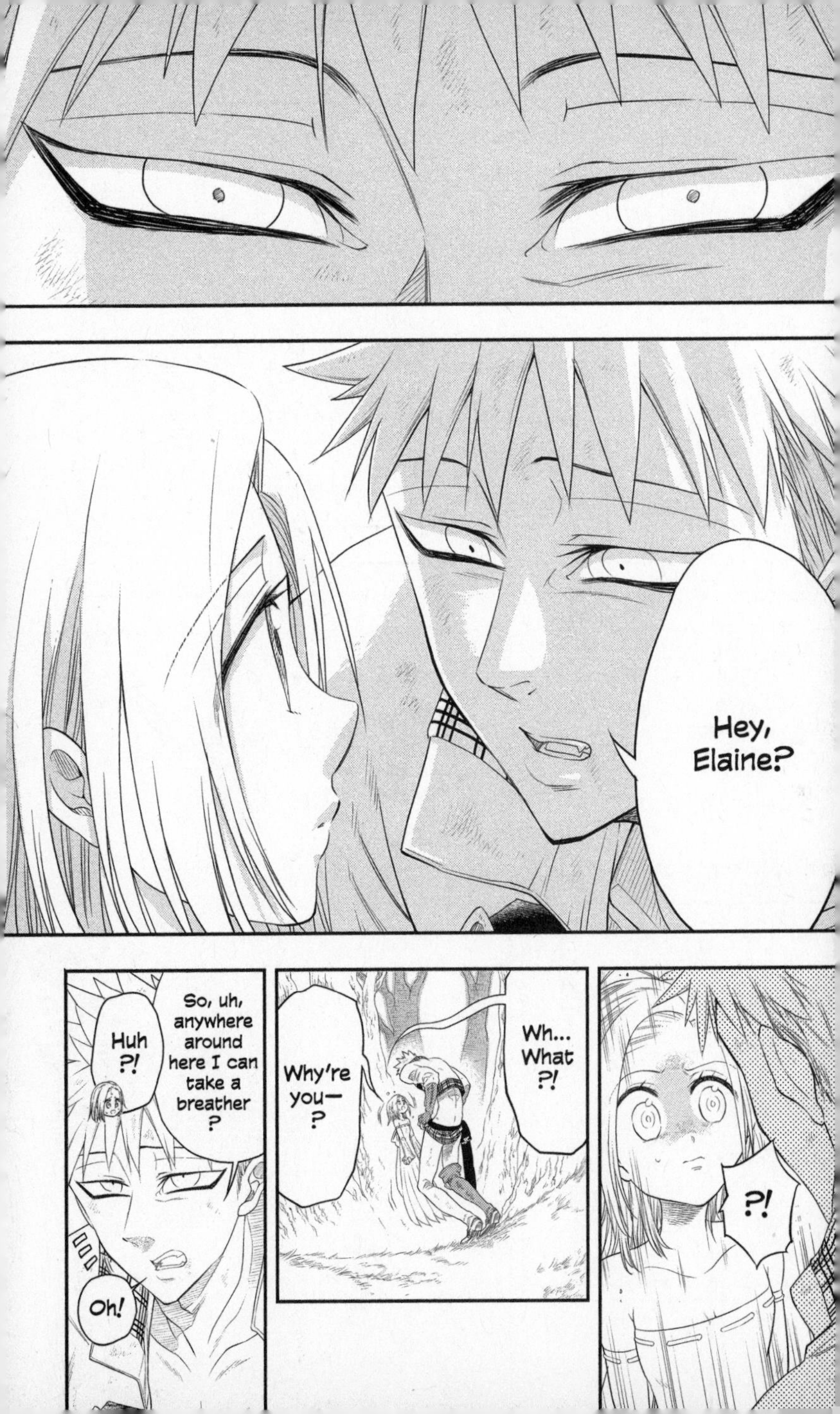
Hey, Elaine?
?!
Wh... What?!
Why're you—?
So, uh, anywhere around here I can take a breather?
Huh?!
Oh!

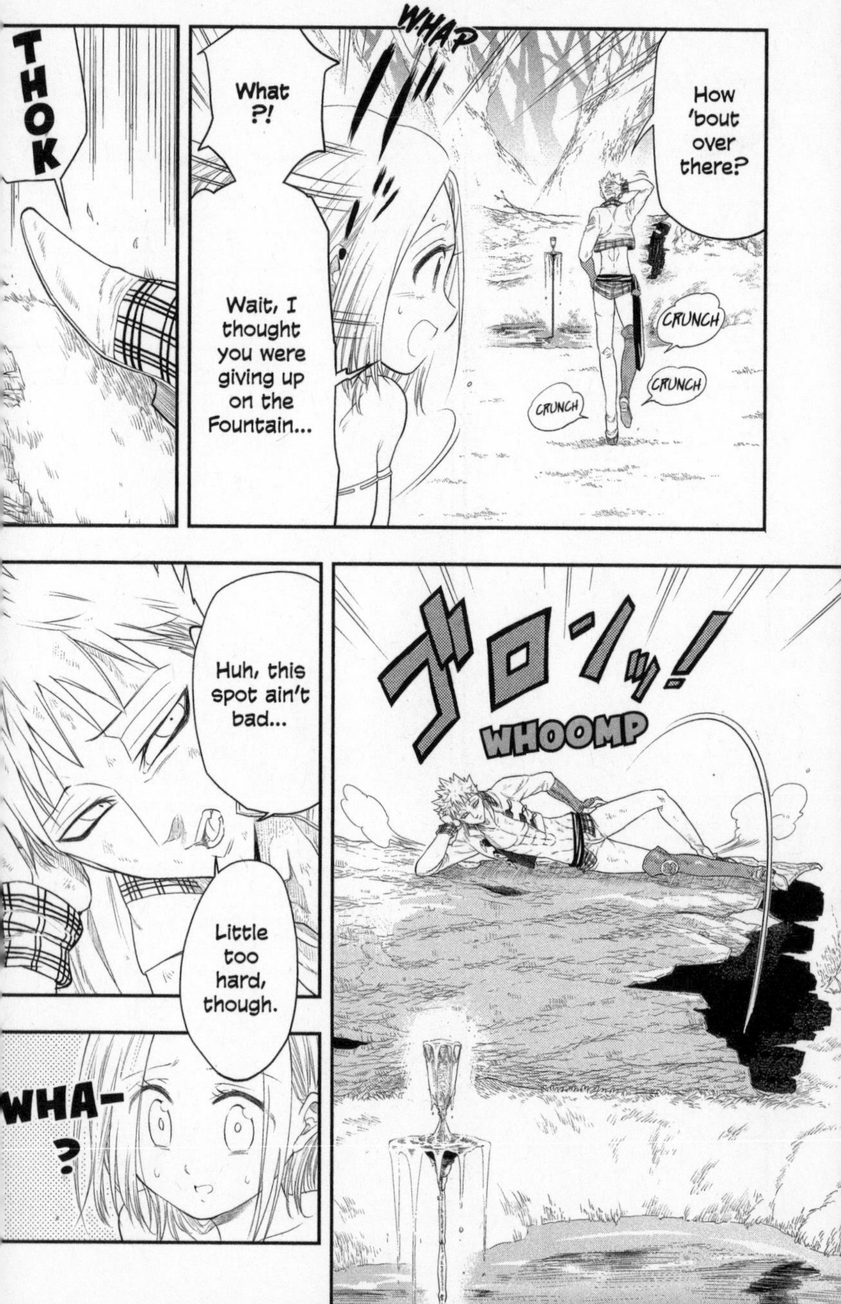
WHAP
How 'bout over there?
CRUNCH
CRUNCH
CRUNCH
What ?!
Wait, I thought you were giving up on the Fountain...
THOK
ゴロンッ!
WHOOMP
Huh, this spot ain't bad...
Little too hard, though.
WHA-?

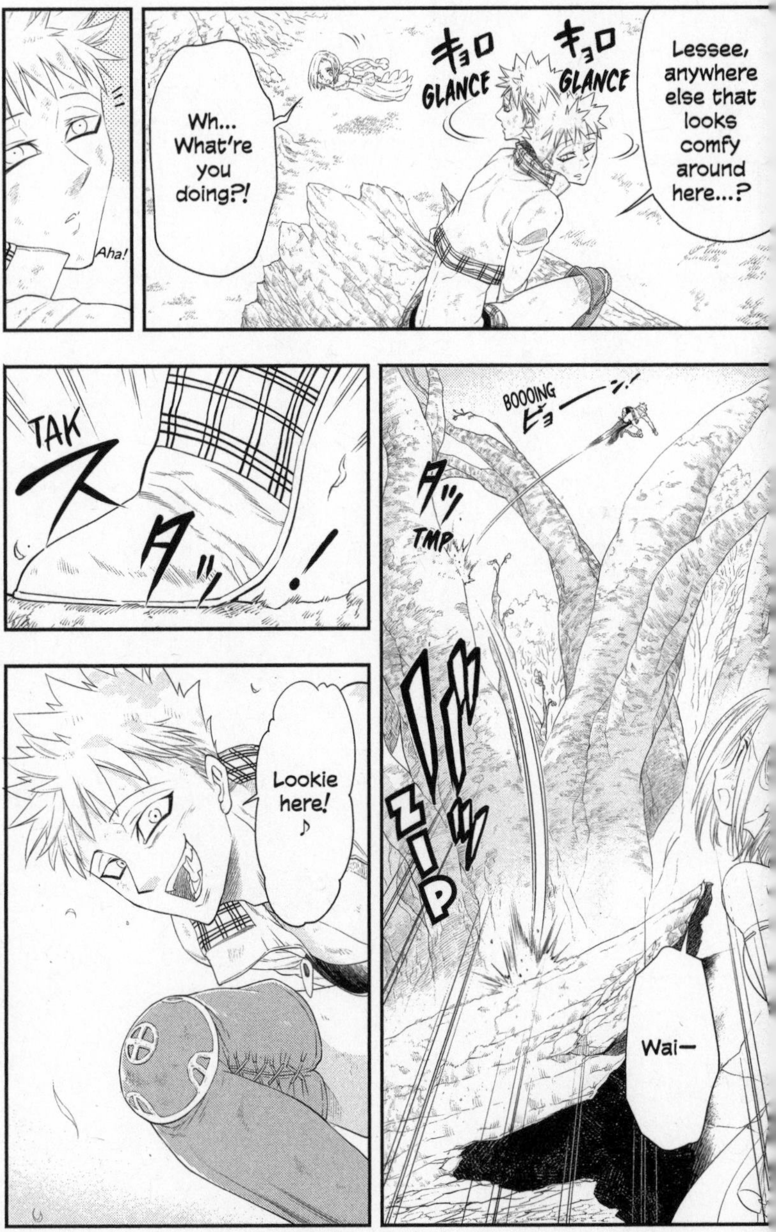
Lessee, anywhere else that looks comfy around here...?
キョロ GLANCE
キョロ GLANCE
Wh... What're you doing?!
Aha!
BOOOING ビョーーン!
ダッ TMP
ZIP
Wai—
TAK ス
ダッ!
Lookie here! ♪

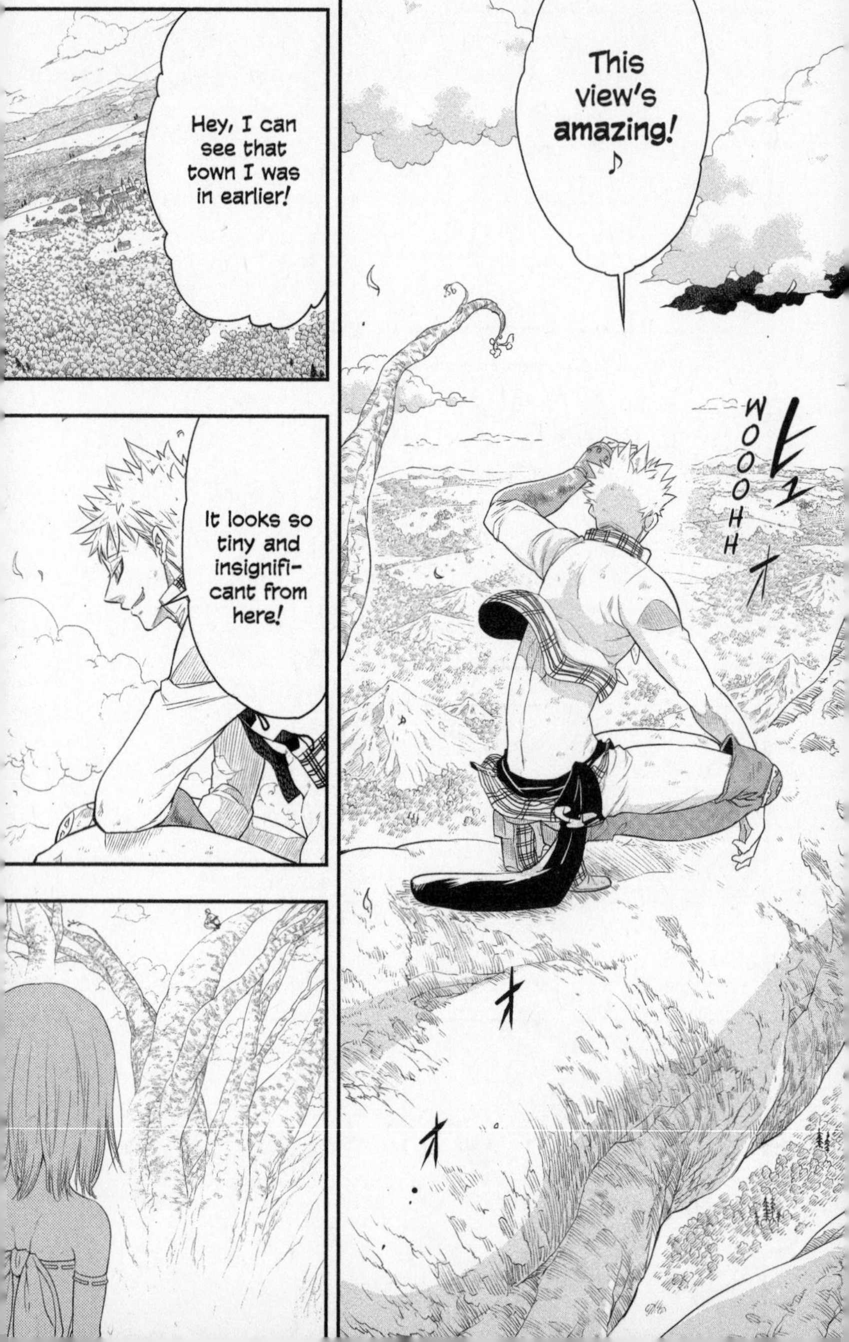
This view's amazing! ♪
WOOOHH
Hey, I can see that town I was in earlier!
It looks so tiny and insignificant from here!

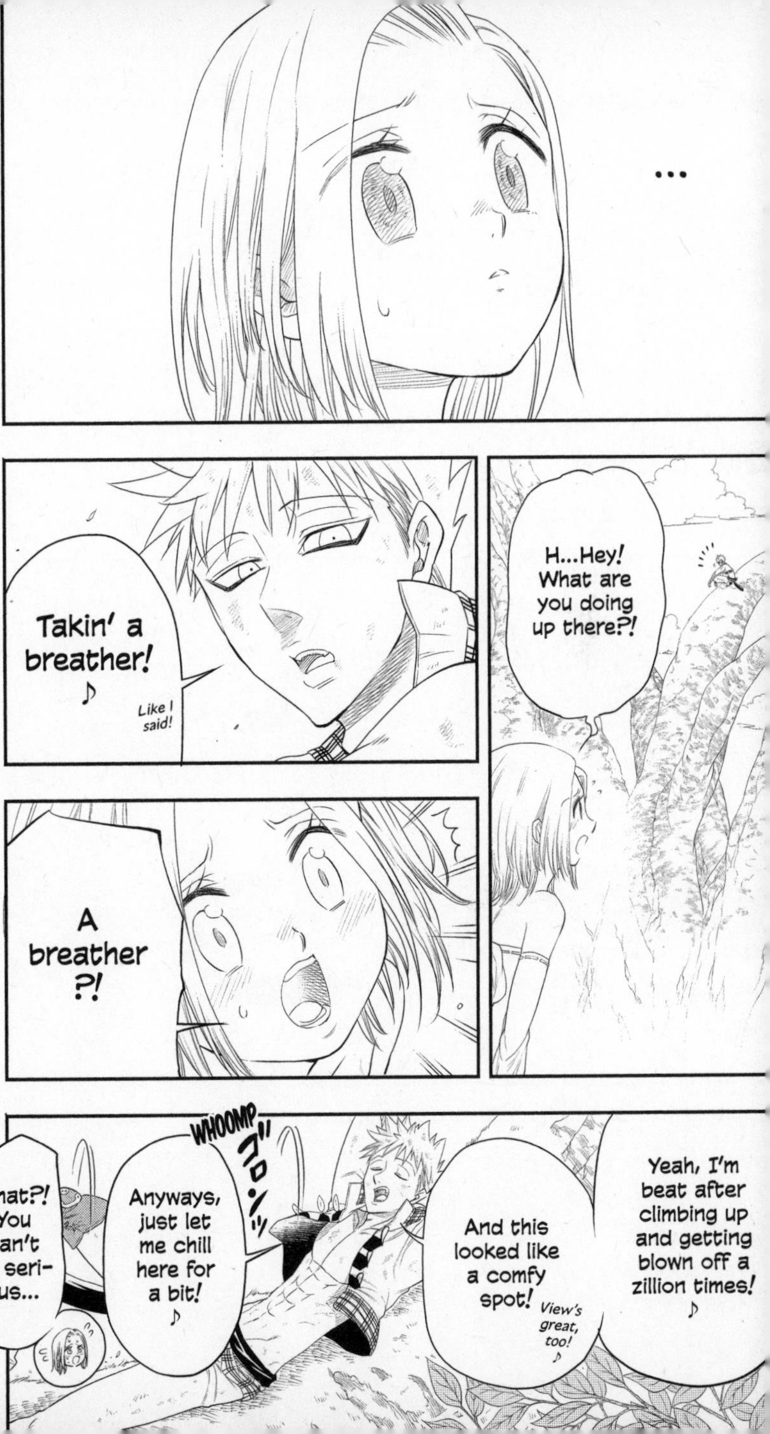
...
H...Hey! What are you doing up there?!
Takin' a breather! ♪
Like I said!
A breather?!
Yeah, I'm beat after climbing up and getting blown off a zillion times! ♪
And this looked like a comfy spot!
View's great, too! ♪
WHOOMP
ゴロンッ
Anyways, just let me chill here for a bit! ♪
What?! You can't be seri-ous...

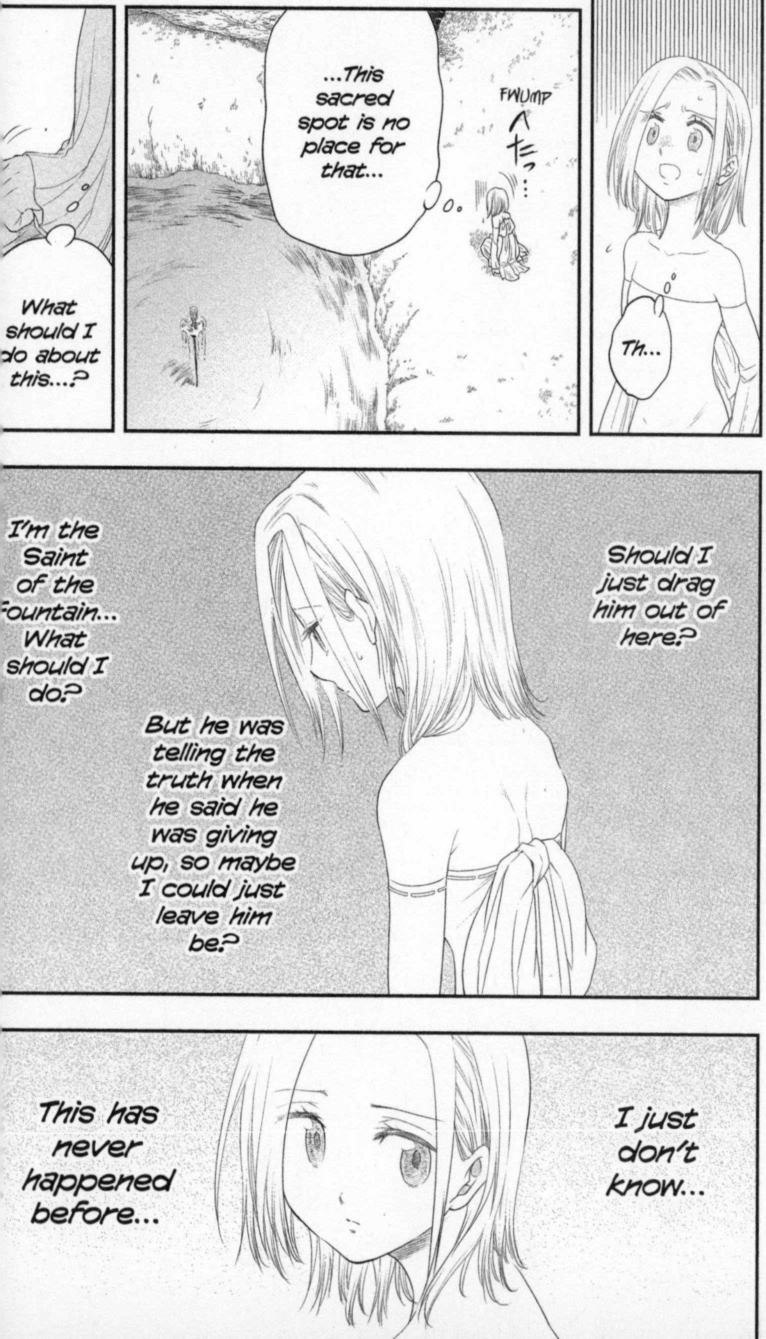
Th...
...This sacred spot is no place for that...
FWUMP
What should I do about this...?
Should I just drag him out of here?
I'm the Saint of the Fountain... What should I do?
But he was telling the truth when he said he was giving up, so maybe I could just leave him be?
I just don't know...
This has never happened before...

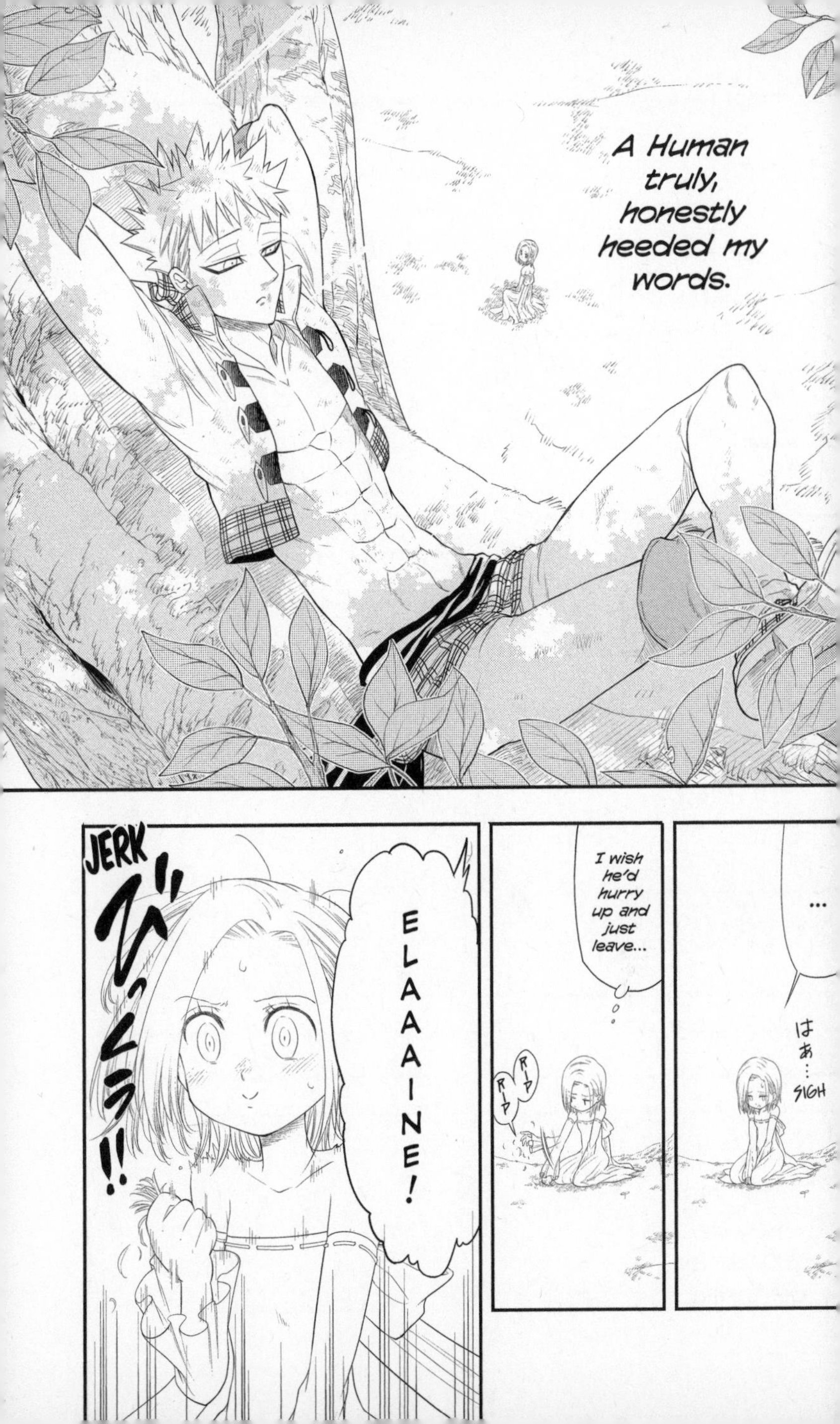
A Human truly, honestly heeded my words.
...
はぁ…
SIGH
I wish he'd hurry up and just leave...
RIP
RIP
ELAAAINE!
JERK
びっくう!!

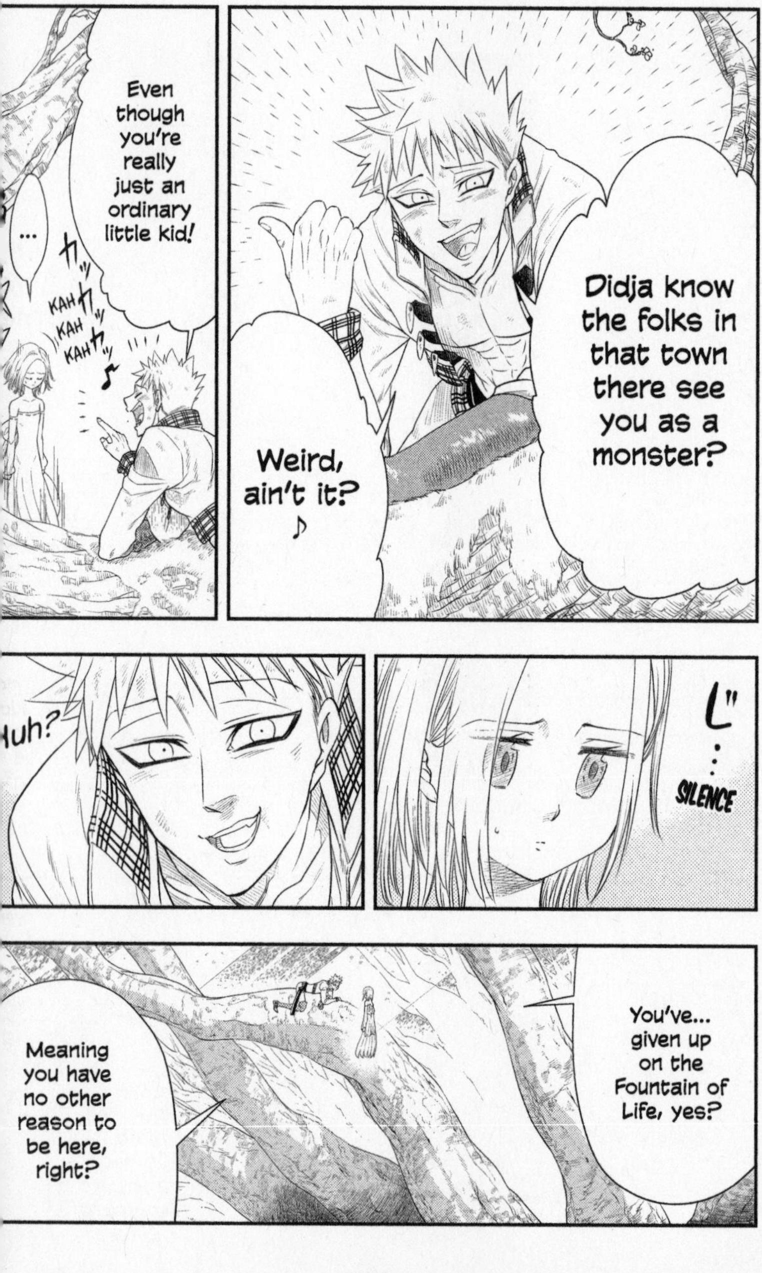
Didja know the folks in that town there see you as a monster?
Weird, ain't it? ♪
Even though you're really just an ordinary little kid!
KAH KAH KAH
♪
...
SILENCE
Huh?
You've... given up on the Fountain of Life, yes?
Meaning you have no other reason to be here, right?

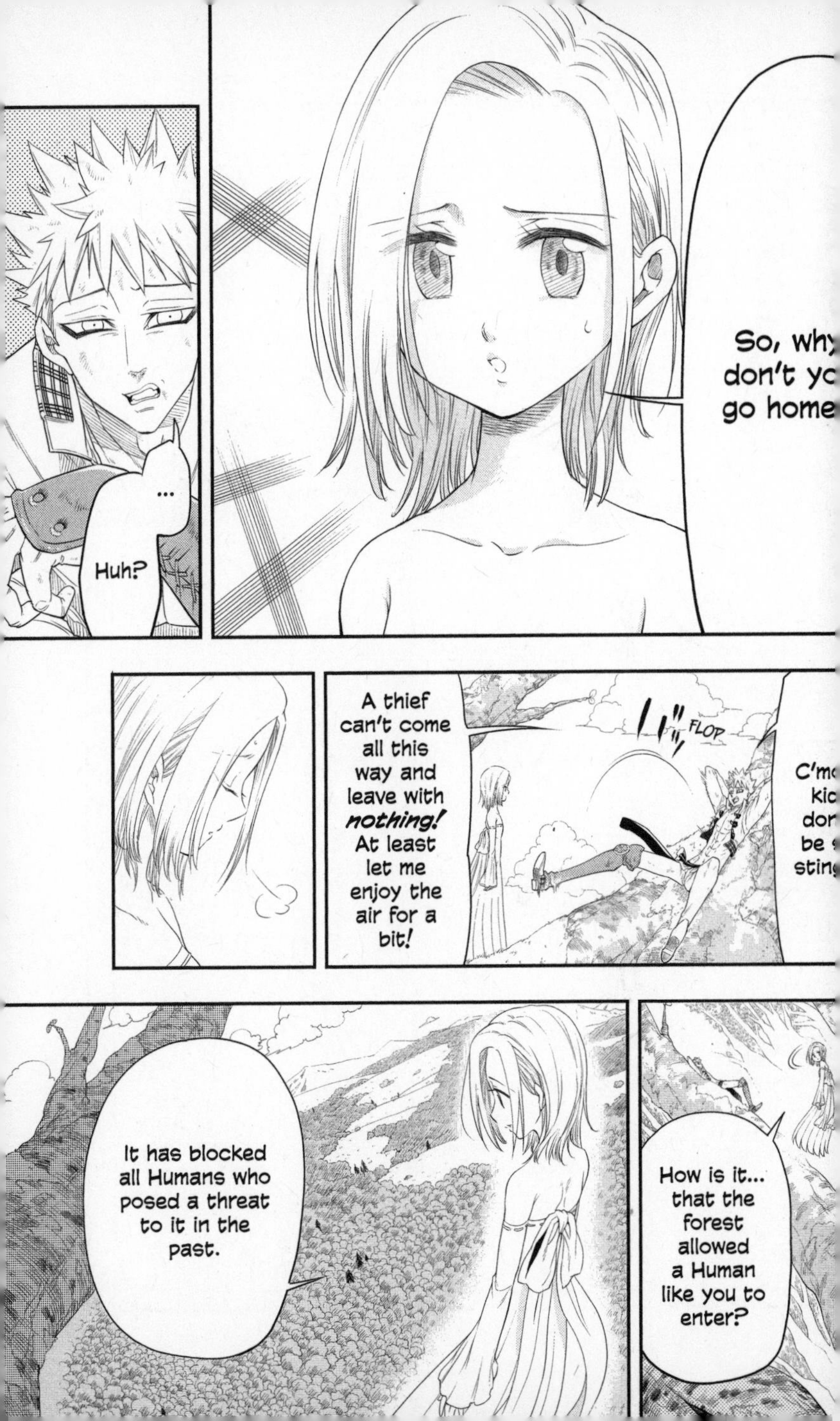

So, why don't yo go home
...
Huh?
C'm kic dor be sting
FLOP
A thief can't come all this way and leave with *nothing!* At least let me enjoy the air for a bit!
How is it... that the forest allowed a Human like you to enter?
It has blocked all Humans who posed a threat to it in the past.

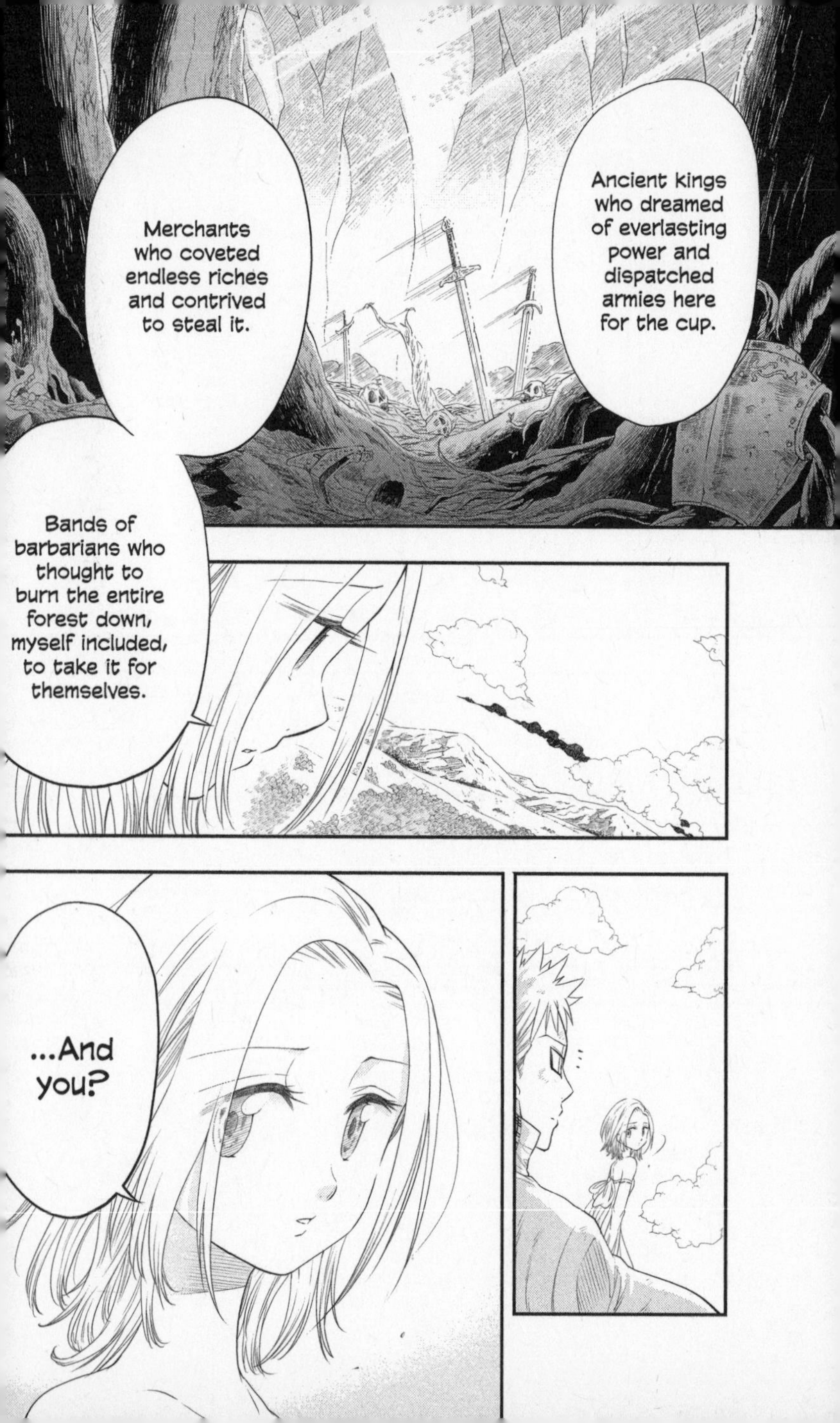
Ancient kings who dreamed of everlasting power and dispatched armies here for the cup.
Merchants who coveted endless riches and contrived to steal it.
Bands of barbarians who thought to burn the entire forest down, myself included, to take it for themselves.
...And you?

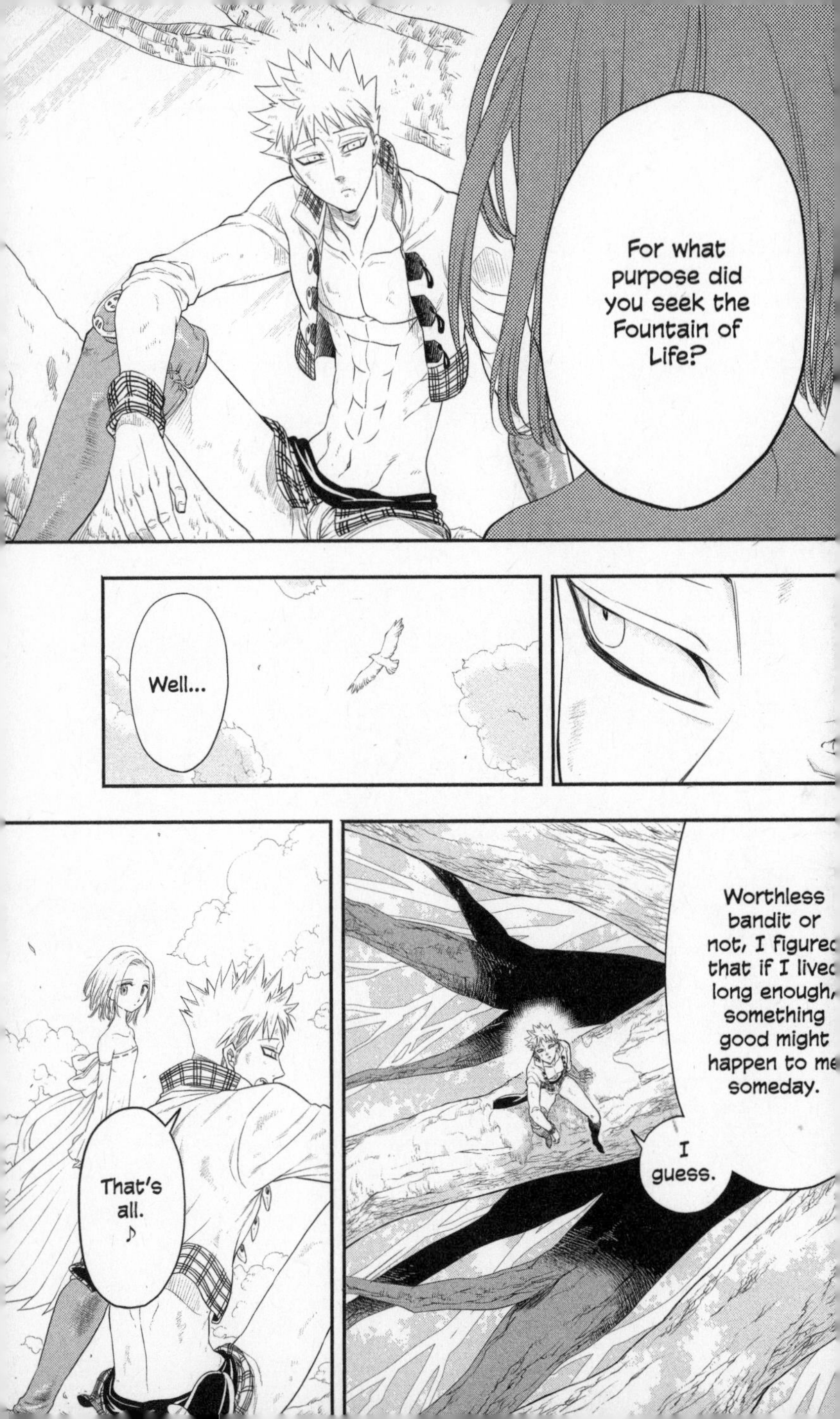
For what purpose did you seek the Fountain of Life?
Well...
Worthless bandit or not, I figured that if I lived long enough, something good might happen to me someday.
I guess.
That's all. ♪

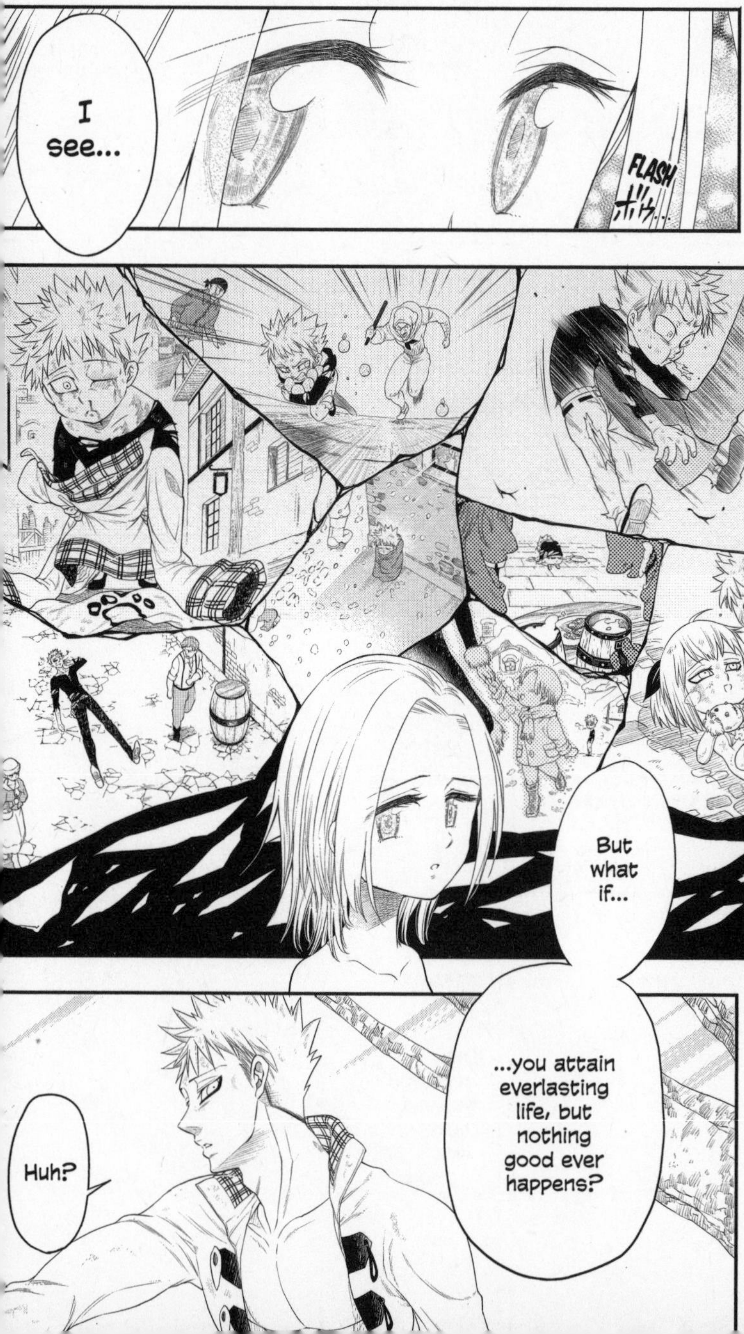
FLASH
I see...
But what if...
...you attain everlasting life, but nothing good ever happens?
Huh?

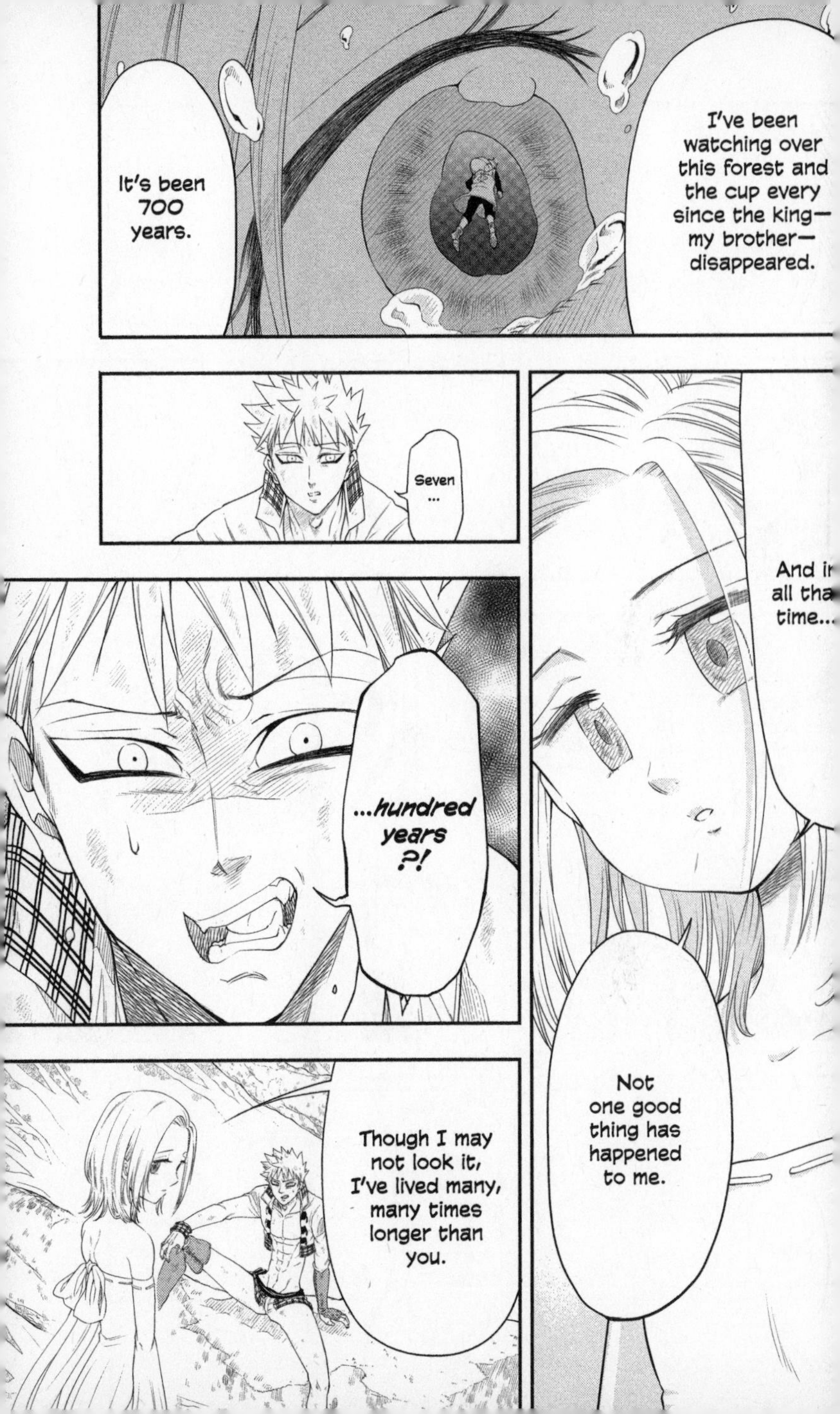
I've been watching over this forest and the cup every since the king—my brother—disappeared.
It's been 700 years.
And ir all tha time...
Not one good thing has happened to me.
Seven ...
...hundred years ?!
Though I may not look it, I've lived many, many times longer than you.

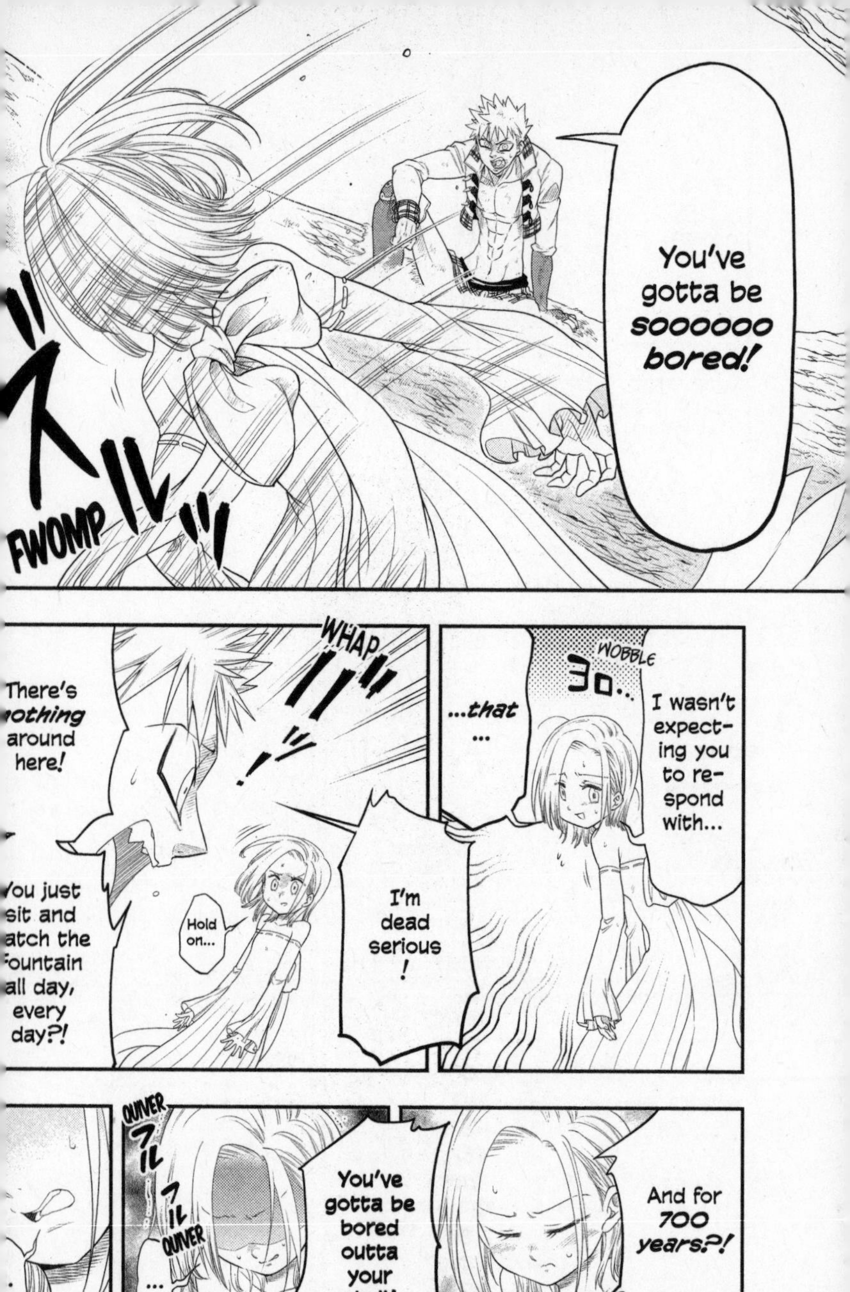
You've gotta be sooooooo bored!
FWOMP
WOBBLE
I wasn't expect-ing you to re-spond with...
...that ...
WHAP
There's othing around here!
ou just sit and atch the ountain all day, every day?!
I'm dead serious!
Hold on...
And for 700 years?!
You've gotta be bored outta your skull!
QUIVER
QUIVER
...

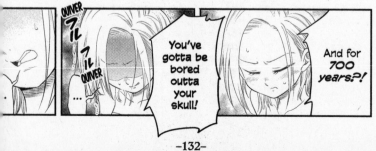

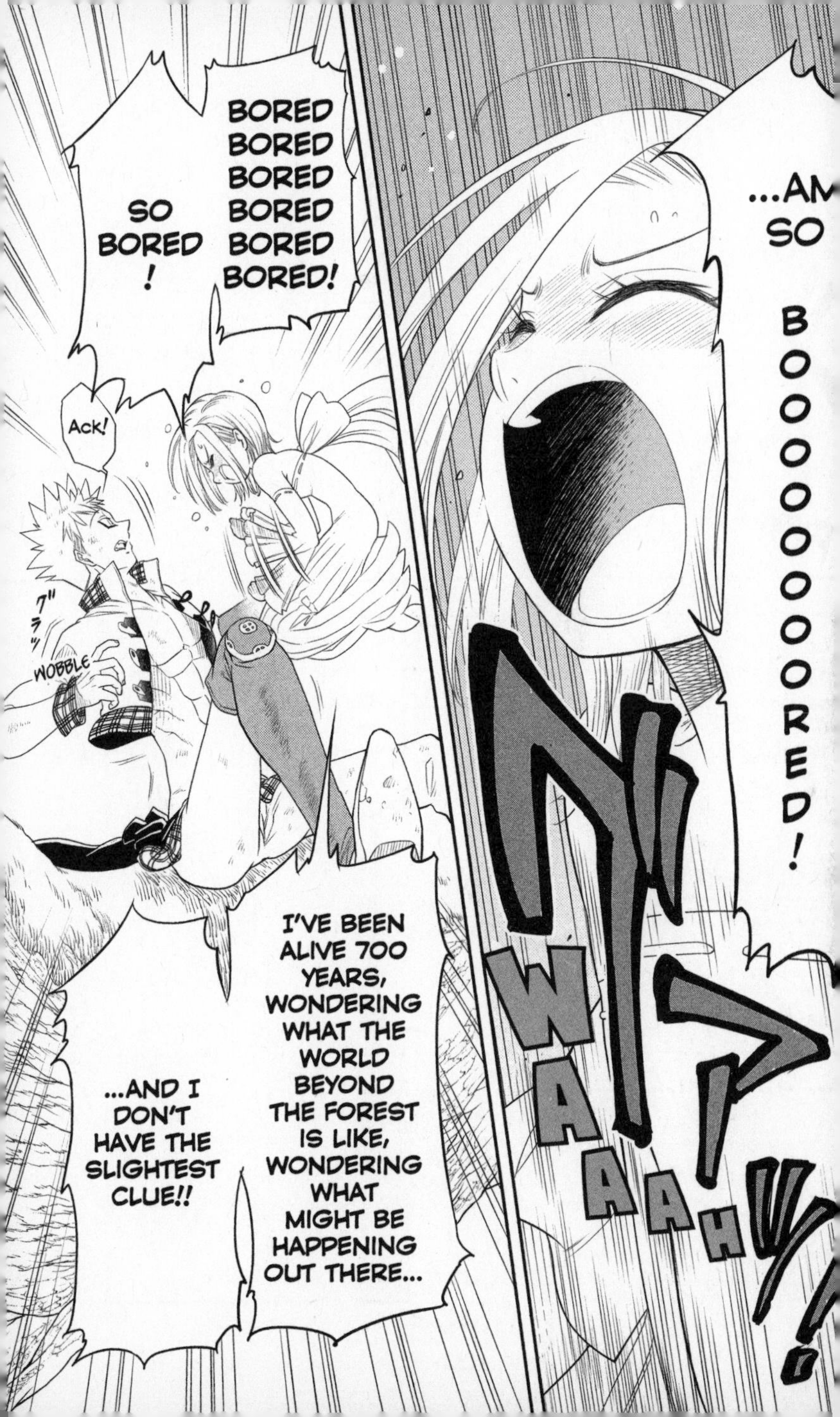
...AM SO BOOOOOOOORED!
WAAAH!!
BORED BORED BORED BORED BORED BORED!
SO BORED!
Ack!
グラッ
WOBBLE
I'VE BEEN ALIVE 700 YEARS, WONDERING WHAT THE WORLD BEYOND THE FOREST IS LIKE, WONDERING WHAT MIGHT BE HAPPENING OUT THERE...
...AND I DON'T HAVE THE SLIGHTEST CLUE!!

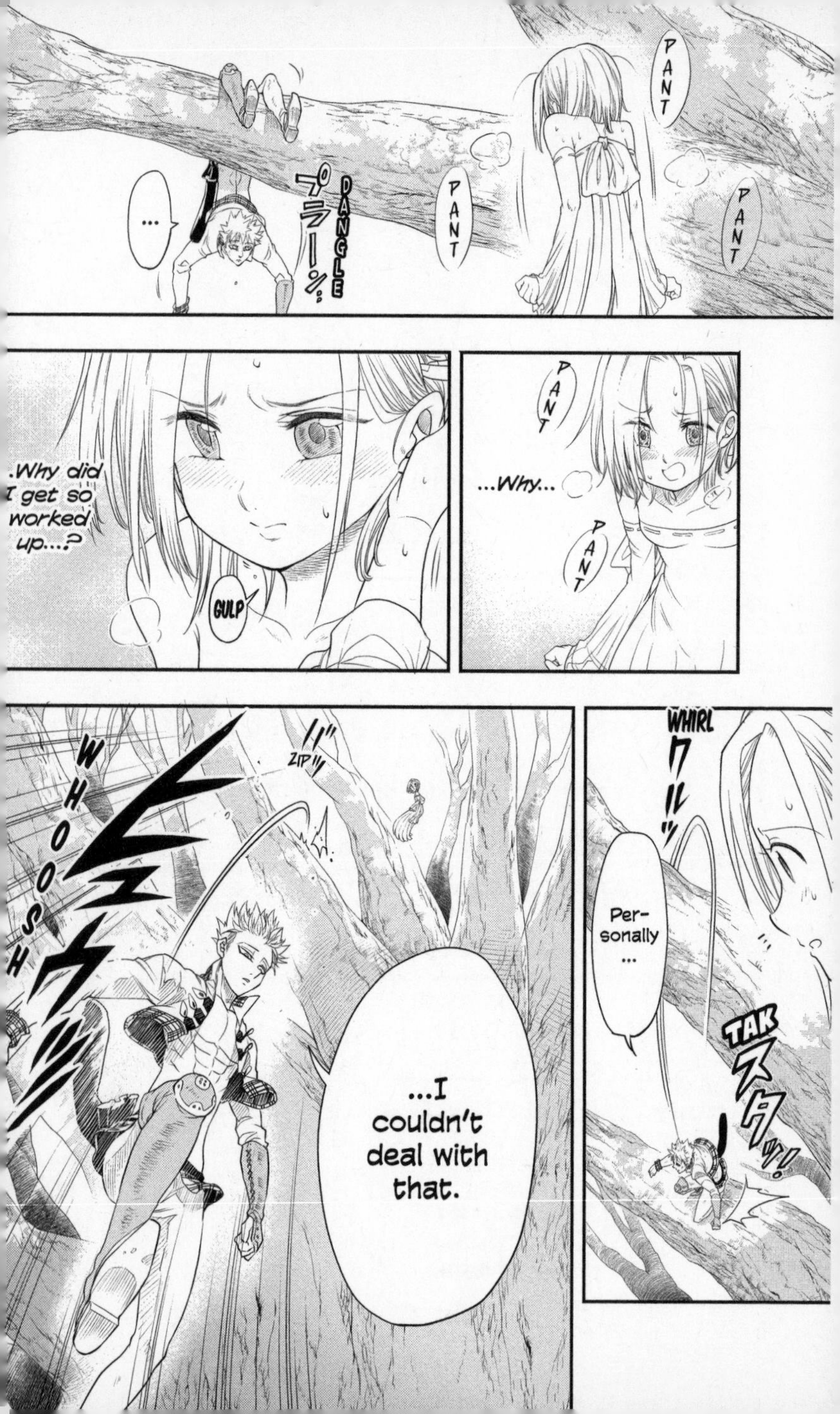
PANT
PANT
PANT
DANGLE
...
PANT
...Why...
PANT
.Why did I get so worked up...?
GULP
WHIRL
Per-sonally...
TAK
ZIP
...I couldn't deal with that.
WHOOSH

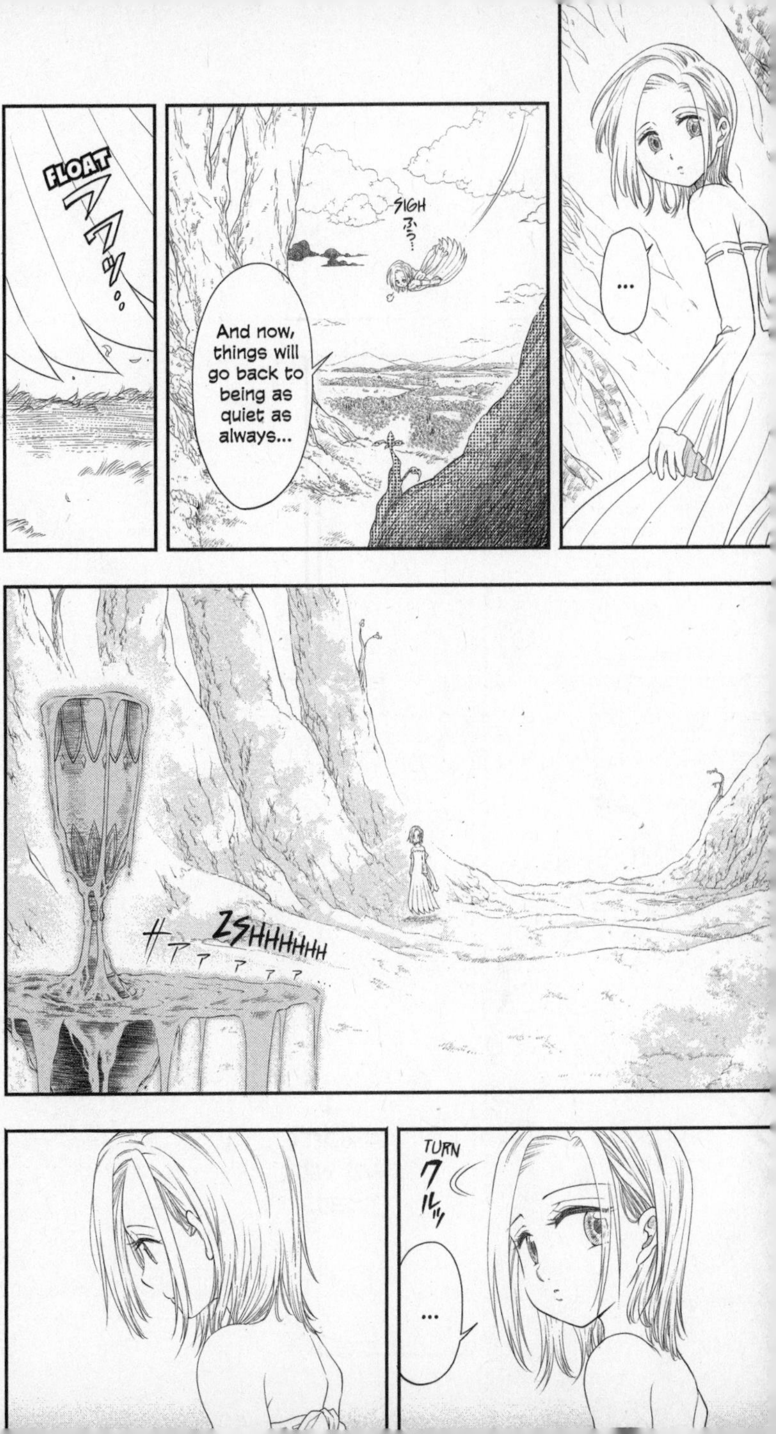

...
SIGH
ふう…
And now, things will go back to being as quiet as always...
FLOAT
フワッ。。
ZSHHHHHH
ザァァァァァ…
TURN
クルッ
...

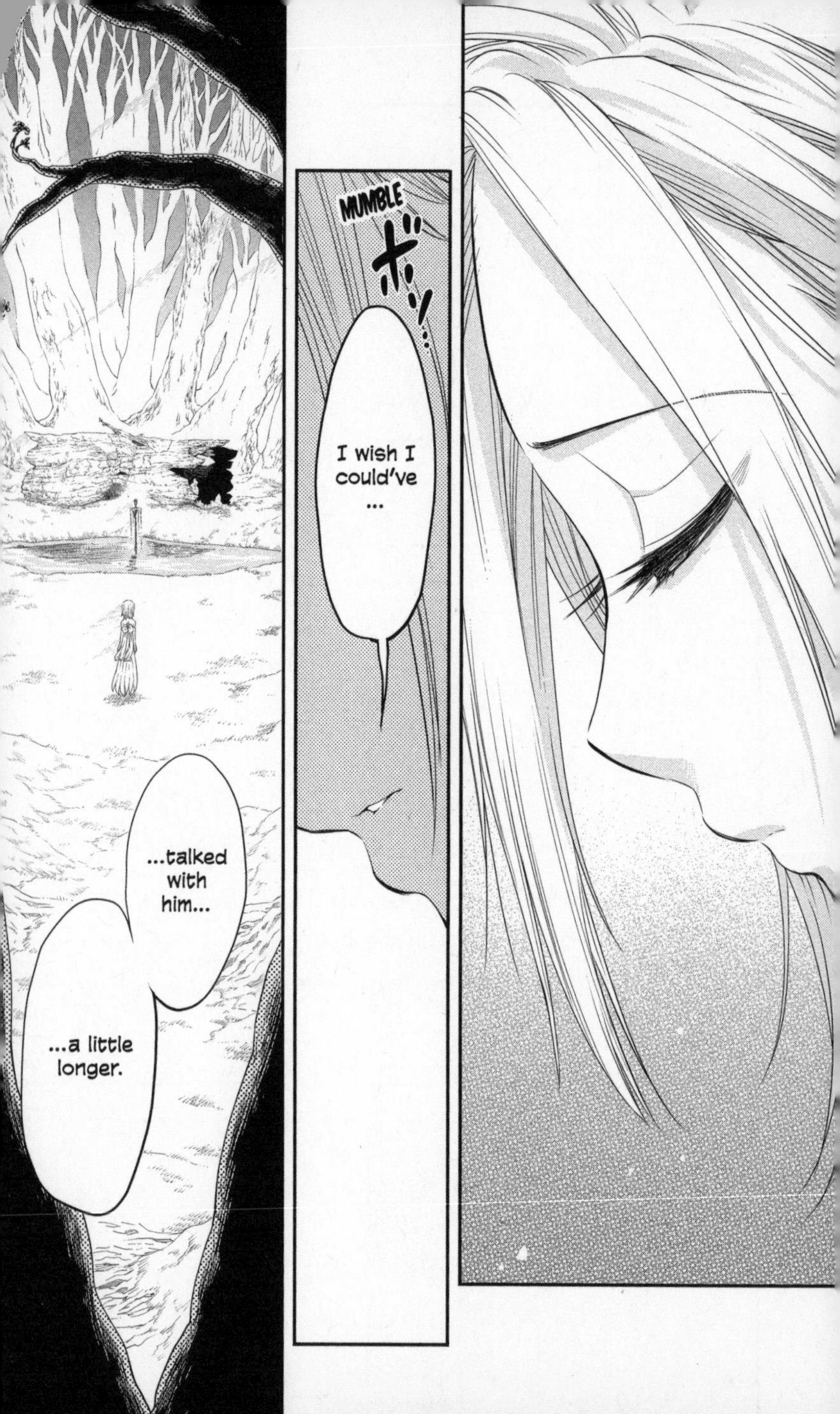
MUMBLE
I wish I could've ...
...talked with him...
...a little longer.

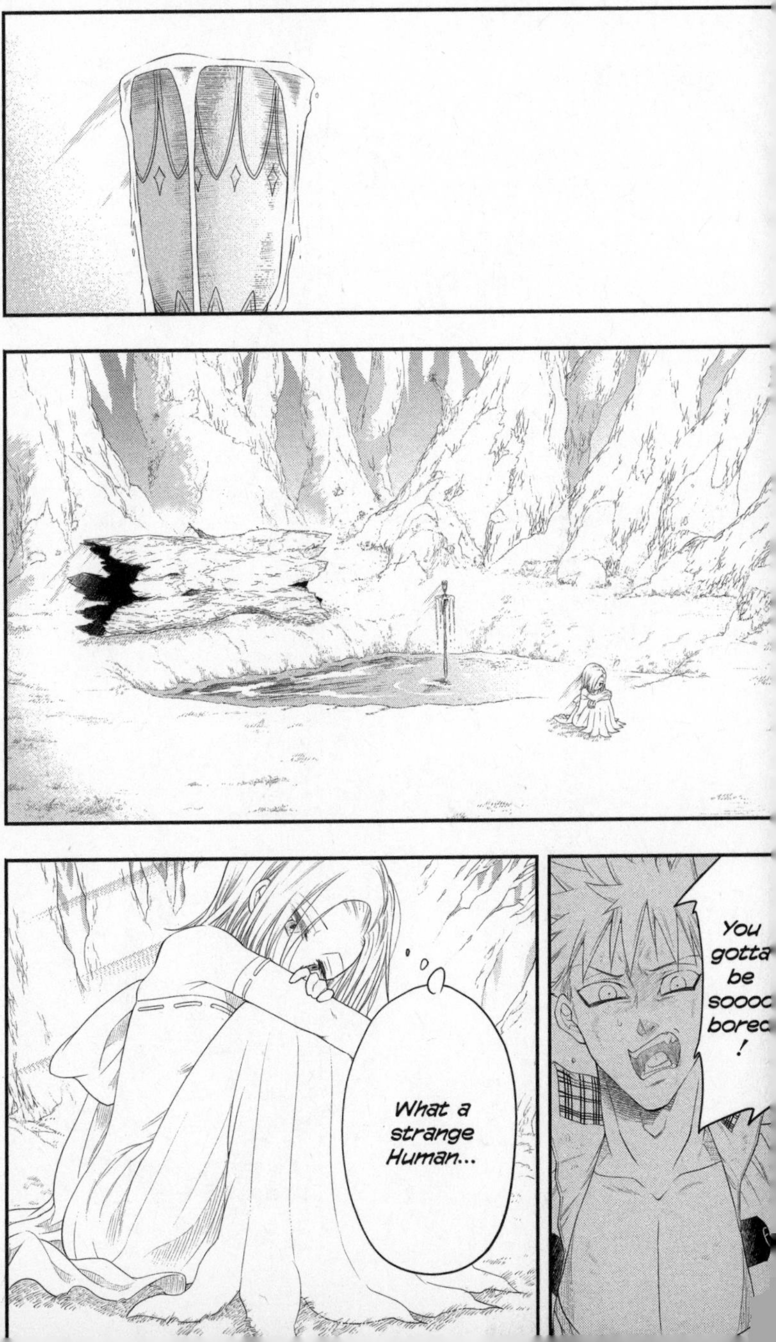
You gotta be sooo bore !
What a strange Human...

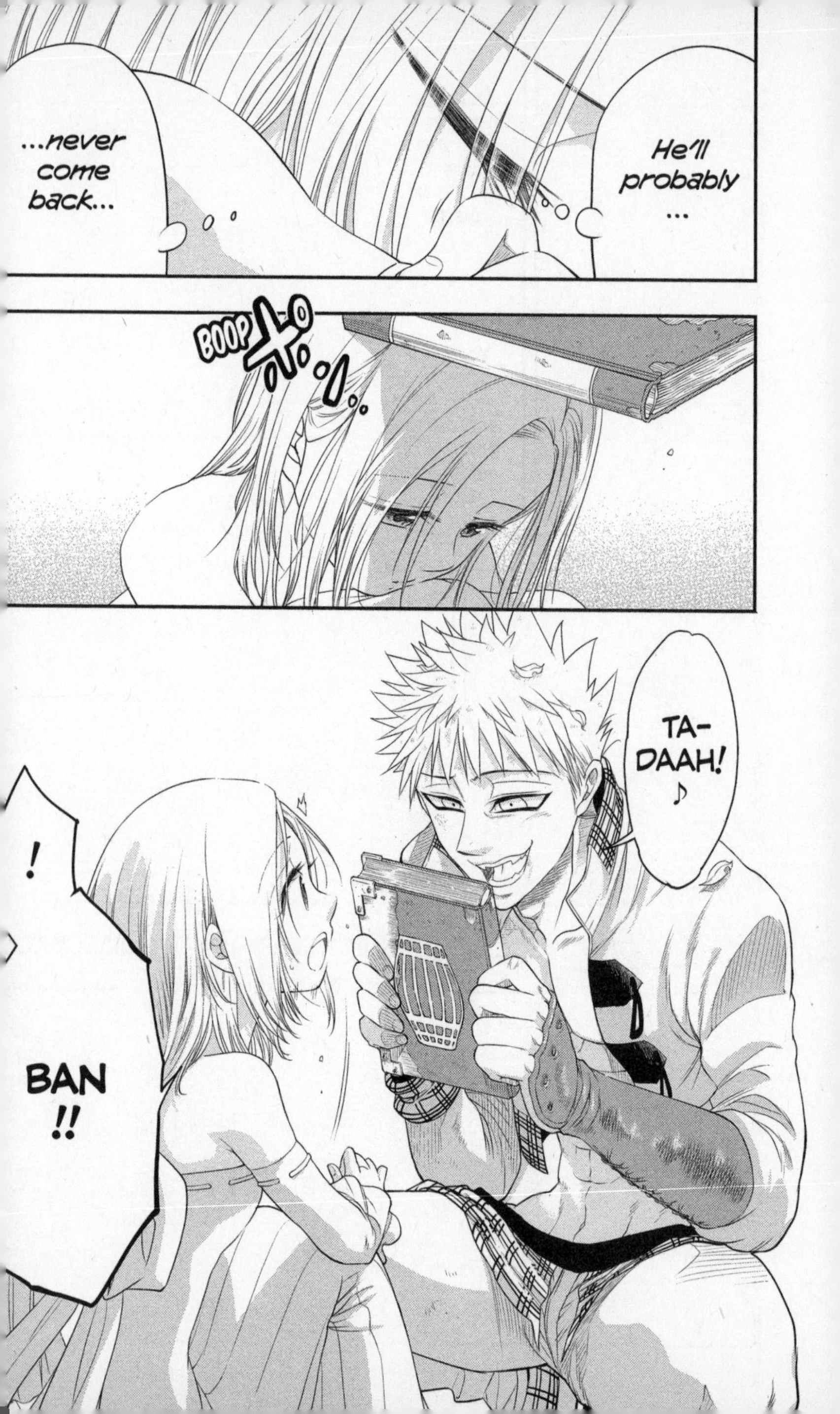
He'll probably ...
...never come back...
BOOP
TA-DAAH! ♪
!
BAN!!

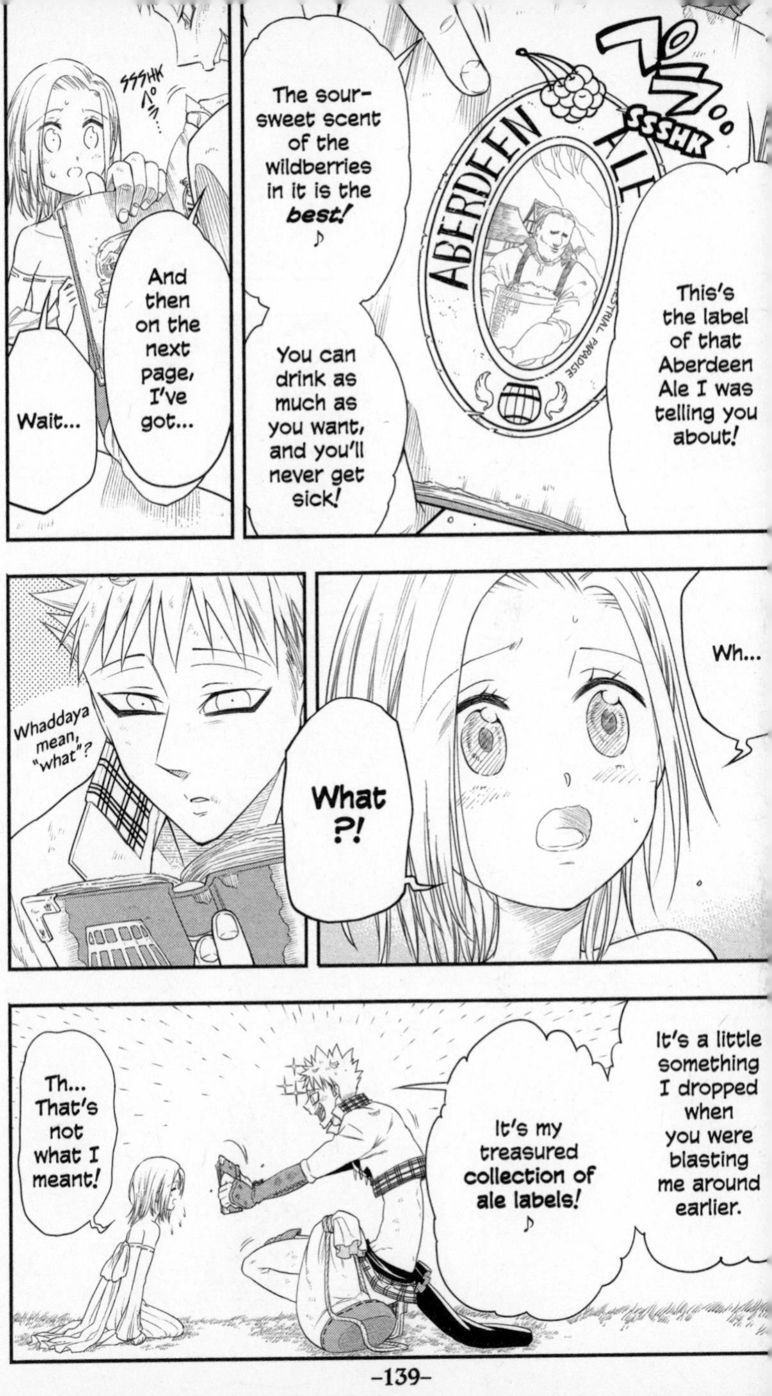
SSSHK
ABERDEEN ALE
This's the label of that Aberdeen Ale I was telling you about!
The sour-sweet scent of the wildberries in it is the *best!* ♪
You can drink as much as you want, and you'll never get sick!
SSSHK
And then on the next page, I've got...
Wait...
Wh...
What?!
Whaddaya mean, "what"?
It's a little something I dropped when you were blasting me around earlier.
It's my treasured collection of ale labels! ♪
Th... That's not what I meant!

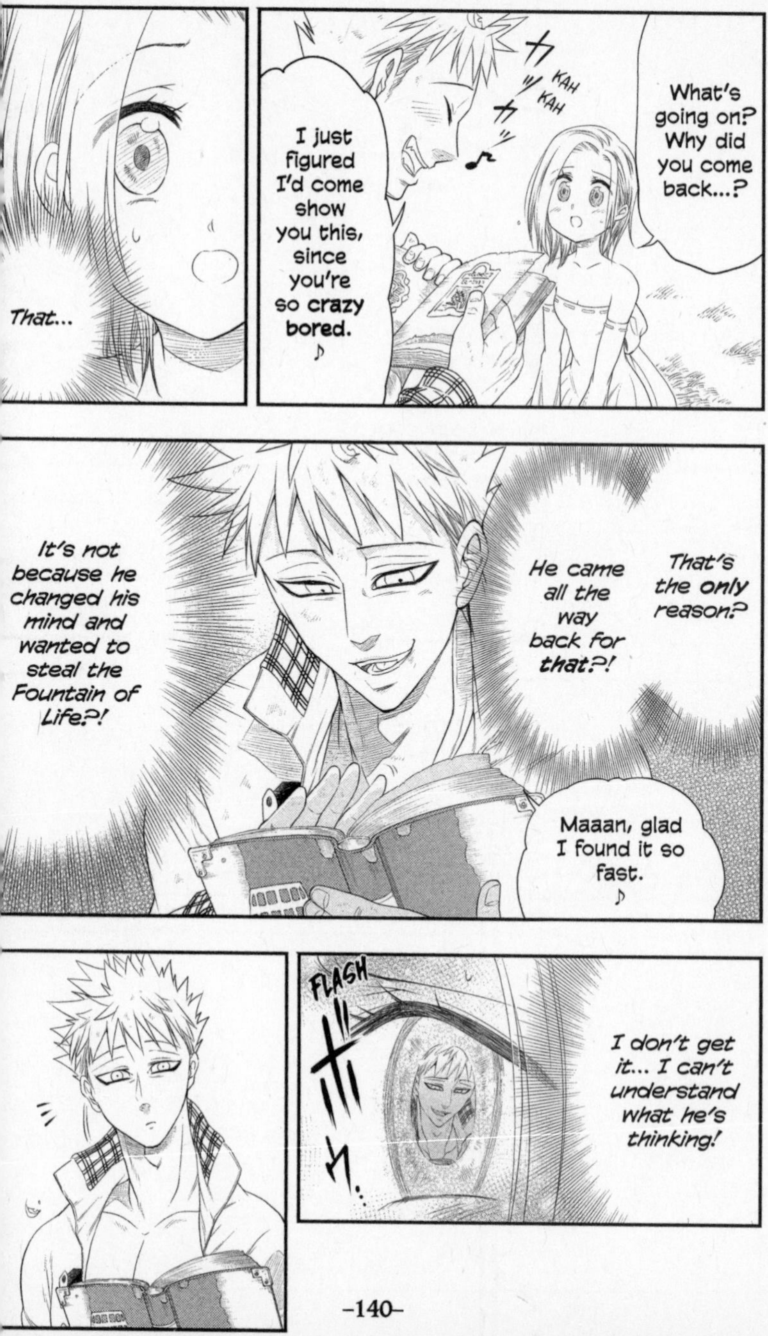
What's going on? Why did you come back...?
KAH KAH
I just figured I'd come show you this, since you're so crazy bored. ♪
That...
That's the only reason?
He came all the way back for that?!
It's not because he changed his mind and wanted to steal the Fountain of Life?!
Maaan, glad I found it so fast. ♪
FLASH
I don't get it... I can't understand what he's thinking!

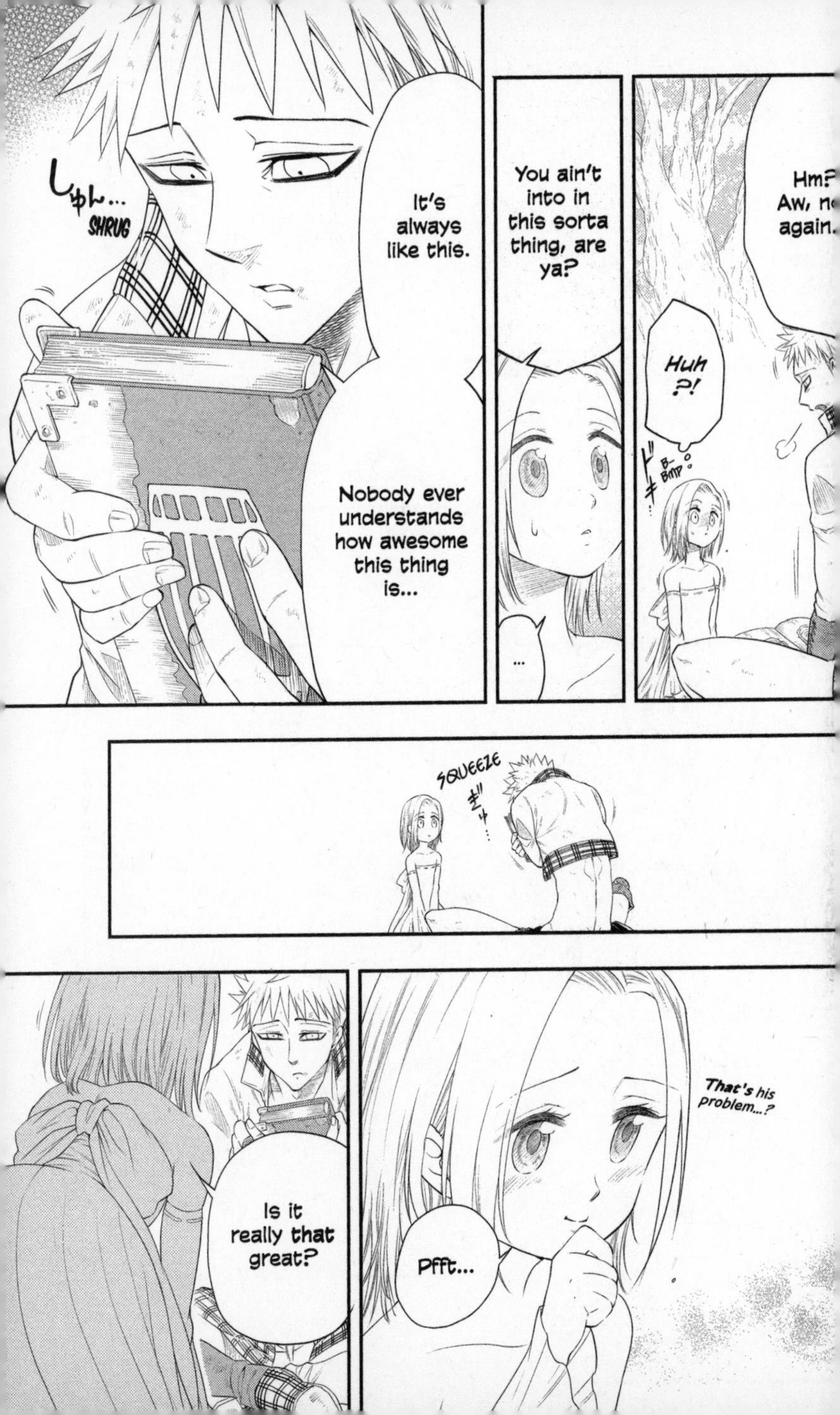
Hm? Aw, n again.
Huh ?!
ドキ
B-BMP
You ain't into in this sorta thing, are ya?
...
It's always like this.
Nobody ever understands how awesome this thing is...
しゅん...
SHRUG
SQUEEZE
ぎゅ...
That's his problem...?
Pfft...
Is it really that great?

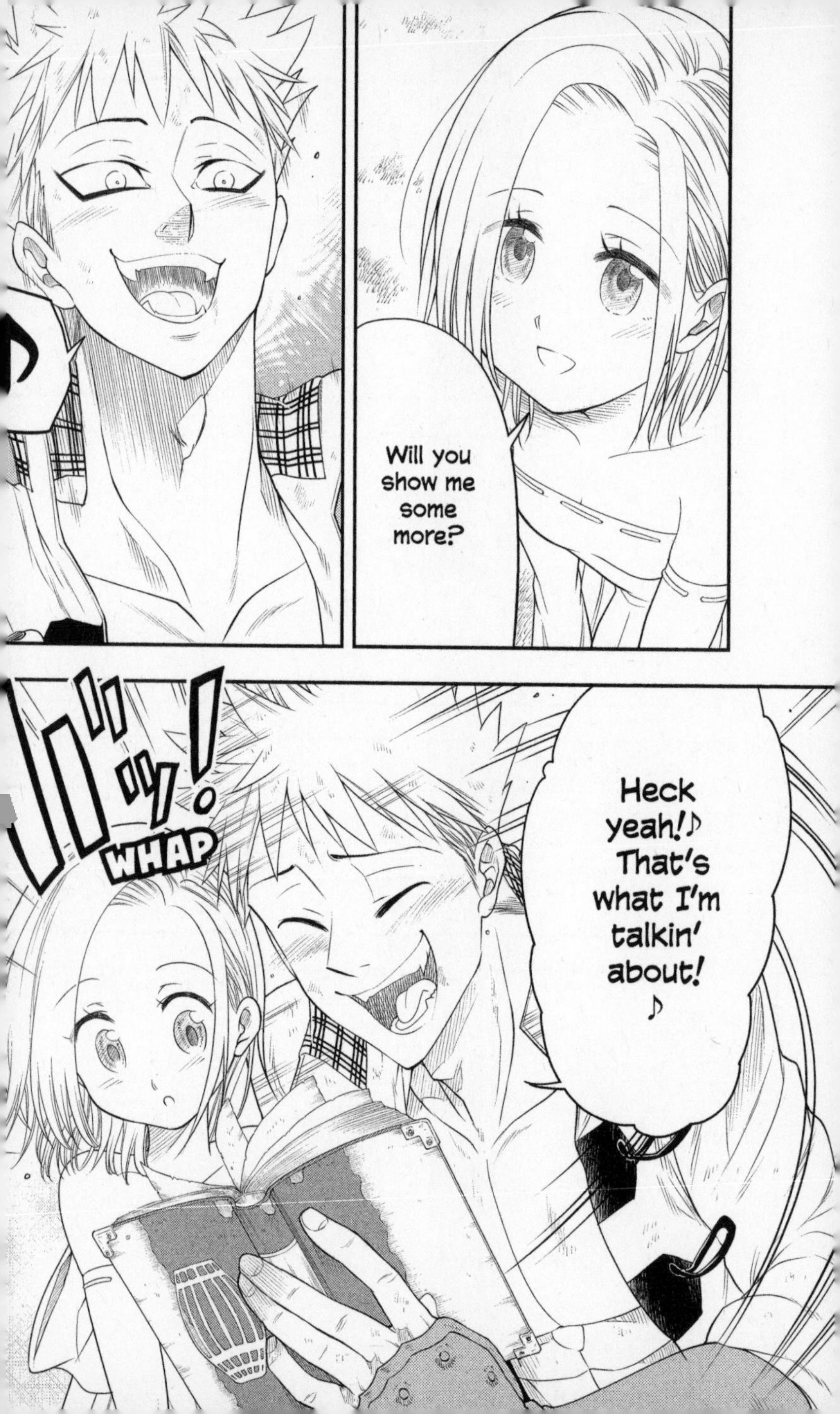
Will you show me some more?
Heck yeah!♪ That's what I'm talkin' about! ♪
WHAP

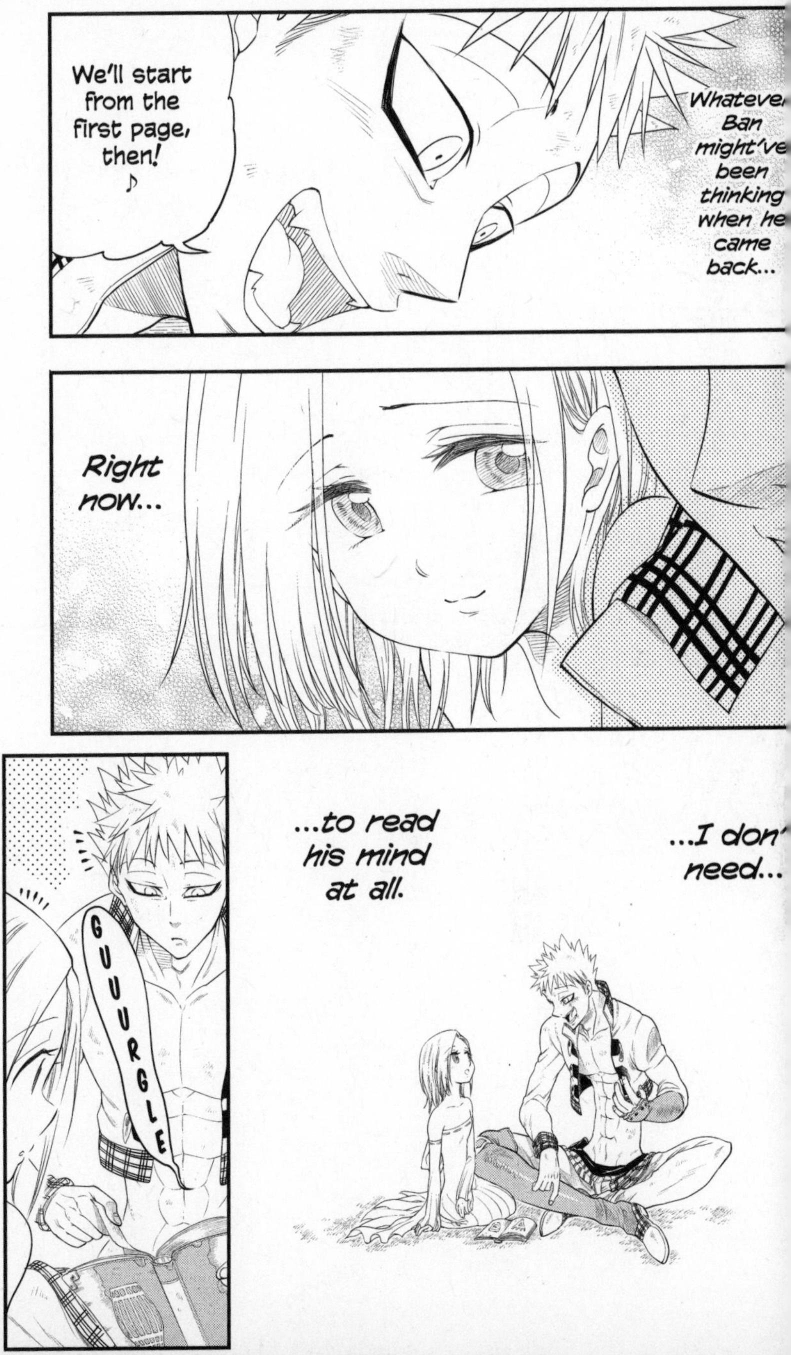
Whateve Ban might've been thinking when he came back...
We'll start from the first page, then! ♪
Right now...
...I don' need...
...to read his mind at all.
GUUURGLE

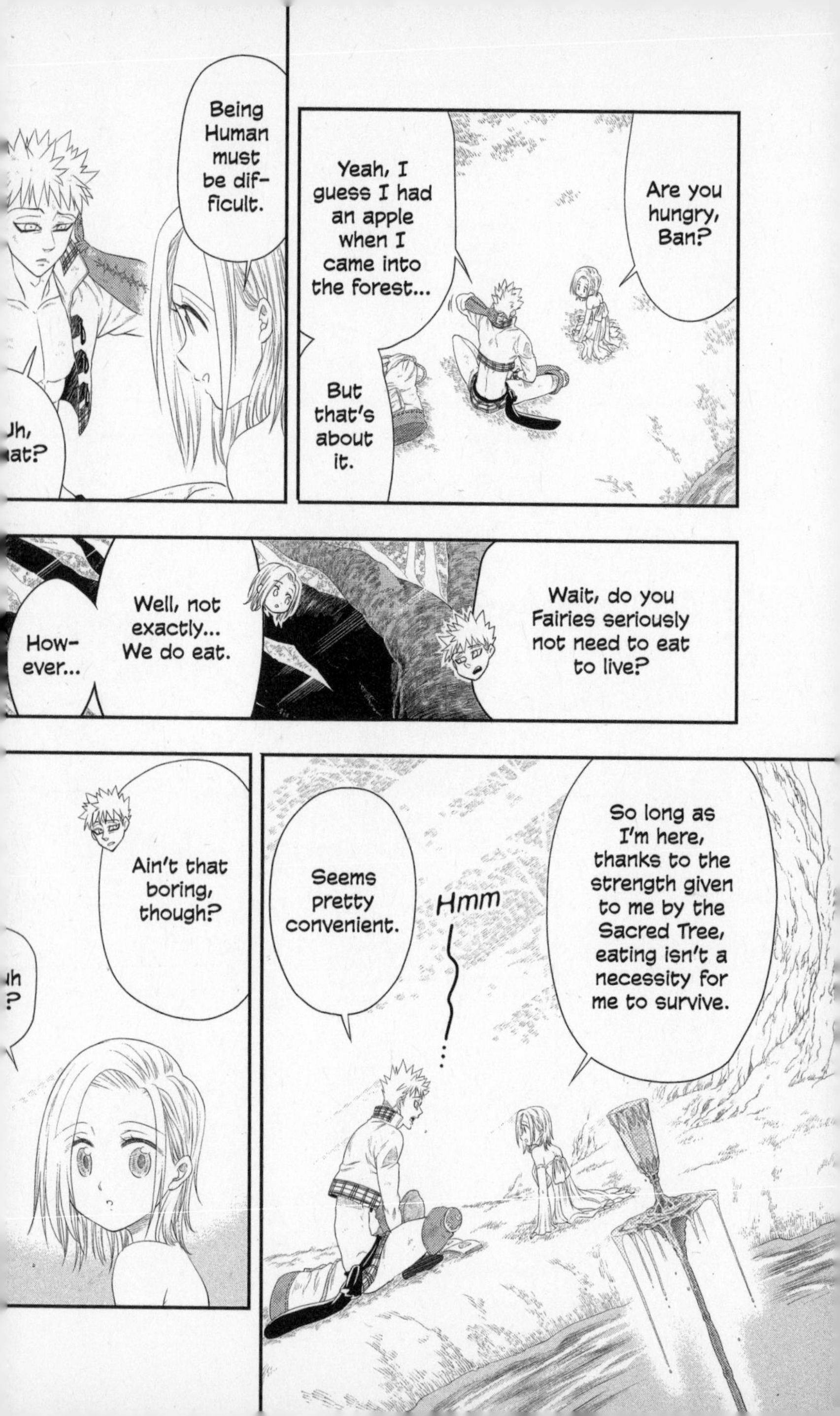
Are you hungry, Ban?
Yeah, I guess I had an apple when I came into the forest...
But that's about it.
Being Human must be dif-ficult.
Wait, do you Fairies seriously not need to eat to live?
Well, not exactly... We do eat.
How-ever...
So long as I'm here, thanks to the strength given to me by the Sacred Tree, eating isn't a necessity for me to survive.
Hmm...
Seems pretty convenient.
Ain't that boring, though?

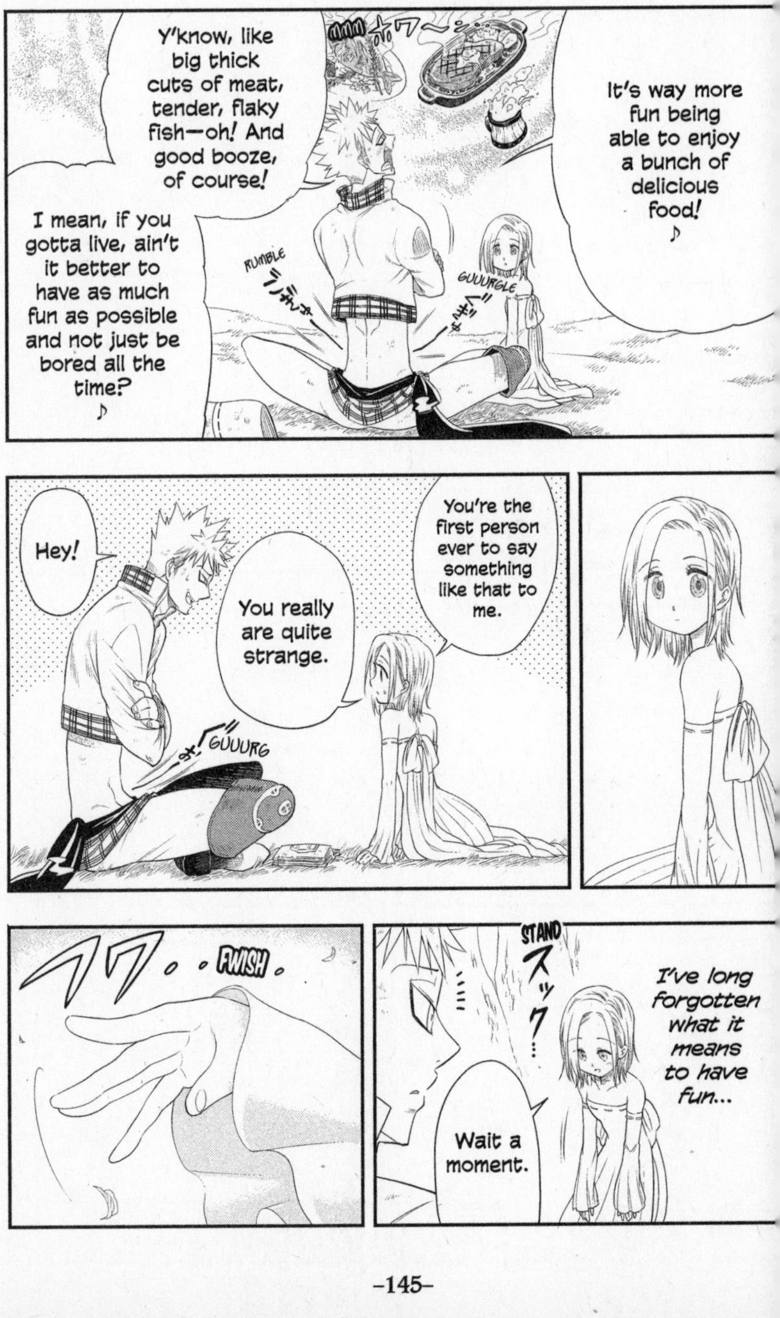
It's way more fun being able to enjoy a bunch of delicious food! ♪
MMM
Y'know, like big thick cuts of meat, tender, flaky fish—oh! And good booze, of course!
GUUURGLE
RUMBLE
I mean, if you gotta live, ain't it better to have as much fun as possible and not just be bored all the time? ♪
You're the first person ever to say something like that to me.
You really are quite strange.
Hey!
GUUURG
STAND
I've long forgotten what it means to have fun...
Wait a moment.
FWISH

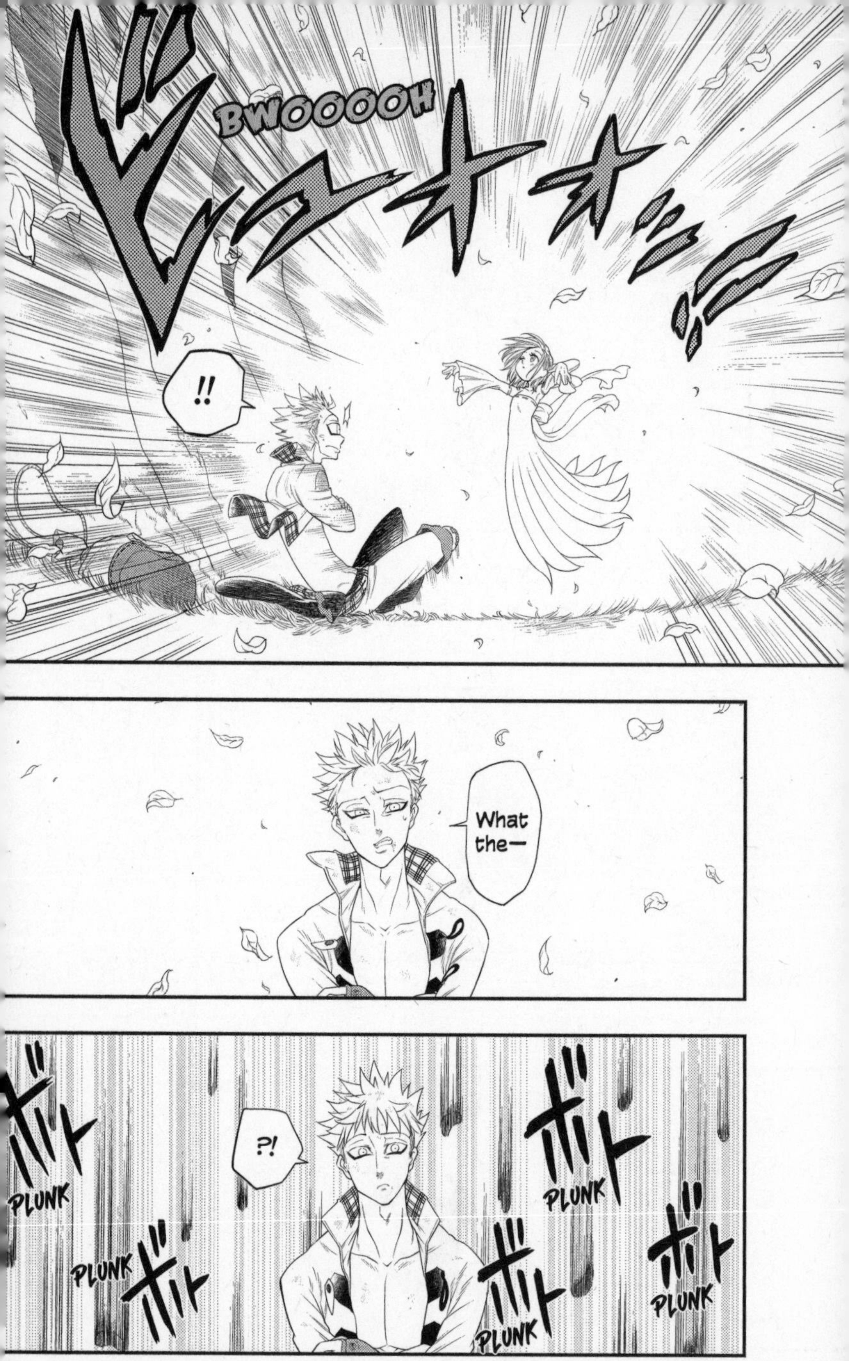
BWOOOOH
!!
What the—
PLUNK
PLUNK
PLUNK
?!
PLUNK
PLUNK

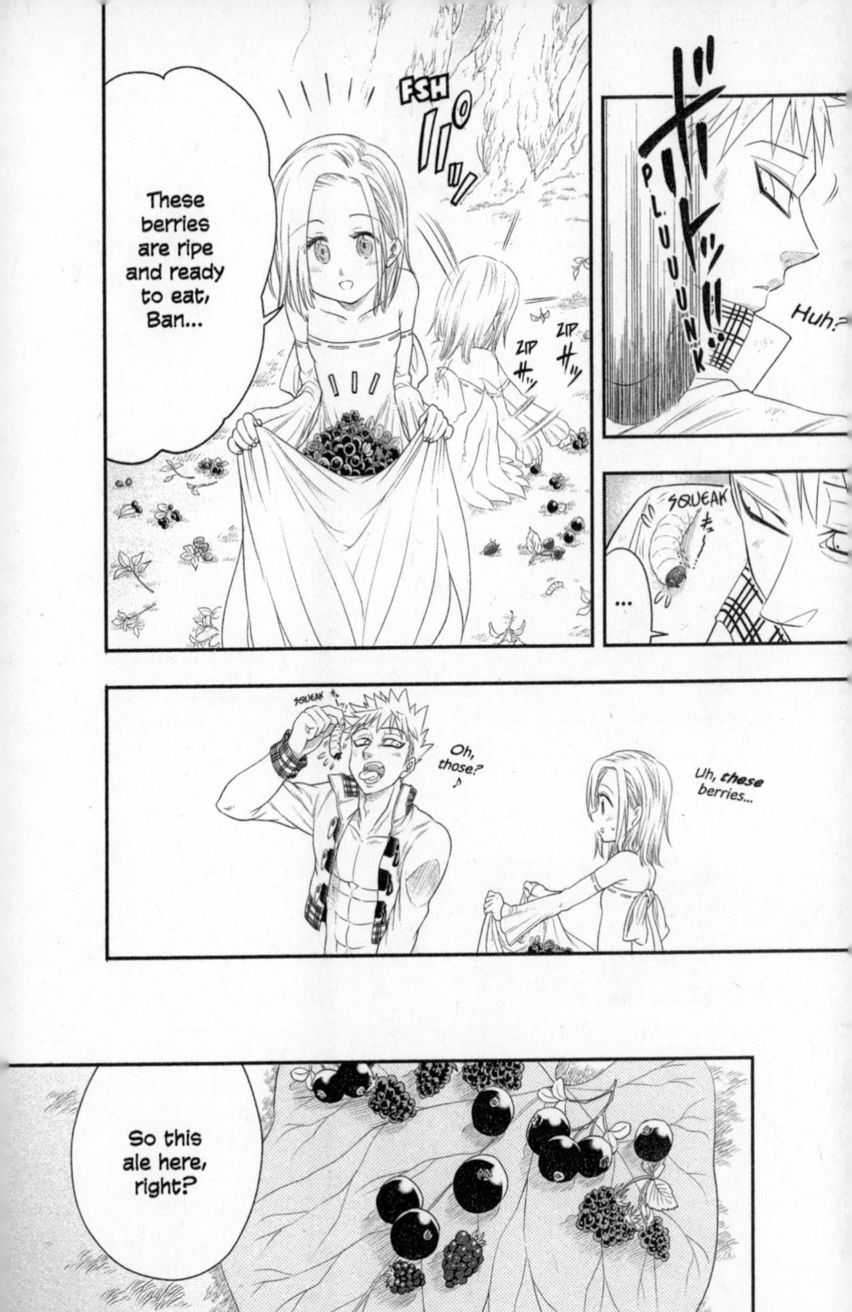

PLUUUUNK
Huh?
SQUEAK
...
FSH
These berries are ripe and ready to eat, Ban...
ZIP
ZIP
Uh, *these* berries...
SQUEAK
Oh, those? ♪
So this ale here, right?

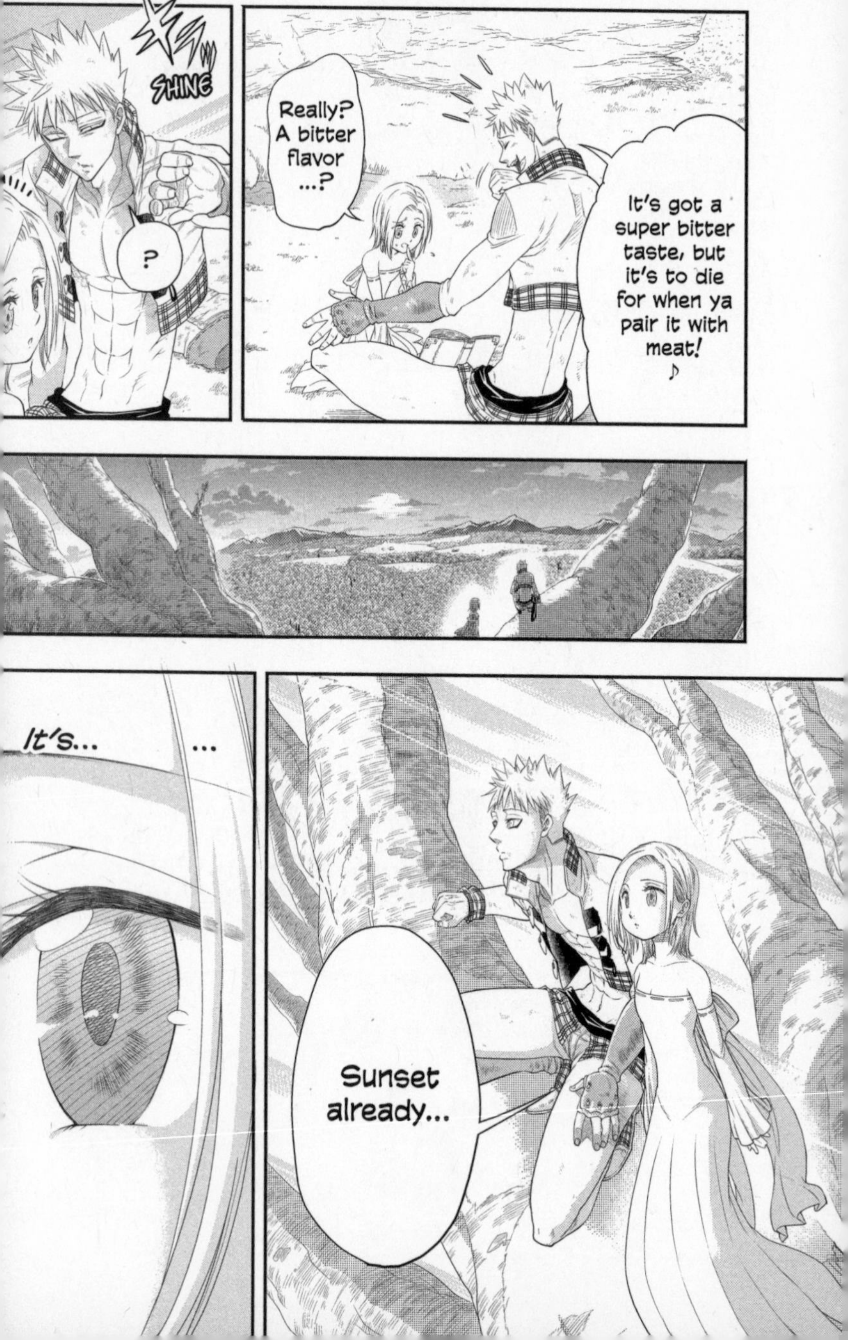
It's got a super bitter taste, but it's to die for when ya pair it with meat! ♪
Really? A bitter flavor ...?
SHINE
?
Sunset already...
It's...
...

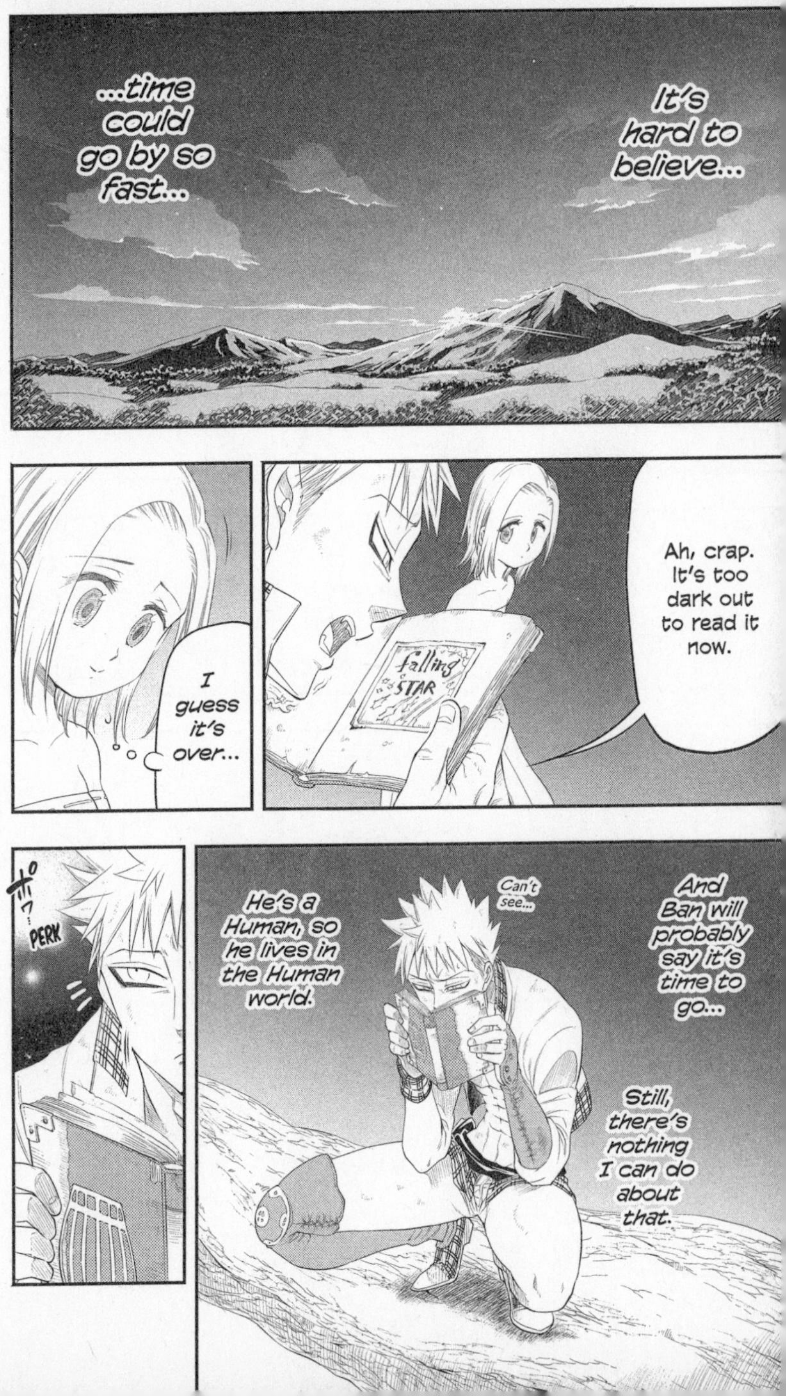
It's hard to believe...
...time could go by so fast...
Ah, crap. It's too dark out to read it now.
falling STAR
I guess it's over...
And Ban will probably say it's time to go...
Can't see...
He's a Human, so he lives in the Human world.
Still, there's nothing I can do about that.
PERK

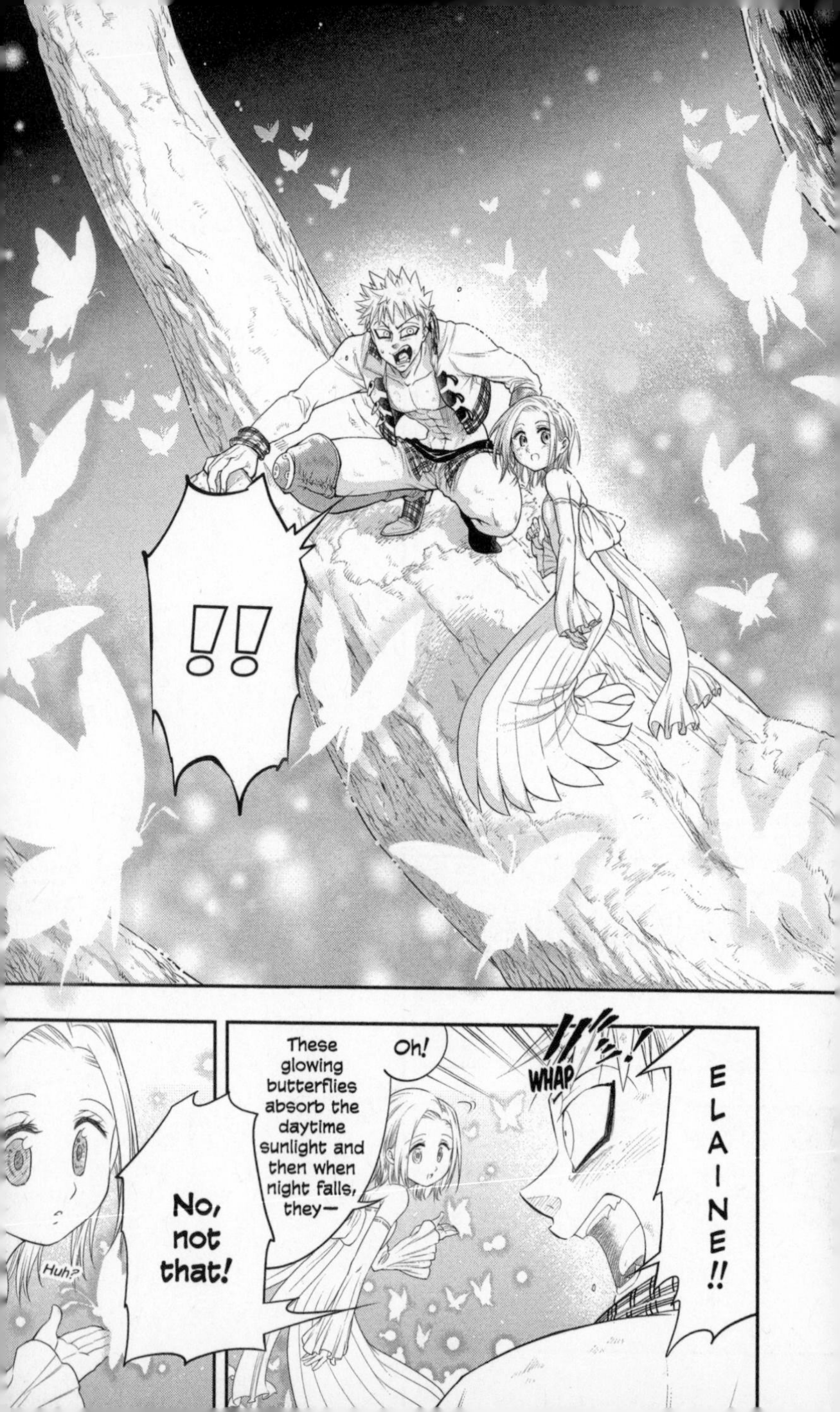
!!
ELAINE!!
WHAP
Oh!
These glowing butterflies absorb the daytime sunlight and then when night falls, they—
No, not that!
Huh?

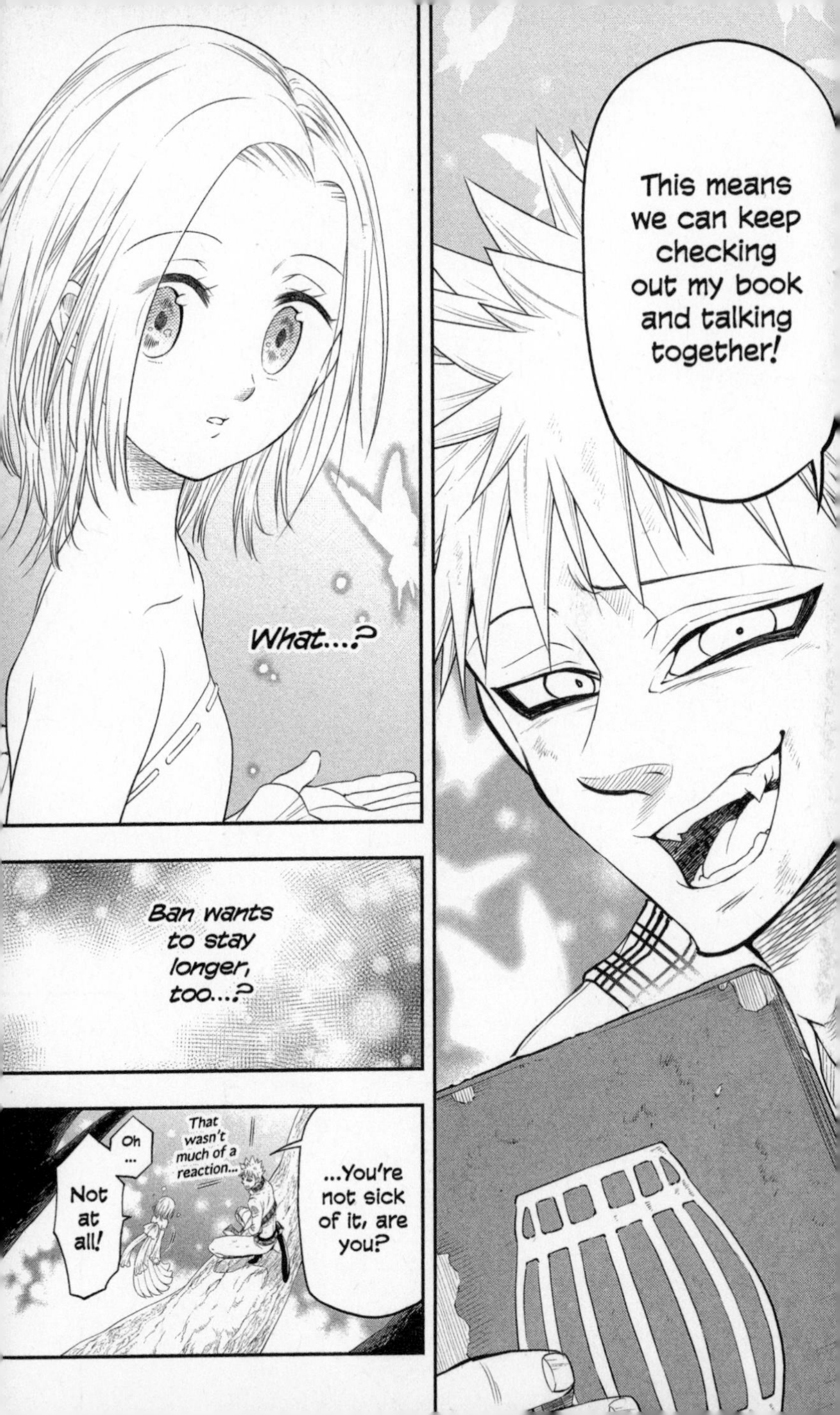

This means we can keep checking out my book and talking together!
What...?
Ban wants to stay longer, too...?
...You're not sick of it, are you?
That wasn't much of a reaction...
Oh ...
Not at all!

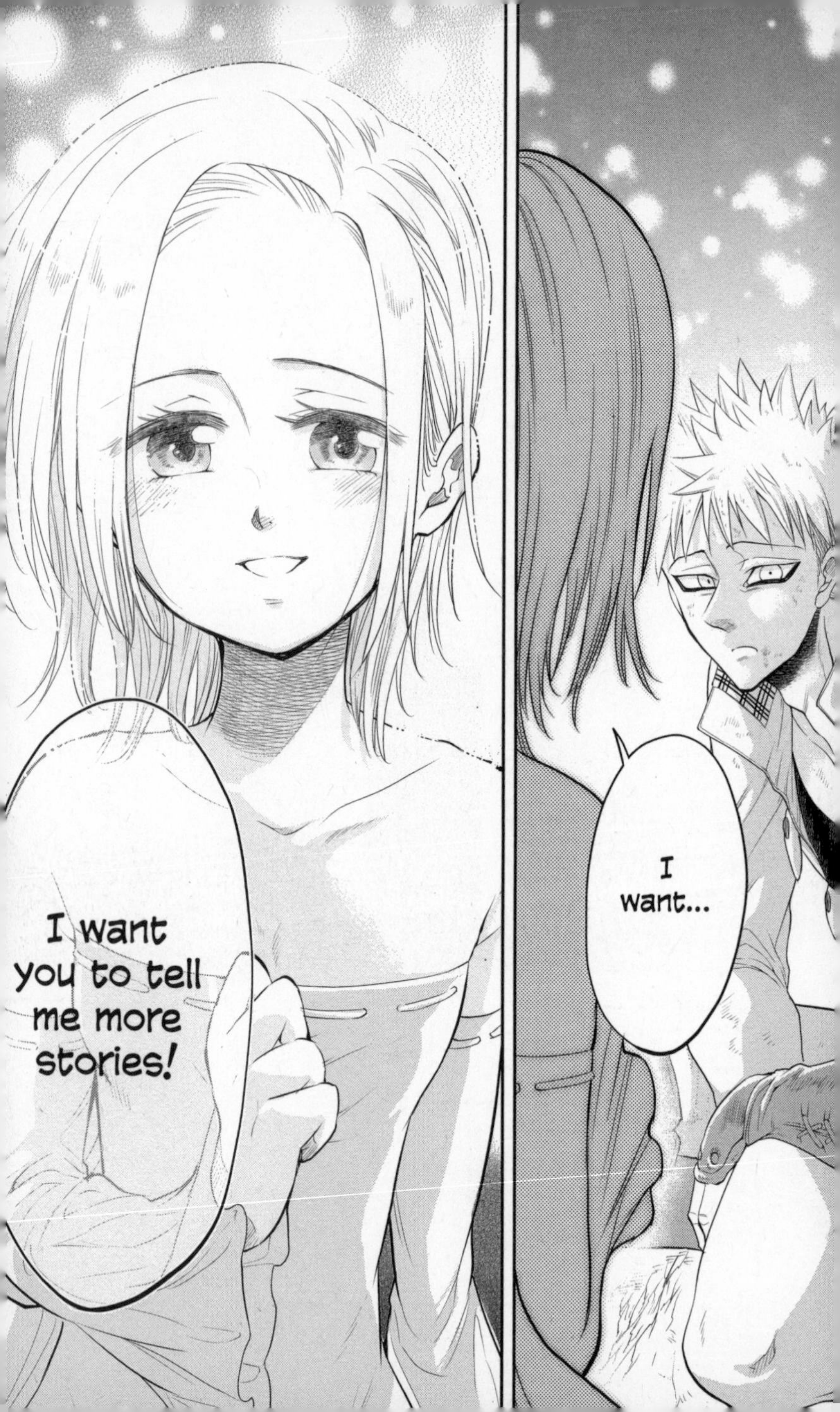
I want...
I want you to tell me more stories!

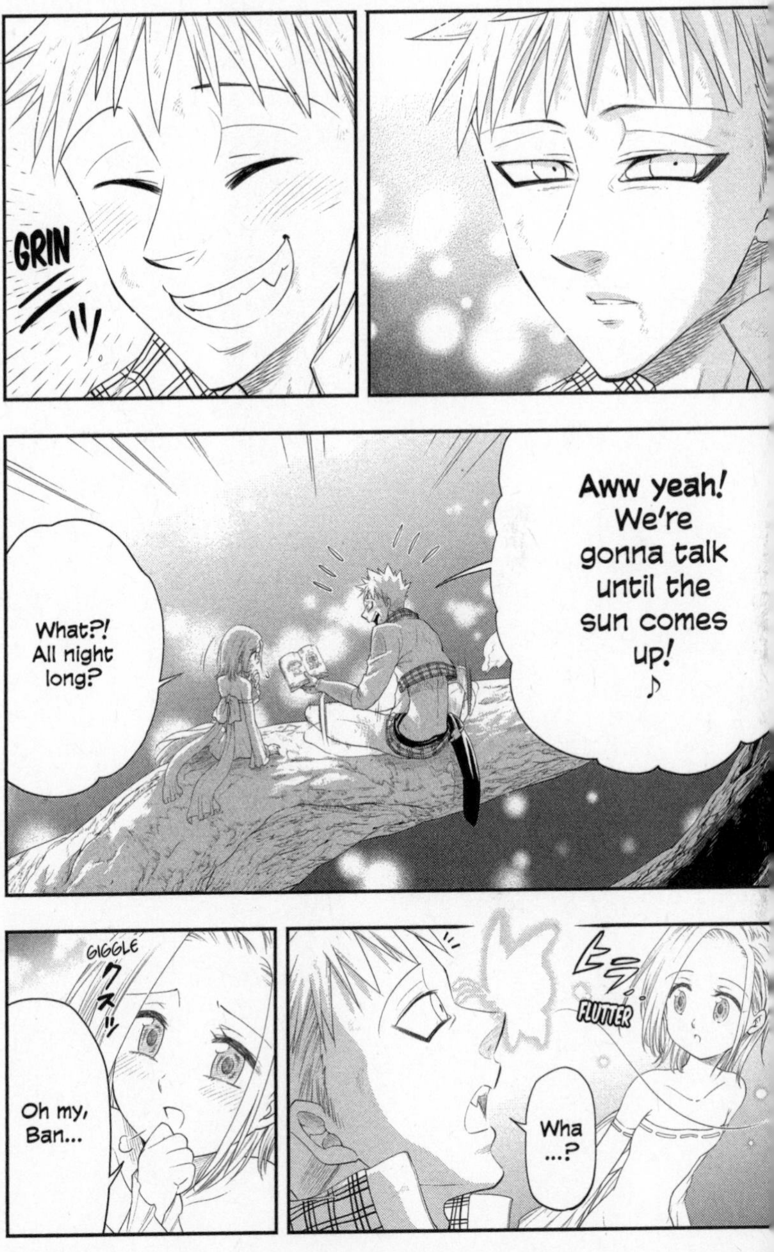
GRIN
Aww yeah! We're gonna talk until the sun comes up! ♪
What?! All night long?
FLUTTER
Wha ...?
GIGGLE
Oh my, Ban...

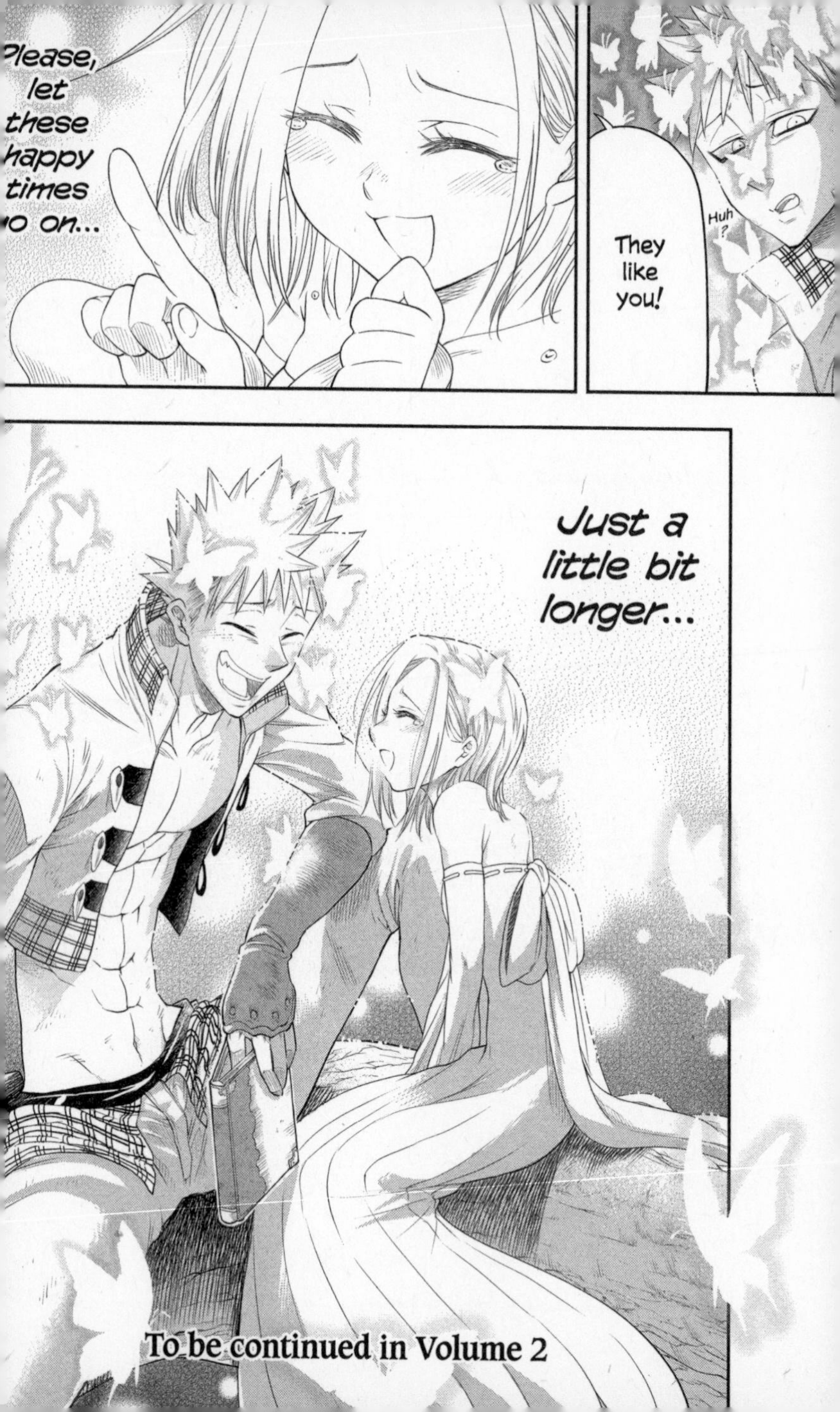
Huh?
They like you!
Please, let these happy times go on...
Just a little bit longer...
To be continued in Volume 2

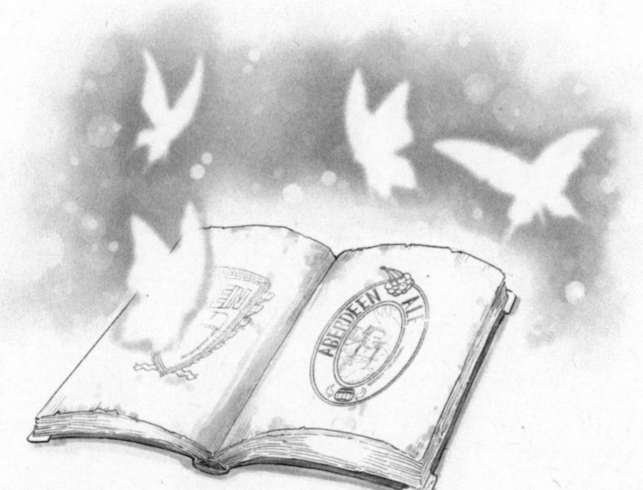
ABERDEEN ALE

Game Time for the Fairies with Too Much Time On Their Hands

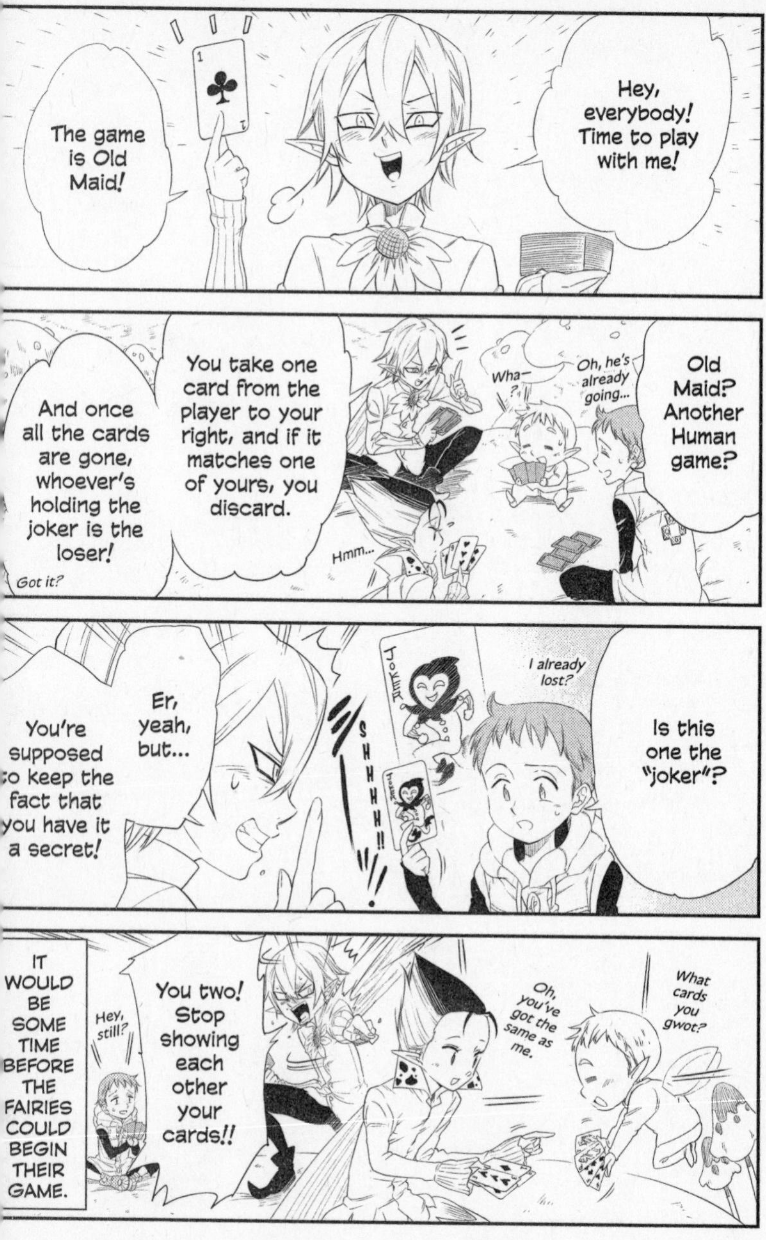
Hey, everybody! Time to play with me!
The game is Old Maid!
Old Maid? Another Human game?
Oh, he's already going...
Wha—?
You take one card from the player to your right, and if it matches one of yours, you discard.
And once all the cards are gone, whoever's holding the joker is the loser!
Hmm...
Got it?
Is this one the "joker"?
I already lost?
JOKER
SHHHH!!
Er, yeah, but...
You're supposed o keep the fact that you have it a secret!
What cards you gwot?
Oh, you've got the same as me.
You two! Stop showing each other your cards!!
Hey, still?
IT WOULD BE SOME TIME BEFORE THE FAIRIES COULD BEGIN THEIR GAME.

Game Time for the Fairies with Too Much Time On Their Hands Part II

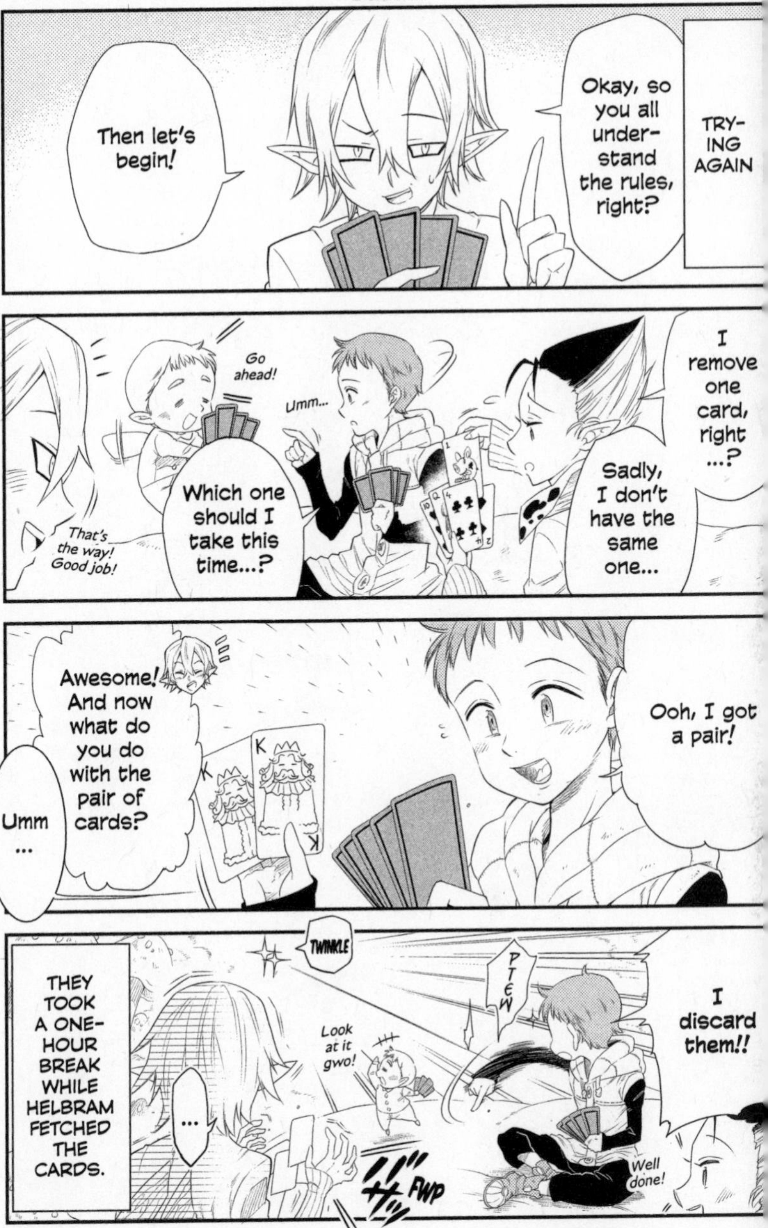

TRY-ING AGAIN
Okay, so you all under-stand the rules, right?
Then let's begin!
I remove one card, right ...?
Sadly, I don't have the same one...
Umm...
Which one should I take this time...?
Go ahead!
That's the way! Good job!
Ooh, I got a pair!
Awesome! And now what do you do with the pair of cards?
Umm ...
I discard them!!
Well done!
PTEW
TWINKLE
Look at it gwo!
FWP
...
THEY TOOK A ONE-HOUR BREAK WHILE HELBRAM FETCHED THE CARDS.

ame Time for the Fairies with Too Much Time On Their Hands: Part III

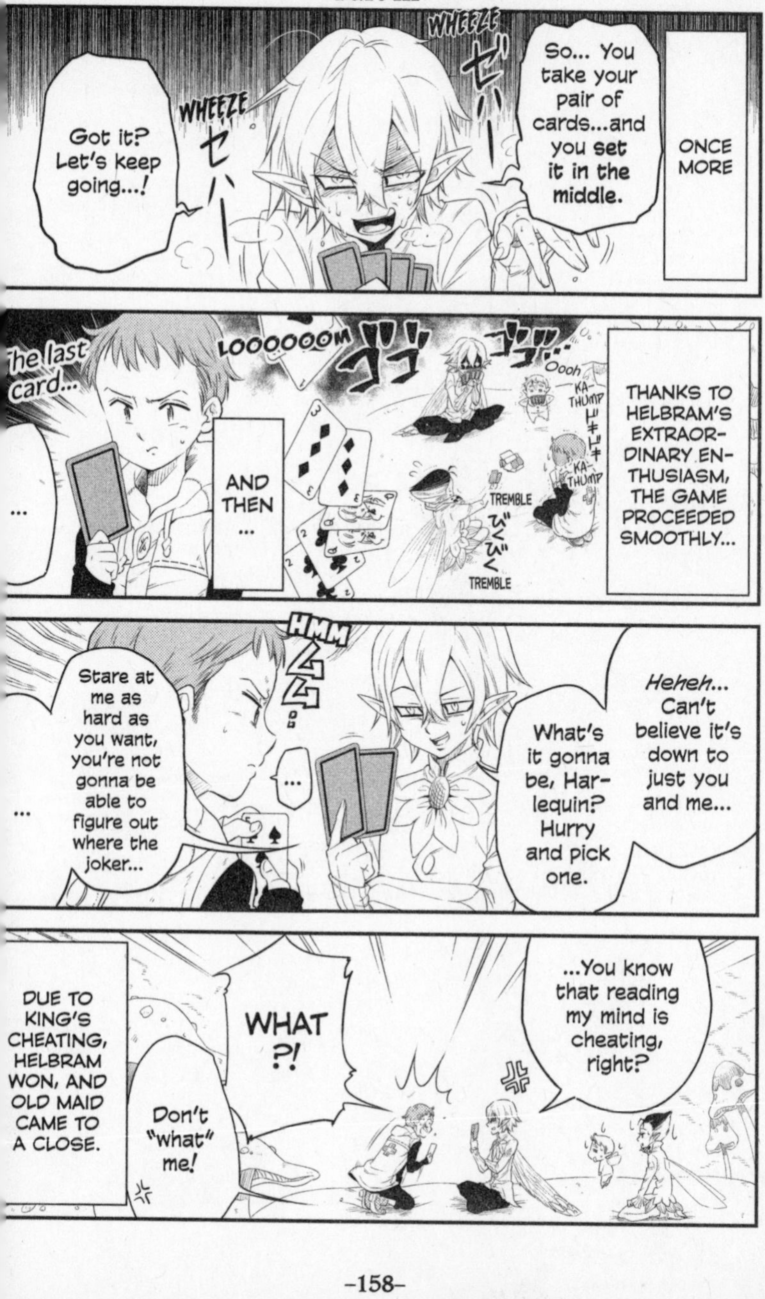

ONCE MORE
So... You take your pair of cards...and you set it in the middle.
WHEEZE
WHEEZE
Got it? Let's keep going...!
THANKS TO HELBRAM'S EXTRAOR-DINARY EN-THUSIASM, THE GAME PROCEEDED SMOOTHLY...
Oooh
KA-THUMP
KA-THUMP
TREMBLE
TREMBLE
LOOOOOOM
AND THEN ...
The last card...
...
Heheh... Can't believe it's down to just you and me...
What's it gonna be, Har-lequin? Hurry and pick one.
HMM
...
Stare at me as hard as you want, you're not gonna be able to figure out where the joker...
...
...You know that reading my mind is cheating, right?
WHAT ?!
Don't "what" me!
DUE TO KING'S CHEATING, HELBRAM WON, AND OLD MAID CAME TO A CLOSE.

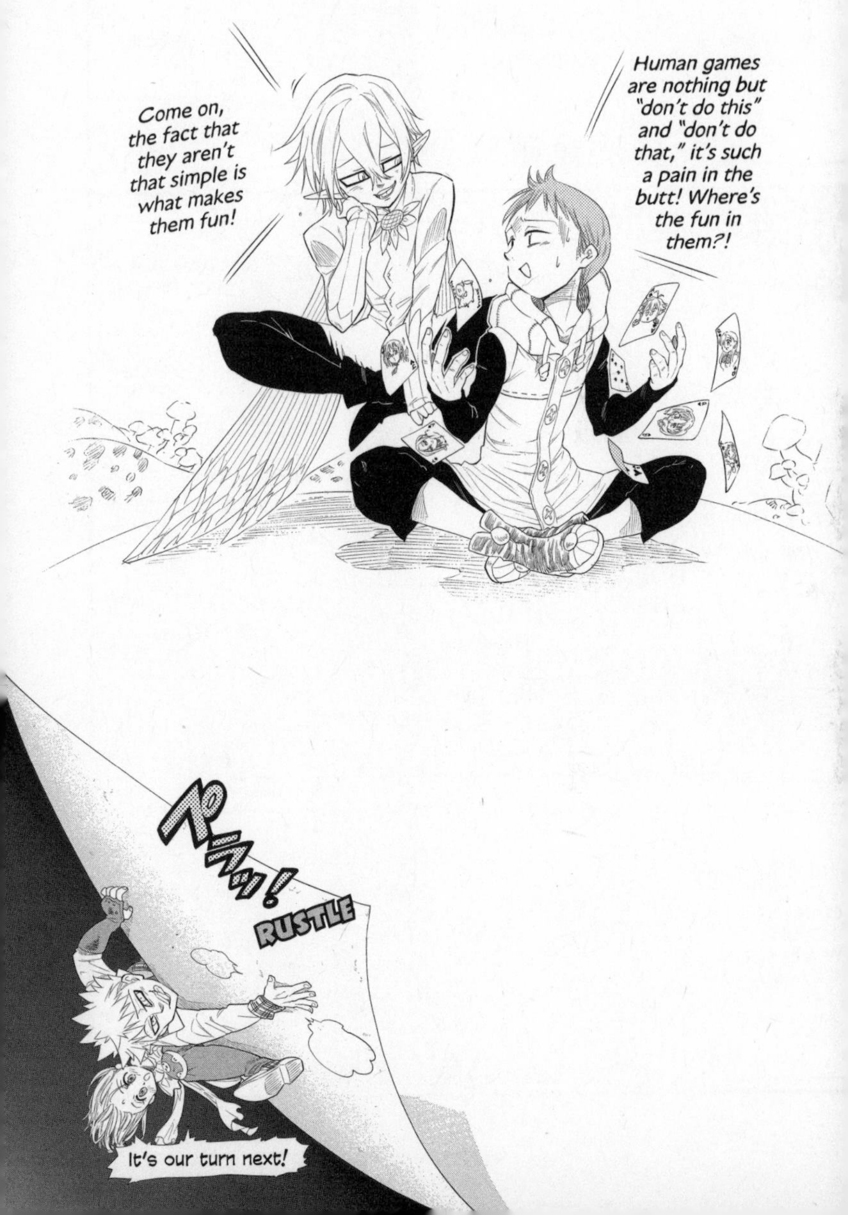
Human games are nothing but "don't do this" and "don't do that," it's such a pain in the butt! Where's the fun in them?!
Come on, the fact that they aren't that simple is what makes them fun!
RUSTLE
It's our turn next!

Sharp Dresser

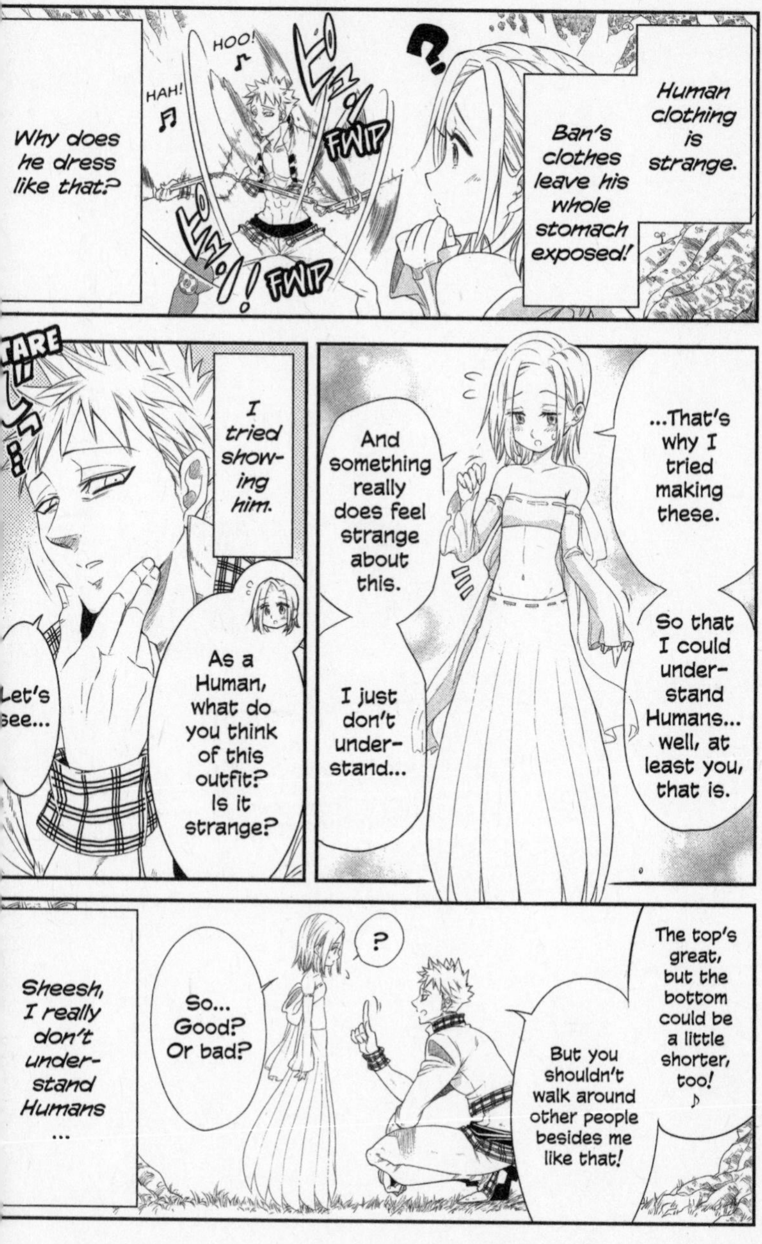
Human clothing is strange.
Ban's clothes leave his whole stomach exposed!
HOO! ♪
HAH! ♪
FWIP
FWIP
Why does he dress like that?
...That's why I tried making these.
So that I could understand Humans... well, at least you, that is.
And something really does feel strange about this.
I just don't understand...
I tried showing him.
As a Human, what do you think of this outfit? Is it strange?
Let's see...
The top's great, but the bottom could be a little shorter, too! ♪
But you shouldn't walk around other people besides me like that!
?
So... Good? Or bad?
Sheesh, I really don't understand Humans...

Princess

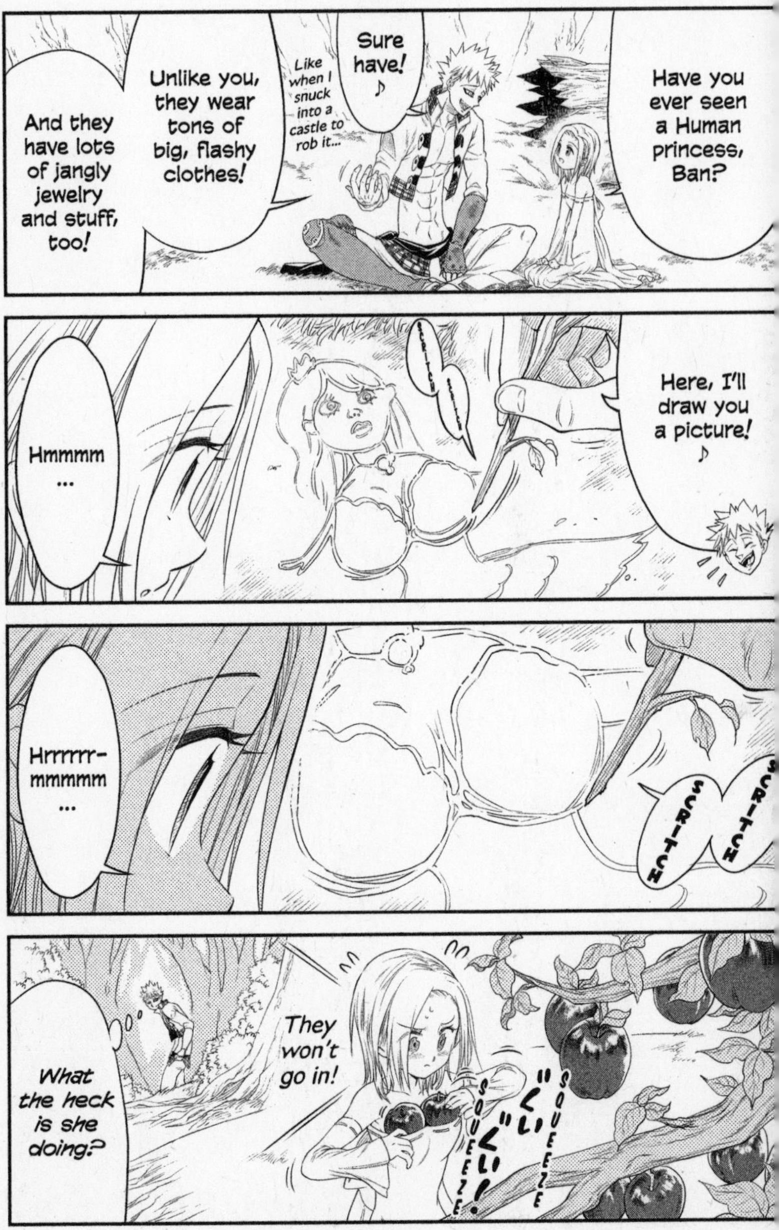

Have you ever seen a Human princess, Ban?
Sure have! ♪
Like when I snuck into a castle to rob it...
Unlike you, they wear tons of big, flashy clothes!
And they have lots of jangly jewelry and stuff, too!
Here, I'll draw you a picture! ♪
SCRITCH SCRITCH
Hmmmm...
SCRITCH SCRITCH
Hrrrrrr-mmmmm...
SQUEEZE
ぐい ぐい!
SQUEEZE
They won't go in!
What the heck is she doing?

Behold!

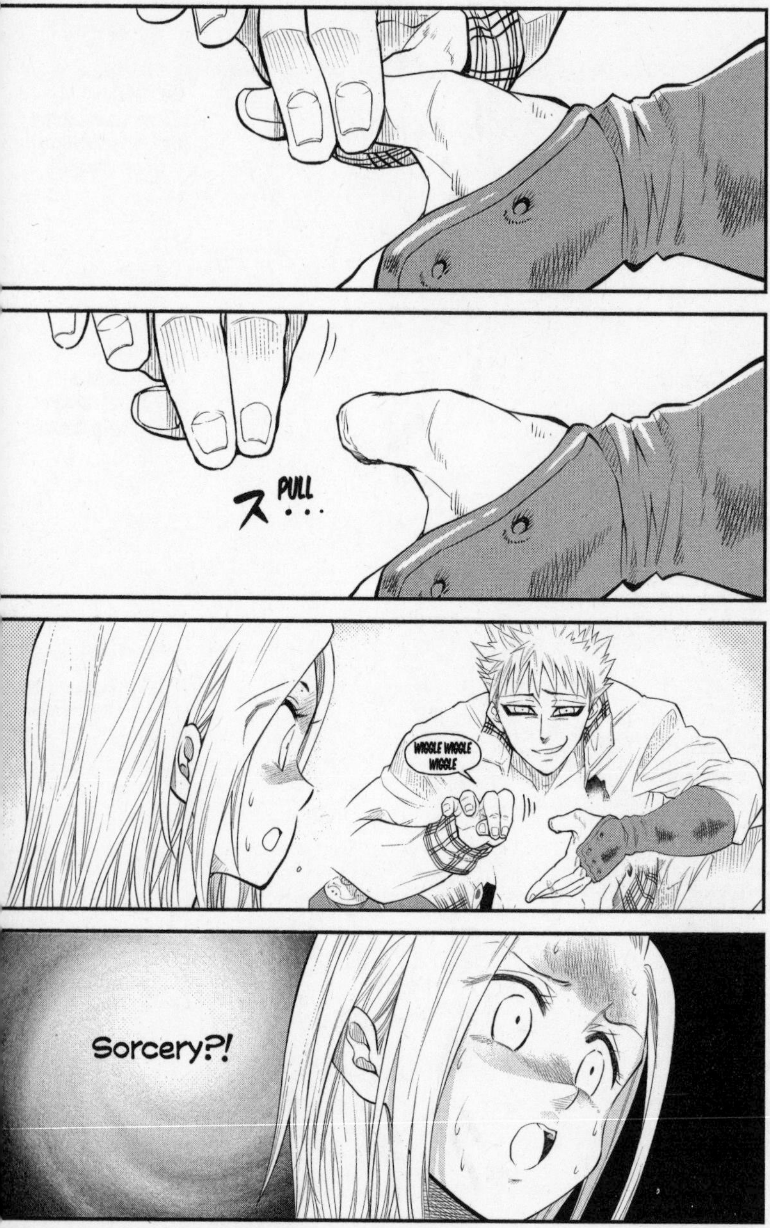
ス
PULL...
WIGGLE WIGGLE WIGGLE
Sorcery?!

My Brother and I

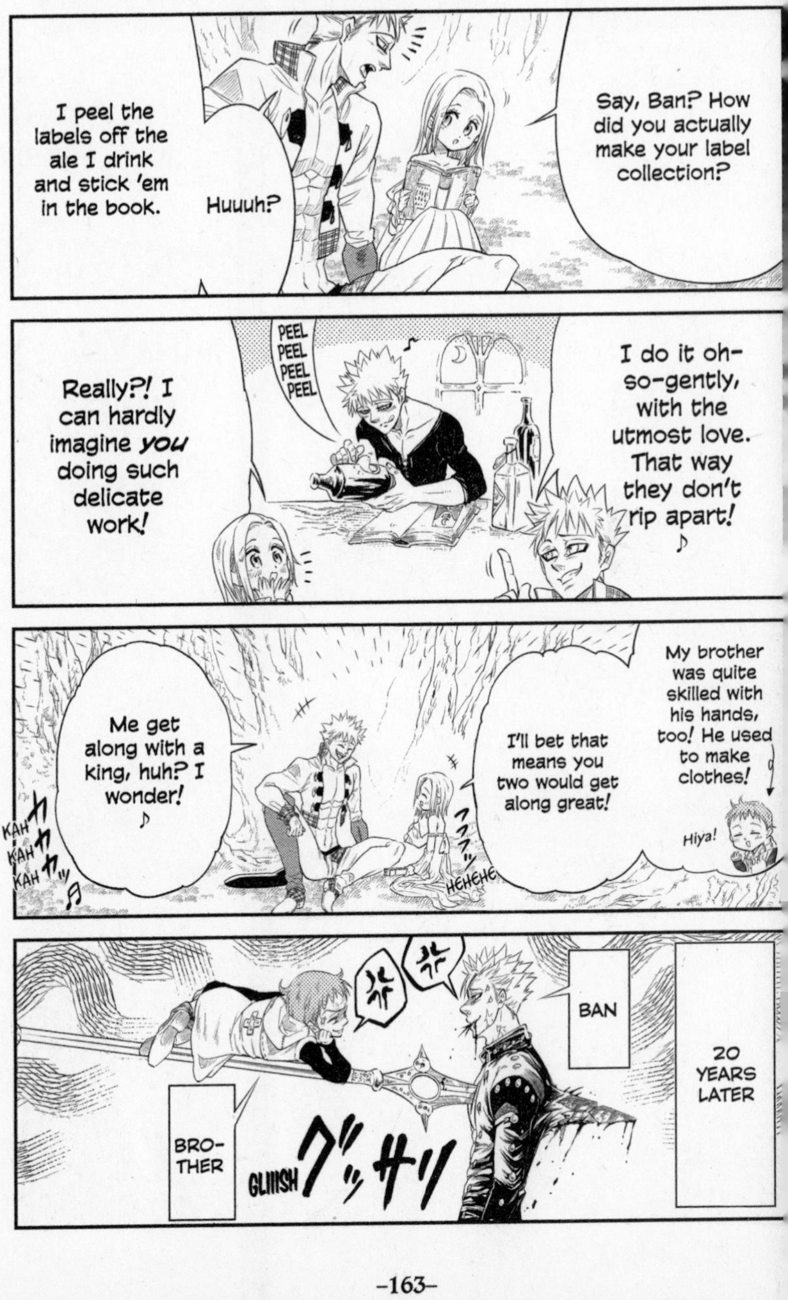

Say, Ban? How did you actually make your label collection?
Huuuh?
I peel the labels off the ale I drink and stick 'em in the book.
I do it oh-so-gently, with the utmost love. That way they don't rip apart! ♪
PEEL PEEL PEEL PEEL
Really?! I can hardly imagine *you* doing such delicate work!
My brother was quite skilled with his hands, too! He used to make clothes!
Hiya!
I'll bet that means you two would get along great!
HEHEHE
Me get along with a king, huh? I wonder! ♪
KAH KAH KAH
20 YEARS LATER
BAN
BRO-THER
GLIIISH

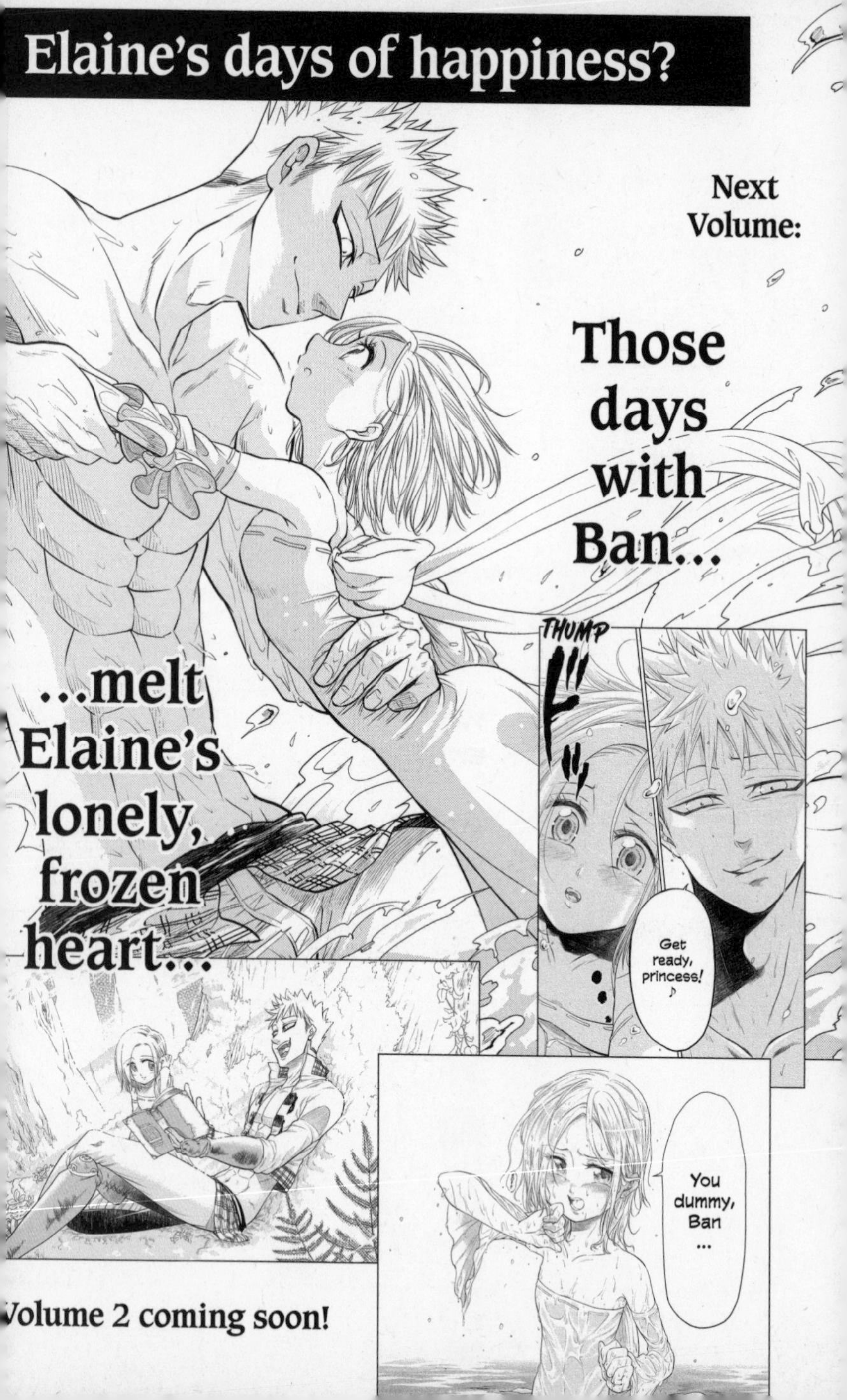
Elaine's days of happiness?
Next Volume:
Those days with Ban...
...melt Elaine's lonely, frozen heart...
THUMP
Get ready, princess! ♪
You dummy, Ban ...
Volume 2 coming soon!

What fate awaits Ban and

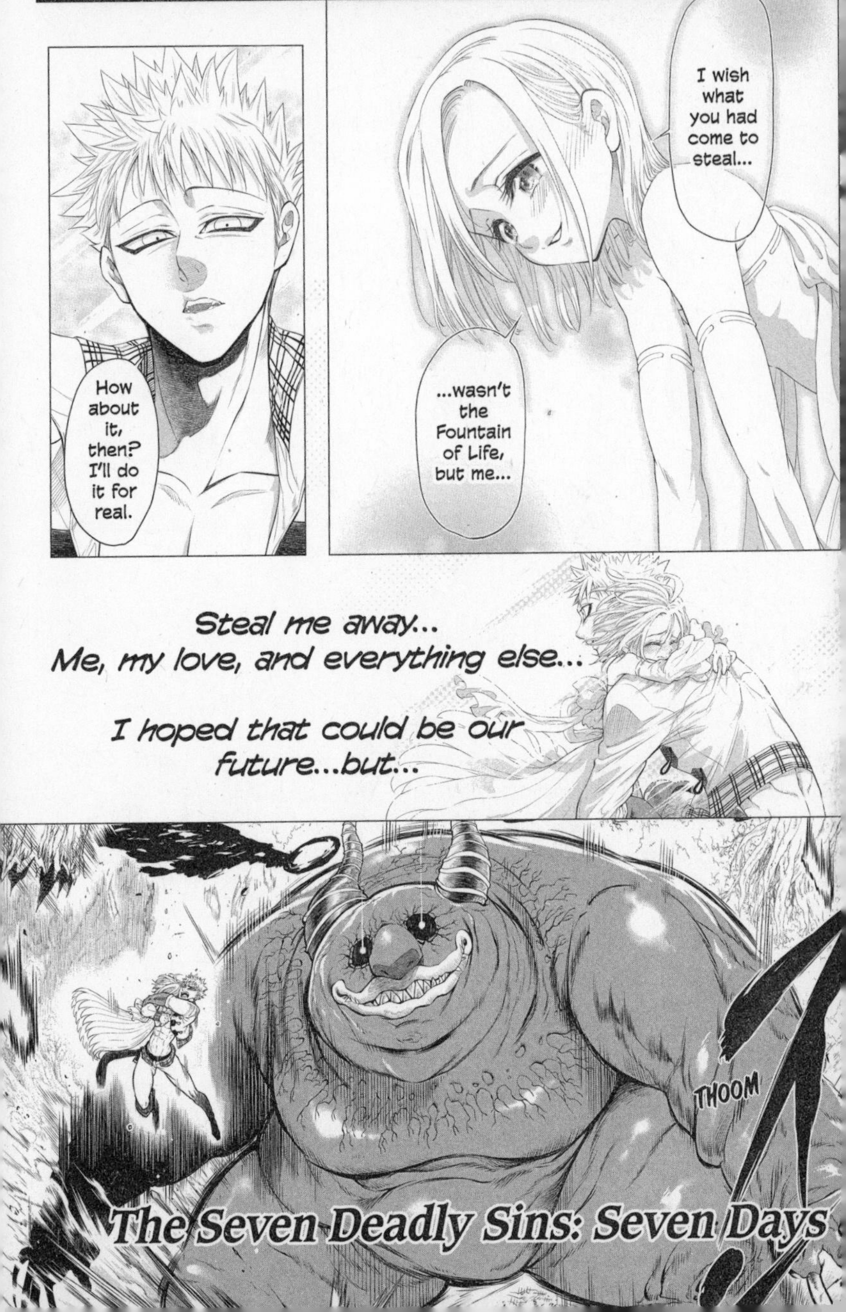
I wish what you had come to steal...
...wasn't the Fountain of Life, but me...
How about it, then? I'll do it for real.
Steal me away... Me, my love, and everything else...
I hoped that could be our future...but...
THOOM
The Seven Deadly Sins: Seven Days

Translation Notes:

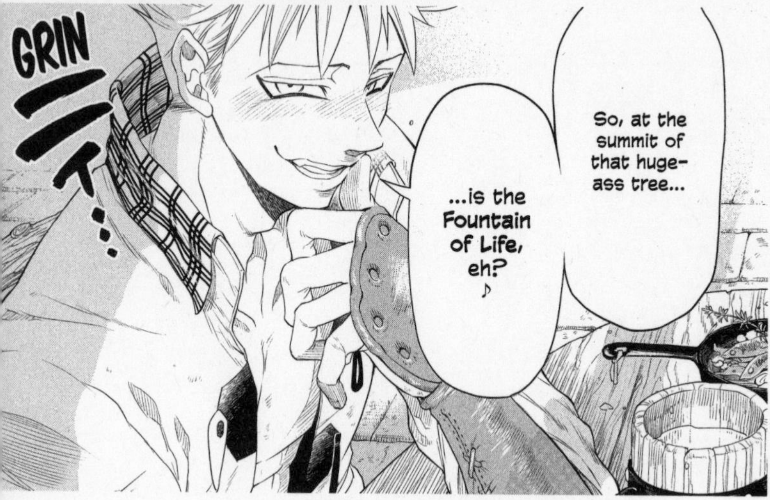
So, at the summit of that huge-ass tree...
...is the Fountain of Life, eh? ♪
GRIN

Fountain of Life, page 10

While this legendary landmark was originally translated as the "Fountain of Youth," the "Fountain of Life" is more accurate for this particular fountain, as it gives life to the forest, and eternal life to whoever drinks it. While there is a Fountain of Life in Christian iconography, it is unclear if it served as inspiration for the fountain that appears in *The Seven Deadly Sins*.

THE SEVEN DEADLY SINS

SEVEN DAYS

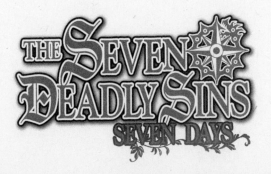

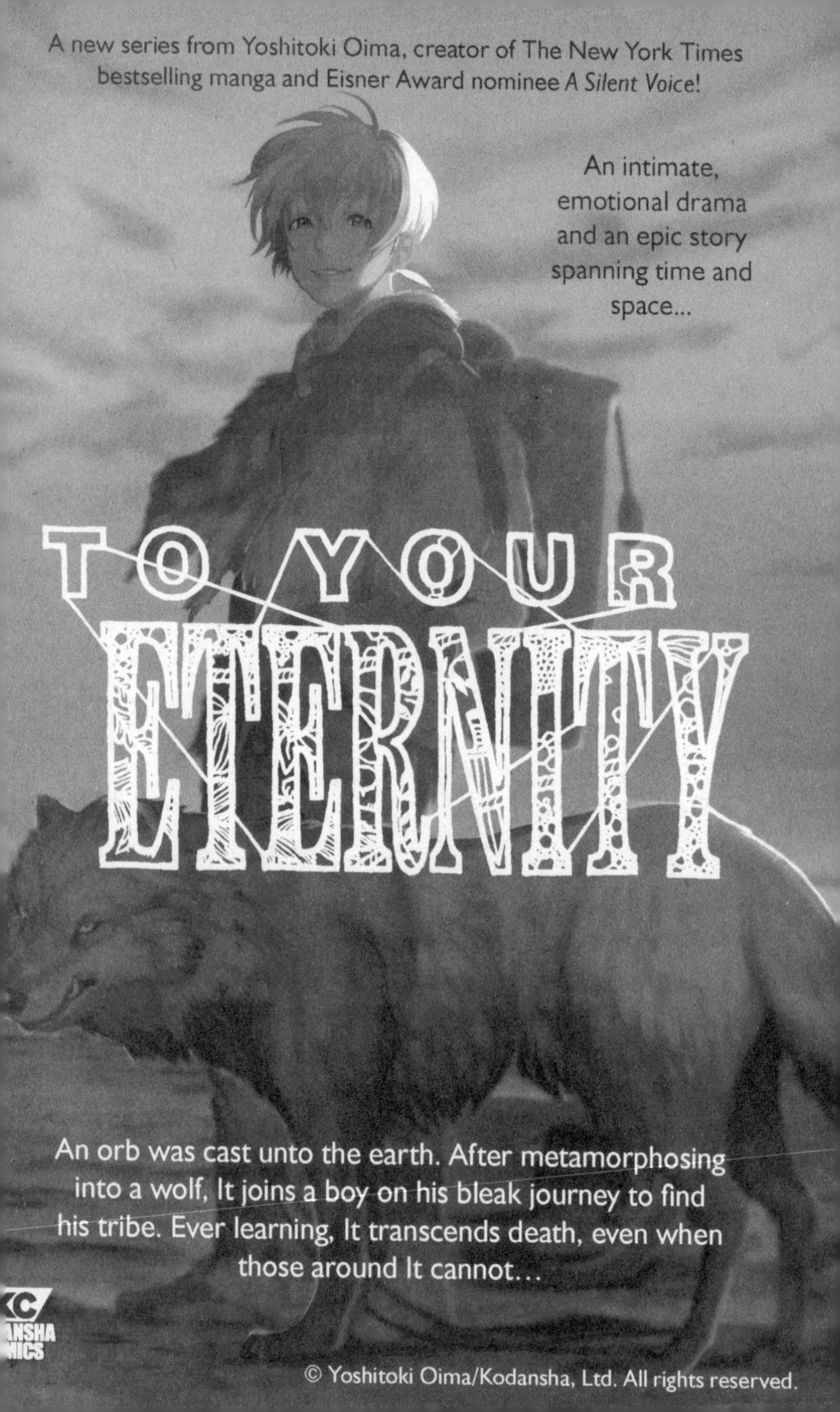
A new series from Yoshitoki Oima, creator of The New York Times bestselling manga and Eisner Award nominee *A Silent Voice*!
An intimate, emotional drama and an epic story spanning time and space...
TO YOUR ETERNITY
An orb was cast unto the earth. After metamorphosing into a wolf, It joins a boy on his bleak journey to find his tribe. Ever learning, It transcends death, even when those around It cannot…
© Yoshitoki Oima/Kodansha, Ltd. All rights reserved.

A beautifully-drawn new action manga from Haruko Ichikawa, winner of the Osamu Tezuka Cultural Prize!

LAND
OF THE
LUSTROUS

In a world inhabited by crystalline life-forms called The Lustrous, every gem must fight for their life against the threat of Lunarians who would turn them into decorations. Phosphophyllite, the most fragile and brittle of gems, longs t join the battle, so when Phos is instead assigned to complete natural history of their world, it sounds like a dull and pointle task. But this new job brings Phos into contact with Cinnabar gem forced to live in isolation. Can Phos's seemingly mundar assignment lead both Phos and Cinnabar to the fulfillment they desire?

17 years after the original *Cardcaptor Sakura* manga ended, CLAMP returns with more magical adventures from a beloved manga classic!

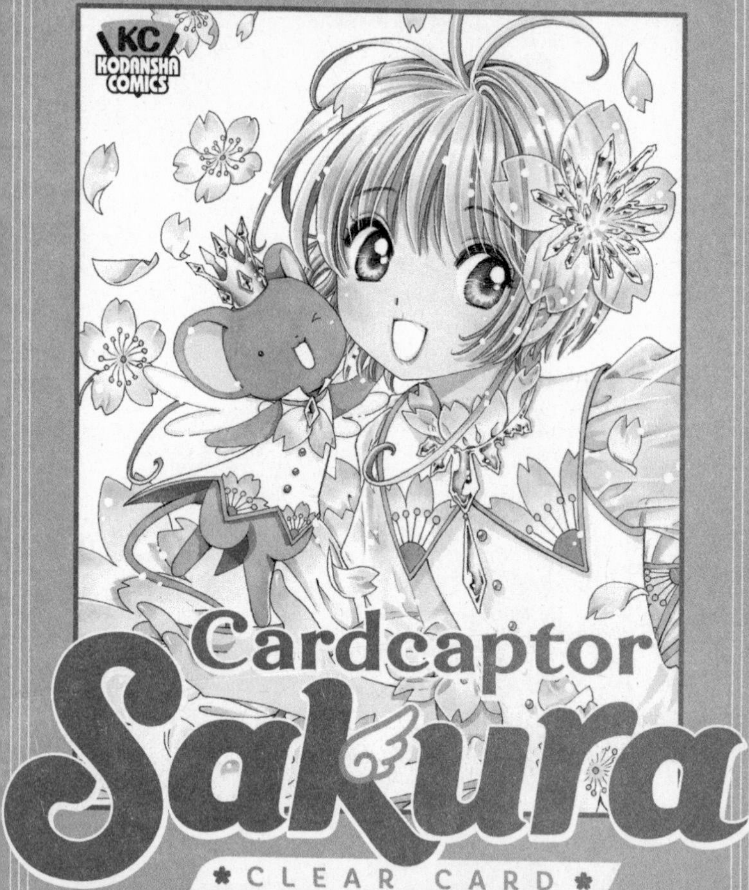
KC KODANSHA COMICS
Cardcaptor
Sakura
CLEAR CARD

Sakura Kinomoto's about to start middle school, and everything's coming up cherry blossoms. Not only has she managed to recapture the scattered Clow Cards and make them her own Sakura Cards, but her sweetheart Syaoran Li has moved from Hong Kong to Tokyo and is going to be in her class! But her joy is interrupted by a troubling dream in which the cards turn transparent, and when Sakura awakens to discover her dream has become reality, it's clear that her magical adventures are far from over...

FAIRY TAIL S

For the members of Fairy
Tail, a guild member's work
is never done. While they
may not always be away on
missions, that doesn't mean
our magic-wielding heroes
can rest easy at home. What
happens when a copycat
thief begins to soil the good
name of Fairy Tail, or when
a seemingly unstoppable
virus threatens the citizens
of Magnolia? And when a
bet after the Grand Magic
Games goes sour, can Natsu,
Lucy, Gray, and Erza turn the
tables in their favor? Come
see what a "day in the life"
of the strongest guild in Fiore
is like in nine brand new
short stories!

KC
KODANSHA
COMICS

A collection of *Fairy Tail* short stories drawn by original creator Hiro Mashima!

ANIME COMING SUMMER 2018

The award-winning manga about what happens inside you!

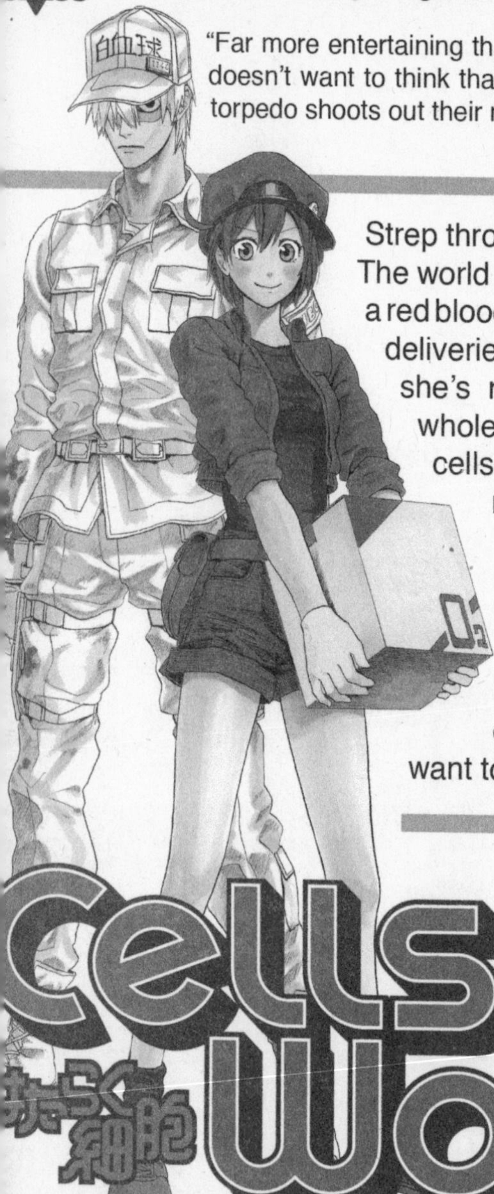

"Far more entertaining than it ought to be... What kid doesn't want to think that every time they sneeze, a torpedo shoots out their nose?"

—Anime News Network

Strep throat! Hay fever! Influenza! The world is a dangerous place for a red blood cell just trying to get her deliveries finished. Fortunately, she's not alone. She's got a whole human body's worth of cells ready to help out! The mysterious white blood cell, the buff and brash killer T cell, the nerdy neuron, even the cute little platelets—everyone's got to come together if they want to keep you healthy!

Cells at Work!

By Akane Shimizu

Japan's most powerful spirit medium delves into the ghost world's greatest mysteries!

Story by Kyo Shirodaira, famed author of mystery fiction and creator of *Spiral*, *Blast of Tempest*, and *The Record of a Fallen Vampire*.

Both touched by spirits called yôka Kotoko and Kurô have gained uniqu superhuman powers. But to gain h powers Kotoko has given up an ey and a leg, and Kurô's person life is in shambles. S when Kotoko sugges they team up to de with renegades fro the spirit world, Ku doesn't have many oth choices, but Kotoko might ju have a few ulterior motives...

IN/SPECTRE

STORY BY **KYO SHIRODAIR**
ART BY **CHASHIBA KATAS**

KC
KODANSHA
COMICS

"I'm pleasantly surprised to find modern shojo using cross-dressing as a dramatic device to deliver social commentary... Recommended."

-Otaku USA
Magazine

The prince in his dark days

By Hico Yamanaka

[D]runkard for a father, a household of poverty... For 17-year-old Atsuko, [mi]sfortune is all she knows and believes in. Until one day, a chance [en]counter with Itaru-the wealthy heir of a huge corporation-changes [eve]rything. The two look identical, uncannily so. When Itaru curiously [goe]s missing, Atsuko is roped into being his stand-in. There, in his shoes, [Ats]uko must parade like a prince in a palace. She encounters many new [ex]periences, but at what cost...?

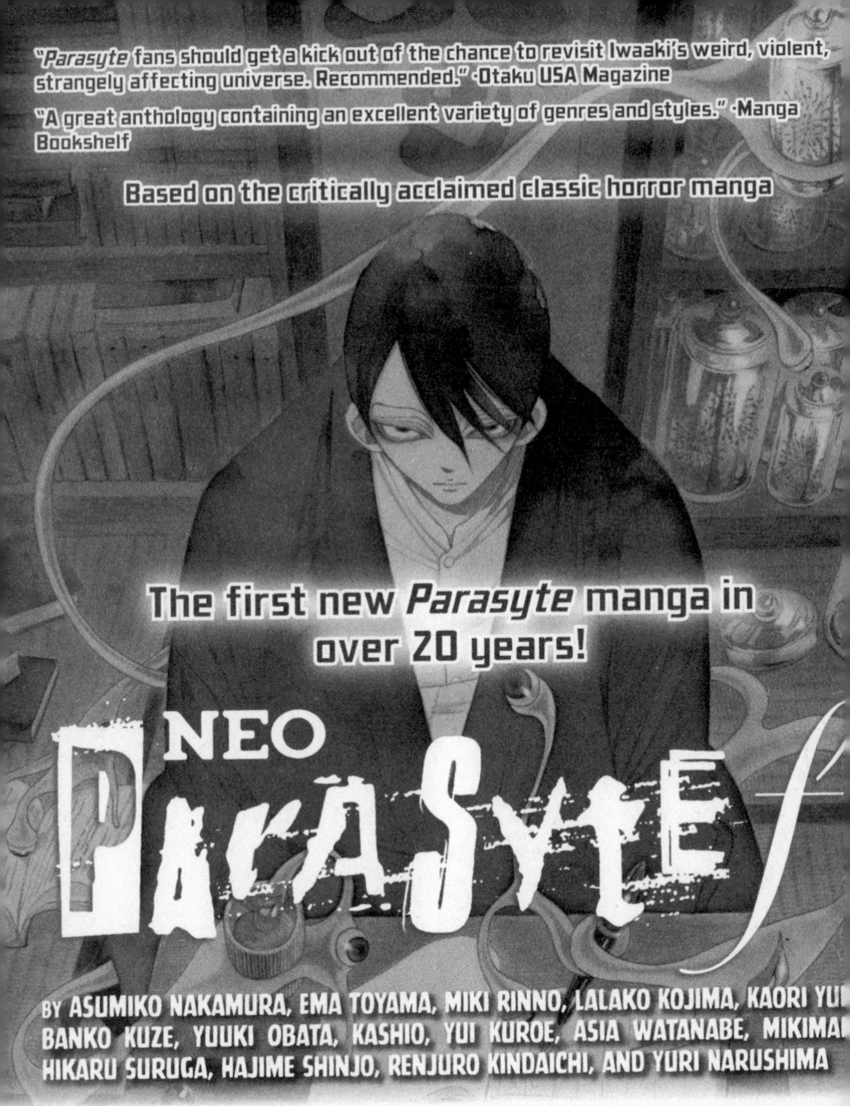

Based on the critically acclaimed classic horror manga

The first new *Parasyte* manga in over 20 years!

NEO PARASYTE f

BY ASUMIKO NAKAMURA, EMA TOYAMA, MIKI RINNO, LALAKO KOJIMA, KAORI YUI
BANKO KUZE, YUUKI OBATA, KASHIO, YUI KUROE, ASIA WATANABE, MIKIMAI
HIKARU SURUGA, HAJIME SHINJO, RENJURO KINDAICHI, AND YURI NARUSHIMA

A collection of chilling new *Parasyte* stories from Japan's top shojo artist

Parasites: shape-shifting aliens whose only purpose is to assimilate with and consur
the human race... but do these monsters have a different side? A parasite become:
prince to save his romance-obsessed female host from a dangerous stalker. Anoth
hosts a cooking show, in which the real monsters are revealed. These and 13 mo
stories, from some of the greatest shojo manga artists alive today,
together make up a chilling, funny, and entertaining tribute to one
of manga's horror classics!

The Seven Deadly Sins: Seven Days volume 1 is a work of fiction. Names, characters, places, and incidents are the products of the author's imagination or are used fictitiously. Any resemblance to actual events, locales, or persons, living or dead, is entirely coincidental.

A Kodansha Comics Trade Paperback Original.

Published in the United States by Kodansha Comics, an imprint of Kodansha USA Publishing, LLC, New York.

Publication rights for this English edition arranged through Kodansha Ltd., Tokyo.

First published in Japan in 2017 by Kodansha Ltd., Tokyo.

ISBN 978-1-63236-761-7

Printed in the United States of America.

www.kodanshacomics.com

9 8 7 6 5 4 3 2 1

Translation: Stephen Meyerink
Lettering: AndWorld Design
Editing: Lauren Scanlan
Kodansha Comics edition cover design: Phil Balsman